Praise for Thomas H. Keith, Master Chief, SEAL Team 2, USN (Ret.)

"Tom Keith was, in a phrase, a phenomenon of understatement and over-achievement. He was the 'go-to guy' within the East Coast SEAL community, and he continues to be 'gone to' wherever he hangs his hat or docks his boat. Tom Keith is the man I wish I were."

—Larry Bailey, Captain, USN (Ret.)

"It is a very special breed who can work and function effectively in the most dangerous environments on the planet. Three tours in Vietnam and many other locations around the globe including Afghanistan and Iraq and being held in the highest esteem by the guys who were there, brothers in arms with him, more than qualifies him as a national hero. It is my privilege to call Tom Keith my friend." —Steve Schwarzer, Master Bladesmith

"From his first day in training until his retirement, Tom Keith always put the team first. As a warrior there were a few men who were his equal, but none who worked harder. Tom always let his actions speak for him, and his actions, on and off the field of battle, spoke volumes. Tom never gave anything less than his best, and his best was as good as it gets."

—Rudy Boesch, Command Master Chief, USN (Ret.)

"It has been my pleasure to know and have associated with Thomas Keith for well for over forty years. He has been a good friend and steadfast teammate. I say, in his case, 'still water runs very deep.' His quiet, calm demeanor works well for him. He participated in and led many dangerous diving missions from UDT 21. He did three action-packed six-month SEAL tours in the Rung Sat, Vietnam. He spent perilous years in Afghanistan and Iraq fighting for their freedom. And, as always, he is the strong, quiet leader who commands the utmost respect. As always, he receives admiration while smiling in the face of adversity. As always, he's the consummate warrior committed to doing the impossible. And, as always, he is a quiet professional."

—Tom Blais, Command Master Chief, USN (Ret.)

SEAL WARRIOR

The Only Easy Day Was Yesterday

Thomas H. Keith
Master Chief, SEAL Team 2, USN (Ret.)

and J. Terry Riebling

Foreword by Michael E. Thornton,
Lt., USN (Ret.), Congressional Medal of Honor Recipient

THOMAS DUNNE BOOKS
ST. MARTIN'S GRIFFIN
NEW YORK

THOMAS DUNNE BOOKS.
An imprint of St. Martin's Press.

SEAL WARRIOR. Copyright © 2009 by Thomas H. Keith and J. Terry Riebling. Foreword copyright © by Lt. Michael E. Thornton U.S. Navy (Ret.). All rights reserved. Printed in the United States of America. For information, address St. Martin's Press, 175 Fifth Avenue, New York, N.Y. 10010.

www.thomasdunnebooks.com
www.stmartins.com

All photos are courtesy of the Tom Keith collection.

The Library of Congress has cataloged the hardcover edition as follows:

Keith, Thomas H.
    SEAL warrior : death in the dark—Vietnam, 1968–1972 / Thomas H. Keith and J. Terry Riebling ; foreword by Michael E. Thornton. — 1st ed.
        p. cm.
    Includes bibliographical references and index.
    ISBN 978-0-312-37904-9
    1. Keith, Thomas H. 2. Vietnam War, 1961–1975—Personal narratives, American. 3. Vietnam War, 1961–1975—Commando operations. 4. United States. Navy. SEALs—Biography. 5. United States. Navy. SEALs—History—20th century. 6. Guerrillas—United States—Biography. 7. Guerrillas—Vietnam—Biography. 8. Guerrilla warfare—Vietnam—History—20th century. I. Riebling, J. Terry. II. Title.
  DS559.5.K395 2009
  959.704'38—dc22
  [B]

2009007825

ISBN 978-0-312-62803-1 (trade paperback)

10 9 8 7 6 5 4 3

This book is dedicated to every warrior who has stepped into harm's way, put his life at risk, and has allowed our nation to survive against what sometimes seemed impossible or overwhelming odds on countless fields of battle.

The warriors who fought with me in Vietnam, including the boat support crews, navy pilots, army helicopter pilots, and, never last or least, my brother SEALs, have all added their personal history to a warrior tradition. No list of names is needed here, they know who they are and the honor they have given me by allowing me to earn their trust and respect. Hoo-Yah!

Contents

Acknowledgments

My mother and dad gave me just about everything a boy, young man, and a man could have been given: their love, strict rules that were to be obeyed, and the desire to carry on what looks like a genetic disposition of the Keith family to serve our country.

My dad served in the U.S. Navy, and fought in World War II and Korea and my Uncle, Richard Keith, served as a U.S. Marine in both Korea and Vietnam, but they were not the first of the family to serve their country.

My grandfather, James Keith, an army sergeant in World War I, fought in France. My great, great grandfather, John B. Keith fought on the Confederate side in the Civil War, and Cornelius Keith fought with Francis Marion, known, as "the Swamp Fox," in the Revolutionary War.

My cousin Brian Keith was always ready to help me with my many computer glitches and researching family history. Brian also checked and double checked dates, names, and all of the details that helped me put the facts in order as I wrote the book.

One of my closest friends, Steve Schwarzer, the master bladesmith, encouraged me to tell the story that would become this book. He also introduced me to Terry Riebling, my coauthor. Starting with just a list of chapters Terry made sure that the book was what I wanted it to be. Thanks to his hard work the book turned out better than I thought it would. Terry has become a close and trusted friend.

I would also like to thank Pete Wolverton, Associate Publisher at Thomas Dunne Books, and our production editor Bob Berkel. They both made this a better book.

Foreword

In the decade following World War II, the attention of the world was focused on the rebuilding of shattered European cities; Southeast Asia was almost forgotten. For over a decade Vietnam smoldered like a tinder-dry forest that had gone too long without rain. Constant brush fires threatened to begin the conflagration that would consume the country. The Vietminh, under the command of General Vo Nguyen Giap, a resourceful guerrilla leader, plagued the French occupying forces by employing hit-and-run tactics that Giap knew would slowly bleed the French dry. The Vietminh were exceptional guerrilla fighters. They chose where and when they would fight; they never stood their ground or fought a fixed battle. Giap changed his tactics in March of 1954 at Dien Bien Phu.

The Vietminh surrounded the three French firebases, which could only be resupplied from the air. They did what the French had thought impossible: They moved their heavy artillery and antiaircraft guns to the tops of the mountains surrounding the bases. Throughout the months of March and April and into early May the French forces were hammered by artillery, almost continuous small-arms fire, and infiltration by sappers. Amid the airfield destroyed by artillery fire, able to be resupplied only by parachute, with all supplies running low, and increasing numbers of

Vietminh fighters surrounding the base, the French were close to being overrun. Commanding officer Colonel Christian de Castries radioed the French HQ in Hanoi, "The Vietminh are everywhere. The situation is very grave. The combat is confused and goes on all about. I feel the end is approaching, but we will fight to the finish."

Seven years after the French defeat at Dien Bien Phu, President John F. Kennedy, an ex–U.S. Navy lieutenant, recognized the clear need for an unconventional warfare capability unlike any other in history. President Kennedy authorized the establishment of the SEALs. At 1300 hours on January 1, 1962, SEAL Team 1 was commissioned in the Pacific Fleet and SEAL Team 2 in the Atlantic Fleet.

The SEALs may have come late to the dance, but we would soon redefine modern guerrilla warfare. Anxious to serve a president who was one of their own, the navy moved mountains of paperwork, searched for and found facilities where these new Sea, Air, and Land Teams would be based, and began a SEAL legacy that survives today—ignoring, bending, or breaking the rules to accomplish their mission.

The navy had decided to do what had never been done before, pull highly disciplined volunteers out of a well-defined command and control structure where everything went by the book and turn them into guerrilla fighters. Before any man could become a SEAL, he would have to prove himself. He would also have to prove that there was a single four-letter word that was not a part of his vocabulary: quit. The teams would be made up of volunteers who had proven their ability to accomplish any mission or die trying.

The small brush fires in Vietnam, fed by Communist China, grew into an inferno that could no longer be ignored. To cut the supply lines, stop the Communist infiltration of South Vietnam, and sustain the balance of power in Southeast Asia, the SEALs would become the unconventional force that could take the battle to the enemy on their own turf. The SEALs would not be another means to use the heavy hammer of American military power. They would be small units of extraordinary men who would become the surgeons of unconventional warfare, going anywhere at any time to take on and defeat any enemy.

To learn how to fight a guerrilla war, the SEAL Teams started with a blank slate. Everything from tactics to weapons was new. Unless we had tried it, tested it, and proven it, we didn't bet our lives on it. There was only one fact that we did bet our lives on. If you were one of us, you were one of the best-trained and toughest fighting men in history. The men who became the backbone of the SEALs were warriors, and warriors can only be forged in battle.

In Vietnam we learned the warrior's craft. We took the battle to the enemy in the jungle, the mangrove swamps, the rice paddies, and on the rivers, the canals, and underwater. As we learned, fought, and reinvented guerrilla war, the men with green faces brought terror to the hearts of the Vietcong.

Throughout my career as a SEAL I had the privilege of fighting beside many good men, but Master Chief Tom Keith, U.S. Navy, Retired, is one of the warriors that made the SEALs what they became: the most deadly, unconventional group of warriors who have ever existed. Tom was, and remains, an operator, one of the very few men who is only fully alive when he is in the bush, jumping out of perfectly good airplanes that are not on fire, underwater, or under fire. When the night is dark, the enemy numbers overwhelming, and the shit is going to hit the fan, Tom Keith is the man I want at my back

—LT. MICHAEL E. THORNTON, U.S. Navy, Retired, SEAL Team 1,
    recipient of the Congressional Medal of Honor

Preface

Our nation was created by men who would have been proud to call Tom Keith their friend. Like Tom, the first Americans who fought for their nation were volunteers—citizen soldiers and sailors, who, when their service was needed, raised their hand, signed their name, or scratched their mark on an enlistment contract that many couldn't read, and left behind their homes, shops, fields, and families to march into harm's way. Most of these volunteers were men, but as we have come to know, women, disguised as men, also fought. War, when we look closely at our history, must be endemic to freedom, for we have been unceasingly at war since long before America, as a nation, existed.

When we speak of "peacetime," what we most often mean is the time between wars that engage us as a nation. When we look outside of this narrow definition, it is difficult or impossible to find even a few weeks of what most would consider "peace."

It is said that if one loves peace, one must constantly prepare for war. It is a fact that the first Americans, the indigenous people who have been called American Indians for centuries, lived at war. They killed their meat, fought their enemies with the best weapons at hand, sired children, and lived from the land. They were, and many still are, exceptional examples of guerrilla warriors. It was from these warriors that the American frontiersmen learned how to fight, and also realized that numerical and technological superiority did not always mean victory. From the beginning, Americans have been at war or preparing for it.

As a people, Americans are unique. Ours is the only nation that guarantees that each citizen has the right to be armed, a freedom exercised by more than thirty million hunters and shooters every year.

America has been called "a nation of riflemen," and I can see little room to debate this. In many communities, schools close for the opening few days of deer season, and twelve-year-old children carrying high-powered rifles sneak into the wilderness to, as the mountain men said, "make meat." Hunting, to some, has become a sport, but every year tens of millions of Americans kill, eviscerate, and drag home the carcass of a deer, elk, moose, or any animal that will feed their family. Perhaps this is why and how American warriors have become the criteria by which all fighting men and women are measured. We are a tough people, and we have never stopped learning the skills that put food on the family table and allow us to be prepared always for war or peace.

If we are very lucky, most of us will live out our lives without facing an enemy in battle. For this, we can offer our thanks to God and to all of the warriors who constantly train for war so that we may have peace.

Master Chief Tom Keith, U.S. Navy, Retired, is a very rare man in the company of rare men. He embodies the honor, courage, and skill at arms that assure America will always be free and ready for war. He has survived in circumstances under which most men, myself included, would have failed, and died. He has trained future warriors, and those warriors have trained more warriors.

I have tried to do justice to Tom and to the other SEALs who served with him through three tours of duty in Vietnam. I have done my best to represent accurately those who fought at his side in and out of the SEAL Teams, dates and times when important, weapons used, and a few of the women who played a part in Tom's life and times. It has been an honor to know Tom, to earn his trust, and to work with him on his first book. I sincerely hope that I have helped to portray the master chief as he is, a man of rare skill, immense courage, and patriotism. If there is any failure to tell Tom's story accurately and well, it is mine.

—J. Terry Riebling

There's but the twinkling of a star
Between a man of peace and war.

—SAMUEL BUTLER,
Hudibras II. Part iii. 957.

Author's Note

This is a true story, though some names have been changed.

SEAL WARRIOR

1

The Fourth of July

It was a moonless night, and seventeen green-faced men were hidden in the bush and along the dikes; we were hunting the Victcong. Fresh, hot intel had come in from the Chieu Hoi camp that had been checked, double-checked, and confirmed by the CIA. We were loaded for bear and ready to let Charlie know that they couldn't hide too deep or too far away. No matter where they went or what they did, we would find them, dig them out, and make them dead.

The VC that had been preying on the local villages, carrying off sons and daughters at the muzzle of an AK-47, and dropping random mortar rounds into cities and towns throughout South Vietnam, would be moving cross-country tonight. We had blown away one of their newly trained mortar teams only a few days ago, and they knew that as soon as we got better intel it would be only a matter of time before we would capture or kill them all. They were running scared, looking for a safe haven where they could train more mortar crews and operate without interference. The VC were hoping that if they moved far enough, fast enough, we would lose their trail, the intel would dry up, and they could continue raining down terror in the form of ChiCom (Chinese Communist) mortar rounds on the helpless villagers and townspeople. They could run, but tonight they couldn't hide.

Motionless, like frozen green statues in the bush and along the paddy dikes, we wouldn't initiate our ambush until the VC were centered in our field of fire. It wasn't long before they came walking down the path that ran the length of the dike between two rice paddies as if they were absolutely sure that they were the only armed bastards in the valley. Even before we could see them, we heard their gear clinking and banging; they were talking and laughing. As they came within about sixty yards of our position, we could hear the slapping of their sandals on the hard, sun-baked mud. It was as dark as it could be on a cloudy, almost moonless night, but their movement and black pajamas, the uniform worn by most of the VC, made them easy targets against the lighter bush and paddies behind them. Even with the minimal illumination from the quarter moon, we could see that their rifles were slung over their shoulders or carried carelessly, almost casually resting on their shoulders. The two RPK machine guns that I could see were useless; they didn't even have ammunition belts inserted into the receivers. That these VC had survived so long could only have been what we called PDL—pure dumb luck. They didn't know it, but their luck was about to go south.

Traveling at the speed of light, the incandescent, blinding flash from the explosion of two claymore mines, each containing a pound and a half of C-4 explosive, was the only warning the VC got when we initiated our ambush. We had carefully placed and secured the mines only a hundred feet from where we waited. Moving more slowly, only at the speed of sound, the concussion from the blast wouldn't reach them until after the two thousand steel ball bearings fired from the claymores went screaming across the dike at three times the speed of sound, shredding tree trunks, flesh, bone, and anything and everything else in their path.

With the sound of the blast still ringing in our ears and the flash of the exploding claymores still burned into our retinas, we opened up with four M-60 machine guns, two Stoner light machine guns, nine M-16 rifles, and two 12-gauge shotguns. Six or eight concussion grenades and two ground illumination grenades exploded, lighting up the sixty-yard-long kill zone in the middle of the paddies. As our red tracers streaked through the darkness, cutting down everything that crossed our field of fire, two white star parachute flares transformed night into daylight. The VC never knew that we were there in the darkness. Two of them lived long enough to get their weapons off of their shoulders, but neither of them lived long enough to pull back the operating handle on the right side of the receiver and get a round into the chamber. In less than a minute the officer in charge (OIC) called a cease-fire. None of the VC centered in the kill zone had fired a single round, and none of them was going to need medical treatment. Bodies, pools of blood, and parts of bodies were strewn across the killing zone. For fifteen or twenty seconds, we could hear a few of the VC moaning in pain. Then we heard the familiar gurgling gasps as their lungs collapsed, they bled out, and the battlefield went silent. Tonight we would not be taking any prisoners back with us for interrogation.

After a security perimeter was set up, a four-man team was sent out into the kill zone to cautiously roll over and check the bodies. With all of the VC confirmed dead, the team searched what was left of the bodies for documents or any other materials that might be useful to the intel people. Once these were secured, they gathered up all of the weapons and munitions so that they could be destroyed. Intelligence gathering was always our second highest priority; staying alive through the use of overwhelming firepower was always our first. We wanted to take prisoners so that we could bring them back and get more actionable, solid information that would lead us to VC even higher up the chain of command. On many of our missions we were successful, but when we staged an ambush we knew that dominating the field of fire was the best and maybe the only way to make sure that all of us would get back to base alive, in one piece, and without any serious injuries. It was our job to make the VC pay the death tax. Only after they had paid that tax could we take prisoners or look for the bloody, sometimes bullet-riddled documents that might lead us to another good operation.

There was also another reason that was always in the back of our minds when we dropped the hammer or fired the claymores that initiated an ambush. In the free-fire zones where we operated most of the time, there were always VC cadres moving men and munitions, or resting up after a march through the bush. Most of these cadres were small groups of ten or fewer men, but when two or three cadres got together to come looking for our usual six- or seven-man squad, they could easily outnumber us six or eight to one. When we touched off an ambush, we wanted it to sound and look like at least a company-sized force was in the area and on the attack. That might make the VC quick reaction forces or individual cadres think twice about charging through the boonies trying to track us down before they had grabbed up the extra men and the heavy weapons they would need to overpower a company. Creating the impression that we were a large, well-armed company gave us just what we needed most after an ambush: the time to search the dead, grab every document we could find, destroy their weapons, and haul ass back to our extraction point before the VC could get coordinated teams assembled and out looking for us.

In only a few minutes the bodies were searched, the weapons destroyed, and our head count complete. With all of our weapons reloaded and the rising moon lighting the way, it didn't take long to hump a couple of klicks back to our extraction point near Quang Tho village.

Just as we started to hear the distant whop-whop-whop of the blades of the helo coming in for our extraction, we saw the first trails of green VC tracers arching up into the sky. Two Seawolf helos that were running interference for our extraction helos peeled off and started their firing runs on the area along the tree line where the muzzle flash from the AK-47s and the tracer fire were concentrated. The Seawolves swept down on the VC, firing volleys of 2.75-inch rockets, and thousands of rounds per minute from their 7.62 miniguns. Both of the door gunners were busy laying down .50 caliber fire from the Browning machine guns. The roar of the guns and the concussion of the rockets exploding drowned out even the sound of their rotors. I remember thinking that all of those red tracers arching down from the sky and explosions lighting up the night was as beautiful as any Fourth of July fireworks display I had ever seen. Even as we prepared for extraction I couldn't stop myself from thinking how lucky I was, and how easy it could have been for me to have ended up someplace else, living a life that I would have never chosen. My father, a navy chief, had taught me more than he would ever know, or admit, and I had almost always gotten lucky when luck was the only thing that mattered. I had a lot of people to thank, but there were two people in particular that I hoped I would live long enough to thank someday.

2

Thank You,
Richard Widmark

The afternoon sun pierced the canopy of the trees, heating the sand under my boots like a blowtorch. Through the dancing waves of heat curling from the trail, I could see the humidity rising from the shallow, cedar-colored water that ran sluggishly between the creek banks. Without the sweat running down my face and body, the heat would have felt good, like a sauna, but the heat and humidity were turning the bush into a stifling steam room.

Somehow the planning for this operation had gone wrong. I met the woman at the right time and place, but the other members of the team never showed up. It was up to me to take the initiative, to move ahead and hope that they would find us in the bush. If they never caught up, it was up to me to get in, accomplish the mission with as little exposure or risk as possible, and get out in one piece.

The young woman ahead of me obviously had been here before. She knew the terrain like the back of her hand and led the way down a well-used animal trail that meandered through the bush that lined the banks of the small creek. Like ghosts, we moved as quickly and quietly as possible, keeping to the shadows to hide our presence. We were hunting, and silence let us get close to the targets before they knew we were there. We spotted our quarry before they spotted us. Each of the high-value targets that we spotted as we approached the staging area was taken with a single round, most with head shots.

Following her through the bush, I couldn't help but notice that under her loose-fitting pants and shirt were curves that betrayed her youth and femininity. She was barefoot and dripping with sweat, but that didn't keep me from realizing that she was very nicely put together.

As we approached the target area, I took stock of what we had accomplished so far. Three raccoons, four muskrats, and a fox had been dispatched and skinned out, their hides hung in the deep shade to cool. In only a couple of hours I had made almost twenty bucks with the expenditure of eight .22 long rifle bullets. My single-shot, bolt-action Winchester was accurate and economical. If I did my job, it was always the same— one shot, one kill.

Lou Ann, the eldest daughter of a local farmer, had led me to the secret swimming hole. At eight feet deep it was the deepest hole in Big Creek, one of thousands of small tributaries that fed the mighty Mississippi. She had carried our cane poles and the tin can full of worms that were fated to be used as bait to catch a mess of catfish and carp. If there was anything better than this, I had yet to experience it. This was how I wanted to spend the rest of my life; a good rifle, good friends, great fishing, and miles and miles of bush full of valuable targets that I could hunt. The cool water of Big Creek was now beckoning us to get the hooks baited and in the water before we waded in and washed the sweat from our bodies. This was the best day of my life so far. I didn't even care that the rest of our gang, local kids that spent most of our time in the Shelby State Forest or somewhere else in the boonies near the Mississippi River, hadn't shown up.

Lou Ann handed me the cane poles and the can of worms. Wanting to get cooled off as soon as I could, I waded into the creek, baited the hooks, and flipped the worms into the slow current. As I turned to hand one pole to Lou Ann, I was struck almost speechless by one of the most lovely images I had ever seen—Lou Ann was standing on a big rock wearing nothing but her bra, her panties, and an inviting smile.

I don't remember taking off my clothes, but by the time I was as naked as a jaybird Lou Ann was attired in her most alluring outfit, nothing but what the genetic wheel of fortune had provided—and from what I could see, Lou Ann had hit the jackpot! I can't swear that this is exactly right, but I think that might have been the afternoon that sealed my fate. That afternoon, without even knowing it, I learned something about myself that would lead me to the SEAL Teams. I liked guns and shooting and was above average in the use of almost every weapon I had ever tried, I was completely at home in the water and wild places, and now I was as sure as I would ever be that girls were the icing, candles, and ice cream on the cake of my life.

I had always been a hardheaded kid, and that didn't change much as I grew up. When I made up my mind to do something, there was little hope that anybody was going to change my mind, slow me down, or get in the way of me accomplishing my goal. Long before I became a SEAL, I learned that both luck and circumstance sometimes play a big part in where you are, where you're going, and how you're going to get there. The first time I knew that I was going to be a frogman was in a dark movie theater. The movie that Saturday afternoon was *The Frogmen*, with Richard Widmark playing the lead role of Lieutenant Commander John Lawrence, the CO of a UDT, an Underwater Demolition Team. Widmark wasn't the biggest guy on the screen, but he sure was the toughest. A Hollywood producer, a friend of his, once said that the actor was "the sort of man who could make you shit just by looking at you." I didn't want to make anybody crap his skivvies, but I sure wanted to be the kind of man that Widmark played in that movie. From that point on, it seems that the stars were aligned in my favor; everything that could have gone wrong went right.

I was born two days after D-Day, on June 8, 1944, in Providence, Rhode Island. I was the eldest son of a navy chief and the grandson of two army men who served in World War I, and I grew up as a navy brat, traveling the world and experiencing military life firsthand. One of my earliest memories was the day that I boarded my first navy transport ship with my mother, sister, and brother. It was 1952, and we were on our way to join my father, who was halfway around the world. It was my good luck that he had been stationed at a naval air station in Rabat, the capital of

Morocco. Our home for the next couple of years was a big house with a thatched roof close to the Atlantic Ocean on Media Beach. With World War II not long over, there were still fields crisscrossed by trenches and barbed wire. There were also signs posted around many of them: KEEP OUT—LIVE MINE FIELDS. Even as a kid, for me war was not an abstraction; war was a very real, ever-present part of our daily lives.

However, there was another side to navy life and Morocco that played an important part in forming the young man who would one day become a SEAL. My father was an avid hunter and fisherman. The Atlas Mountains were crawling with partridge that tasted as good as any Cornish game hen, and when we wanted freshwater fish, the largemouth bass were there for the catching in the lakes hidden deep in the cool mountain valleys. For two carefree years I tried my best to live the life of Tom Sawyer and dogged my father's footsteps as he taught me the skills and tricks of the hunter.

In 1954 new orders arrived. I wouldn't be spending any more time with my father roaming the Atlas Mountains, we were going back to the United States. It seemed as if it happened almost overnight; we packed up the house, said our good-byes to friends, and boarded a transport plane headed to the Naval Air Station in Millington, Tennessee. My father was now posted as an instructor in the aviation metalsmith school. Tennessee wasn't Morocco, and I wasn't sure I was going to like it all that much until I met Lou Ann and the gang of kids that would be a part of the best adventures a ten-year-old boy could ever dream about. Still, there were a few rough spots that I had to get over. For some reason known only to mothers, I was now expected to become a model student and respectable member of the community.

For the next seven years I did my best to make my parents proud, or at least to keep them from restricting me to base. I never much liked stiff collars and shiny shoes, or any shoes at all, for that matter, and school was never one of the highlights of my young life. School was that interminable part of the day when I couldn't hunt, fish, and wander unfettered around the wildest places I could find. I was never much of a bookworm, unless the book happened to be about American history, U.S. naval history, or some other subject that caught my interest, but I was always, because my mother and father expected it, a solid B student. Maybe I spent too much time in the boonies when I should have been studying, but it seemed to me, and still does, that anybody who listened, paid attention in class, and did the homework could learn all that classroom stuff. When, at the age of seventeen, I decided to join the United States Navy, it didn't come as much of a surprise. My father, Chief Thomas H. Keith, swore me in.

Boot camp at the Great Lakes Naval Training Center was probably tough for some of the men who hadn't spent their time sneaking through the wilderness, tracking animals, playing sports, exercising, or building muscle. For me it was really enjoyable. The physical side of boot camp— sit-ups, push-ups, jogging, running the obstacle course, all of the work that the instructors put us through to get our bodies shipshape—was actually fairly easy, and the training manuals and books that many of the recruits found difficult or impossible to grasp were not much of a challenge for me. Boats, ships, guns, aircraft, radios, explosives—you name it, if the U.S. Navy had a training manual about it, it caught my interest, and since I was a navy brat I was ahead of the curve when it came to naval regs. By careful observation of my father I had already learned that it was almost always possible to do what you wanted to do when an officer told you that it just couldn't be done. This was another of those life lessons that has never let me down: When it can't be done—get stubborn, never give up, and if possible get the help of a navy chief.

These lessons, my stubbornness, and some help from a few old friends of my father's would soon play a big part in my being accepted into UDT Class 30 and becoming a U.S. Navy SEAL. I only forgot these rules once, and without some luck or divine intervention it could have cost me my career in the SEAL Teams.

I was planning on getting myself transferred to Underwater Demolition Team replacement school at the Little Creek Amphibious Base in Norfolk, Virginia, as soon as possible. I was told that before I could even request the transfer I needed two years of sea duty, and even then there was no guarantee that my request would get me the transfer. My orders sent me to the USS *Robert A. Owens*, a destroyer escort homeported in Norfolk. I spent my first year as a navy enlisted man on the *Owens*, six months of that time on a Caribbean cruise. With a year of solid sea duty under my belt, I asked for and got a transfer to the USS *Forrestal*, an aircraft carrier also homeported in Norfolk. I was assigned to the guided missile division and soon had accumulated three green stripes on my left sleeve that designated me as an airman E-3. The U.S. Navy thought that I was on my way to becoming an aviation ordnanceman; I guess that I may have been the only E-3 aboard the *Forrestal* who hadn't forgotten why I had joined the navy. I was going to somehow, by hook or by crook, become a frogman.

My first deployment on the *Forrestal* was a six-week workup, followed by a six-month cruise in the Mediterranean Sea. We were showing the flag, and I was expanding my knowledge of other cultures, taking advantage of liberty call whenever possible. As a representative of my country and the U.S. Navy, I could do nothing less than my level best to ensure that the loveliest young ladies of each port became intimately aware of the many skills that even a young E-3 on his first European cruise had learned.

At the end of what seemed to me to be a very short six-month cruise, the *Forrestal* headed for home port, and I started thinking, planning, and trying to figure out how I was going to get around that second-year requirement and get myself reassigned to UDT. Before I could come up with a plan, we were approaching Norfolk and I got the first of several surprises that would change my life in the next couple of weeks.

Waiting for us on the dock was one of the biggest crowds of waving and cheering people I had ever seen outside a football or baseball stadium. My father, mother, brother, sister, and new brother-in-law were, like the other thousand or so family members of the *Forrestal* crew, waiting to celebrate their sailor coming home from the sea.

Like most navy families, my family was always tightfisted with the little money we did have—we never spent a dollar when a dime would do—so it didn't come as much of a surprise that my parents were staying with old navy friends, Bob and Ann Grayson. I remembered them both well because they lived across the street from us in 1959 when I was fifteen years old and my father was based in Norfolk. Not only did Bob and Ann welcome my family into their home, they insisted that our family reunion would be held at their house that evening. As lucky as I had always been, this was one of the luckier days of my young life. Bob, whose nickname in the teams was Archie, was a navy frogman with UDT 21 stationed at Little Creek Amphibious Base. I figured that this would be a great opportunity to learn as much as I could about the Underwater Demolition Teams from Bob and maybe find a way to shorten my wait to sign up for a transfer to UDT school.

I didn't even have to ask Bob about UDT training. I am still not sure if my father had asked for Bob's help and set everything in motion, but Bob took the initiative and asked me how my UDT request was going. When I told him about the two-year sea duty requirement, he laughed out loud and told me that he would pick me up the following morning and take me to meet a friend of his, Chief Ben Sulinski, the chief in charge of UDT training. When Bob told the chief that the two-year sea duty was a problem and Aviation Ordnanceman Keith would like a somewhat expedited transfer to UDT, things got moving along smartly. Like my father had taught me, when you want to get something done in the navy—get a chief on your side.

Chief Sulinski spoke to the OIC, Lieutenant Jim Tyrie. He had me fill out a special request form for screening and physical fitness tests that were necessary for acceptance to a UDT class beginning in three weeks. I hand-carried the paperwork to my division chief, got his signature, returned the paperwork to Little Creek, and a week later found myself one of thirteen men being evaluated for entry to UDT class. This was the first time I saw how the navy really got things done. Officers make the decisions, but if you need to move a mountain, find a way to get running water to supply a small riverine base halfway around the world, or get a skinny young E-3 into UDT school fast, you need a chief on your side to start paving the way and pulling strings.

3

Blood, Sweat, and Sand

My orders to report to UDT replacement school were cut, and, like most of the hundred or so members of Class 30, I arrived two weeks early. For those two weeks our instructors ran us through a daily PT (physical training) routine that got us in better condition than any of us had ever known was possible. I was already in very good shape because I had established a personal regimen of PT while on board the *Forrestal*, but the UDT instructors knew what it would take for us to survive in real combat. They pushed each of us to the highest level of physical condition that any of us could achieve. Man by man they tested us, pushed us, and made us so physically tough that we had the physical tools we had to have in order to develop the mental toughness and endurance that they knew would keep us alive when nothing else would. UDT school was hard, harder than anything I had ever attempted. To this day I thank God that I went through the summer class, and I have a lot of respect for the men who survived the frigid waters of the winter class.

We did PT all day, every day. During beach runs, I thought about what was to come and ticked off the days until the official beginning of training for Class 30: June 1, 1963. World War II–era barracks, five identical wooden buildings with fifteen bunks and wall lockers along the right and left walls, a five-foot-wide aisle down the center, a head and shower, and doors at both ends, would be home for the next six months. After what seemed to be an eternity, Class 30 started with our first muster at 0600. There were 105 students in green fatigues and white T-shirts, boondockers on our feet and red helmet liners on our heads. For some of us those red helmet liners would become our personal badge of honor and commitment. Our first activity as a class was a mile run to breakfast. I think that night was the first time I heard somebody say that yesterday was the easy day. We all knew that Hell Week was coming, when we would be forced to face our own weaknesses and mortality in ways that we couldn't even dream up in our nightmares. Until then it was the instructors' job to push us harder than we had ever been pushed before.

It wasn't long before we saw our first men quit. In a way, to some students, quitting early made sense. If you were going to fail, you might as well pull the plug now; just take that damn red helmet liner off, drop it on the ground, the pain was over, and you were gone. If you knew in your gut that you couldn't make it all the way to the end, no matter what, come hell, high water, or World War III, why push yourself another minute? No more sleep deprivation, no more pain from muscles screaming that the well was dry and there was no more to give. It would be wonderful to wash the sand out of every orifice and off of every inch of your body in warm, soapy water. All you needed to do was drop that helmet liner.

Two weeks into the course, with only a week left before Hell Week started, Class 30 was shrinking fast. More than half of the men had been injured too badly to continue, found themselves unfit, or had done their best and failed. I didn't know how the other students were dealing with the mental challenge, but I had my own coping mechanism. If anyone tried to take that red liner off of my head, I would kill him where he stood. I was going all the way, and nobody, nothing, nohow was going to stop me. I always was a hardheaded kid, and I guess somewhere along the line I had become a hardheaded man.

Hell Week is suffered, endured, and overcome by individual men who put aside their own egos and become a part of a team. Nobody, and I mean nobody, believe me, will ever survive Hell Week who isn't willing, trained, and ready to do anything that the team needs to have done whenever the team needs it done. Nor did it matter much how well we had trained before we arrived at Little Creek, or how tough or well prepared we thought we were. Not one of us would have survived Hell Week without the three weeks of what we thought was hard training before we got to Hell Week.

The instructors always did their best to make sure that we couldn't expect what would come, or allow ourselves to slip into a routine. As each day leading to Hell Week passed, and more and more men dropped their red liners, nothing, not even muster at 0600, could be taken for granted.

Morning muster came at 0530, and the day started with an hour of PT: jumping jacks, push-ups, sit-ups, eight-count body builders, chase the rabbit, flutter kicks, and whatever other torture the instructors could dream up to start us off loose, limber, and on the right foot for the day. After breakfast we were ordered to fall out and assume the leaning rest position until everyone was accounted for and ready to get back to work. A brisk jog to the training area was followed by another round of PT and a quick six-mile run—and quick was important. The first five men to finish got to sit in the shade while everyone else got to practice climbing fifty feet up the two-and-a-half-inch ropes that were attached to one of the six climbing towers right next door to the instructors' hut. Sitting in the shade while everyone else busted their hump was what the instructors meant when they told us that it paid to be a winner.

With the rope climb complete, we assumed the leaning rest position until everyone was mustered and accounted for. Then we were given time off until the next muster at 1130, when we would do another rope climb, twenty minutes of PT, then jog in formation to the chow hall for lunch. We learned that it was a good idea to eat fast and to shovel in as many calories as we could. We would need all the energy that we had because we would burn those calories fast when we were introduced to the O course.

The base obstacle course consisted of twenty-two different grueling stages that required climbing, balance, running, crawling, jumping, more running, and swimming if you fell off of the fifty-foot-high, hundred-foot-long slide for life. The course was to be completed in sequence, and we had fifteen minutes to get it done. (After running that bastard every day for three or four days, I started trying to cut that fifteen minutes in half, and I got close. My best time was nine minutes.)

Now the instructors thought that it would be an instructive and valuable experience for us to jog down to the beach and have our first taste of Mt. Suribachi, a large, steep sand dune that doubled as the backstop for the base rifle range. The race up and down Mt. Suribachi would be another of many of those "It pays to be a winner" races, and I moved my boondockers as fast as I could, hoping for another five minutes of relaxing in the shade while the slower guys busted their asses. As I came flying down the other side of the dune, I could see the jeep the instructors used to follow us on our little outings cruising through the soft sand. On the hood there were half a dozen new ornaments: red helmet liners. I didn't have time to wonder who had reached the end of their endurance and quit, and it didn't really matter too much—I wanted to be one of the three "winners."

With Mt. Suribachi conquered, and our boots now completely full of sand, we formed up and continued our run down the beach. We followed one, two, and sometimes up to four instructors, who made running through the surf, soft sand, and sand dunes for an hour a several-times-a-day diversion from other nasty things they had dreamed up. I don't know how, but they made it look easy, and I knew that it wasn't even close to easy.

When we were about a half mile from the training area, we were turned loose to race back. I sprinted to the head of the line and hoped I could finish in the top three and get a rest. I came in third, but that was good enough. I sat myself down in the shade to wait for the rest of the guys to finish the race, but I didn't get to sit there for very long before I learned another of the important lessons taught by our instructors. Ensign Larry Bailey pointed out that we are all a team and that for some men to slack off while other members of the team were still busting their ass was just not the way UDTs worked. He was right—the team always comes first, so I assumed the leaning rest position and waited for the rest of the team to finish the run. Nobody rests until everyone is back safe and the team is ready for our next challenge. It was an important lesson, and maybe that was why Bailey was senior man in our class.

The jeep, following the last men back to the training area, now had at least fifteen red ornaments on the hood, and there were even more in front of the hut. As we lined up for our next rope climb, Chief Jim Cook, one of our instructors, stepped out of the instructors' hut and rang the bell seventeen times, once for every red helmet on the jeep. This sure wasn't getting any easier.

As the last peal of the bell faded into the distance, Instructors Tom Blais and Bernie Waddell strolled casually over to the rope towers and let us know that from here on out we would not be using our legs in any way to climb the fifty-foot rope, and we couldn't use them to break our slide or slow our descent when coming down. They both suggested that it would be a great time to place our helmet liners in a nice neat line. Three men who hadn't even tried to climb that rope did just that. The line of red seemed to be growing by the minute. All I wanted was to be the guy who never even thought about dropping his helmet and finish Hell Week alive.

Climbing that rope without using our legs took just about everything that we had, but nobody else quit. We were told that we would muster at 1600 hours and were dismissed. As I lay on my bunk, getting as much rest as I could while trying to figure out how I could master the O course and cut my time, I heard the brass bell chime out two more times. I guessed that once those two guys had time to think about what was coming while they were in a dry bunk, they figured that they were never going to stick it out to the end. At 1600 there were forty-three red helmet liners in a row in front of the instructors' hut.

At 1600 we started what seemed like endless push-ups, sit-ups, duck-walking, pull-ups, rope climbs, and long runs around the amphibious base. We ran on hard, paved roads, up and down Incinerator Hill (where all of the base trash was burned every day), in the soft sand of the beaches, in the surf, through the dunes, and up, over, and around Mt. Suribachi. Distance didn't matter; now we were running against the clock. Speed and endurance were all that counted. We ran for an hour, then two hours. We followed the instructors, hoping that they would get tired and head for home. Day after day the routine got tougher and faster. On our Saturdays and Sundays off, it took every minute to rest our muscles and to start healing our now shredded skin. It seemed like we never had enough time to get ready to start all over again on Monday morning, and Hell Week hadn't even started.

Our last Friday before Hell Week brought a new revelation. We still had a whole day ahead of us before we could rest when our kind instructors introduced us to the IBL (inflatable boat, large). The IBL was a large rubber boat that would hold ten men and their gear, and the damn thing was heavy. These 375-pound boats would become our almost constant companions in a couple of days.

After morning PT, introduction to the IBL, running through the sand, and climbing ropes, we paused just long enough to get as many calories into us as we could. After lunch we mustered up at the training area, and our instructors, Chuck Newell, Tom Blais, and Jim Cook, led us in the longest nonstop run so far. Down the beach, over Suribachi, down the jetty, around the golf course, back to the beach, and around the jetty again. After three hours of slogging through the sand, pounding our feet on hard roads, and charging up and down Suribachi, we headed into the home stretch toward the instructors' hut. As the hut appeared in the distance, one of the instructors, or maybe all three, gave us the signal to turn around and yelled out, "Halfway point, let's do it again." Four red liners hit the ground and four more men were gone. Blais started laughing and picked up the liners. "Just kidding, men. Run's over for the day." Our instructors had taught us another valuable lesson: You never know when it is going to get harder or easier, nobody has a crystal ball. At the exact moment when you think that it can't get any worse, that you can't take any more, it can get worse. That's when there is only one thing that you can do, reach down inside of yourself and find that you can do what you never thought you could. Then again, as I learned later in Vietnam, it can also get better. In more firefights than I can remember, it looked like we were SOL—shit out of luck—and were going to be toast. We were low on ammo, the VC were shooting at us from every tree and paddy dike, and I was hoping that our close air support would get there in time to save at least some of the team. Then the Seawolves or Black Ponies came out of nowhere and pulverized the VC, and it got real quiet in a couple of heartbeats. In minutes all the VC were dead, dying, or running for their lives. I almost couldn't believe I was still alive and without any big holes anywhere. Our instructors showed us again and again that we could do anything that we wanted if we wanted it bad enough, even the shit that we thought was impossible. In two days I was going to find out how much I could take and just how far I could push myself.

Hell Week would start at one minute after midnight on Sunday. I had almost two whole days to eat, sleep, rest, and recuperate. Sunday came around too quickly, and I hit my rack wearing my fatigues, with my boon-dockers (thin-soled boots) tied tight and my red helmet liner tucked under my right arm. If I had learned nothing else, I had learned to be prepared for the worst. Our instructors didn't let us down—they gave us their worst from the get-go.

At midnight the world suddenly stopped. Whatever I was dreaming about was gone in an instant. Lights were blaring, whistles were blowing, the shit cans (metal trash cans) were being beaten into submission with baseball bats, and the instructors were throwing boondockers, clothing, and anything not nailed down all over our barracks. One of the instructors was screaming through a megaphone, "All you pollywogs fall out—stand by your boats."

With only fifty-five people left in the class, we were split into seven- and eight-man boat crews. In addition to wearing our red helmet liners, each boat crew now carried an IBL almost everywhere we went. With those boats upside down on our heads, we looked like a herd of turtles. Now we actually started to like our red hats. Those lousy helmet liners were beautiful things; they were the only thing that kept the sand stuck to the bottom of the IBL from eating a hole right through the top of our skulls. This was the first time I realized that at 5' 10", being a little shorter than my teammates was a real bonus. The taller guys took most of the weight and punishment doled out as we ran as fast as we could go with those heavy boats bouncing up and down on our heads.

For the next week, the only thing that I could do was will myself to keep moving. I might have not been moving as fast or as powerfully as I would have liked, but I managed to keep myself upright, mostly unin-jured, and not dead. That just had to be enough because I didn't have anything else to give. No matter what the instructors threw at me I was going to prove to them, and myself, that I was one no-quit, hard-ass team-mate whose helmet liner would never hit the ground.

For the next seven days, we couldn't waste any energy thinking about what the instructors were putting us through; we just had to do it. It took everything that we had just to stay awake, to keep moving forward, and to not let the other members of our boat crew down. We didn't know what the instructors were doing or why they were doing it, but they knew precisely. They were engineering the best warriors possible, pushing us to and sometimes over the edge that we thought we could survive. They were testing each of us to destruction.

When engineers design a machine, they don't start throwing parts together and hope that the machine is going to work. Before they start building, they figure out what is possible, and what would be an acceptable performance level that the machine must meet. It could be a number of operations per hour, the number of parts the machine can make, the accuracy of the final result of the use of that specific machine, or several different criteria put together. In weapons systems design, the engineers can calculate everything, but no matter how well they calculate everything, they only really know what a weapon can do when it finally fails in testing. To find out what a weapon can do, how far beyond the specs it can go and still function, the engineers keep increasing the demands made on the system until it finally comes apart at the seams. Our instructors were the engineers, and the boat crews were the machines that they were going to test to the edge of destruction. Most of the men who started training either failed due to injuries or just couldn't take one more step and quit. Hell Week was the last test we had to survive.

To the rest of the world, and sometimes to the men who looked like turtles running around carrying the IBL on their heads, it seemed that our instructors were sadistic psychopaths, that all they wanted to do was make us fail. They made us repeat the same drills over and over. They turned us into "sugar cookies"—made us run into the surf, then roll in the sand until we were well covered—and then we would run the beach carrying our IBL over our heads. Our wet uniforms, covered inside and out with sand, were like sandpaper. The sand that was stuck to the inside of our uniforms and boots ate away our skin and wore through our elbows and knees. We learned that if we tried to move our bodies inside the uniform, without actually touching it, it hurt a lot less. We looked a little funny, but that was better than bleeding. Later we found out that this was so common that the instructors called it the "Hell Week Shuffle." We never stopped; we shuffled everywhere, carrying the IBL on our heads.

Our boots were tied as tight as we could get them without cutting off circulation, and they still filled up with sand. Our instructors ran us until we had bleeding, infected blisters on our feet. We didn't understand anything more than going as fast as we could to accomplish whatever the instructors told us to do, but they knew what every man who graduated learned in that one long week. They knew that if they did everything possible to make us quit and we still made it to graduation, they had built us into warriors who could only fail by destruction. If we were alive, we would be in the fight. There was nothing that could stop us.

There had been a time when I thought that I knew what pain was. Our instructors got that idea out of my head in just one day. I wanted sleep, dry clothes, and anything warm to drink or eat. I was dehydrated, I hurt in places that had never hurt, I hated the IBLs that we carried on our heads, and patches of my skin had been worn off. I was bleeding, and we were going to have to finish a boat race and two trips around the training area before breakfast. With each boat crew under their IBLs, and the men on the sides holding on to the rubber handholds, we jogged as fast as we could. The winners would be allowed to sit on their boat until the rest of the teams finished the race. It was still dark, and the instructors, bless their black hearts, were running in between the boats trying to push them off of our heads. We dropped our boat only once, but some of the teams lost theirs more than once. First to finish was Ensign Bailey's boat; they sat while we all stood, boats on our heads, waiting for the last team to straggle in. The last boat is given an honor for being last to finish, they would be doing a "loser's lap" and, because they finished first, Bailey's team would have the privilege of going along, doing the whole run again, just for the fun of beating them twice.

With the morning boat races done, we were expecting breakfast, but our instructors thought it would be a good idea for all of us to work up an appetite first. After forty-five minutes of PT, push-ups, eight-count body builders, and sit-ups, the sun was just beginning to crawl over the horizon.

We were already soaked in sweat, covered with sand, tired, and dehydrated, and our day had just started. With our boats back on our heads, we were lined up and marched to the special wing of the chow hall where they feed the dirty, sand-covered, bleeding people. We lined up our boats along the front of the building and hit the chow line. Hot coffee, hot food, a chance to stretch our legs and twist and turn our necks to try to get those neck muscles and vertebrae straightened out. *This may not be as bad as I thought it was going to be,* I thought. *Heck, maybe Hell Week is just one of those myths, like the boogey man, used to scare away the people who are easily scared.* My belly was full and I was in a good mood until we all fell out and realized that some asshole had let the air out of all of our boats. Not only did we look stupid, but Newell and Blais were now screaming at us for being so damn dumb that we didn't leave a guard to watch our boats. This was another valuable lesson learned during Hell Week: Never leave your boats, or your back, exposed. That kind of sloppiness in a war can lead to death, and if you are dead you can't accomplish your mission or help your team carry your body back to base. My fun meter was about to hit the red line. The punishment this time was only that we had to carry the deflated IBLs a mile back to the training area where they could be inflated again.

With the boats all reinflated, it was time to pay the piper and learn that lesson again. We were going to have a race around the training area, about the same size as a football field. The whole class was going to duckwalk, with our boats on our heads, all the way around it. Nobody can duckwalk that far nonstop. It took two hours for the entire class to get it done. Our class leader, Ensign Dailey, insisted that we all finish as a team. There were no winners in that race. After doing that duckwalk we had learned another lesson that we couldn't forget; we would never, ever leave our boats where the enemy could disable them. As we mustered at our boats, I noticed that there were two new hood ornaments on the instructors' jeep. Two of our team had decided to stop the pain and call it a day. That damn boat was going to be a lot heavier with two fewer men heaving it up and carrying it along.

We formed up and, with the IBL on our heads, started another run, only to be interrupted by our instructors. They had decided that with two fewer men to help us carry it, the weight of the boat was probably too much for us to hump on our heads, and they didn't want anyone to break his neck. Thus began our introduction to the unique pain of extended arm carry. Carrying an IBL with your arms extended as far from your body as possible is a great way to create an exquisite level of pain. Even at a slow jog the pain shoots up your arms as if someone is slowly driving a very cold ice pick into your shoulders, elbows, and wrists. I couldn't wait to get that damn boat back on my head. Long before we arrived at the O course, all of us had started to think that carrying an IBL on your head was really not all that bad. In fact, it was a piece of cake.

Ensign Blais informed us that there was a reward for the team that finished the O course first. With three days of Hell Week behind us, all of the teams had become competitive. Anything that wouldn't get somebody really hurt was fair. Tripping a competitor, pushing him off a log, or walking right over him in the water-filled mud pit underneath the slide for life was justifiable mayhem. Any dirty trick played that would let your team have an advantage was just fine if it meant that your team would have a few minutes of R&R while everybody else was still struggling to get it done.

Even the instructors joined in the fun. They would grab one or both of the lines that run up to the tower that supports the slide for life. While we were holding on to the top rope and walking down the bottom rope, trying to get to the ground and avoid the mud pit, they were shaking and pulling the rope around trying to get us to fall off so that we'd have to do it all over again. I got halfway to the ground before they shook me off.

We had slept about six hours in five days and now were well into So Solly day, the last day of Hell Week. There were no men left who wanted to quit, or who would quit easily. We ran up and down Suribachi like it was nothing more than a bump on a log; we didn't even know that it was there. We belly-crawled through the mud while artillery simulators blasted in our ears. We crawled through every water-filled ditch and culvert on the base and across and through the infamous Mud Flats. Mud Flats was covered with six-foot-high johnsongrass and smelled worse than we did, like a badly clogged sewer—but deep in that six-foot-high grass was hiding a prize of great value. Ensign Bailey had sent one of his team, Bud Thrift, to requisition a whole case of cold beer that they shared with us. We didn't finish first, but I believe that those beers, and the memory of those beers, made it worth coming in second just that one time.

With the beer gone, we dragged ourselves out of the grass and a hundred yards down through the sand to the barbed wire. There we were handed some C-rats and told to eat as we crawled under the rows of wire stretched fifteen inches off the ground. That sounds easy, and it could have been if our wonderful instructors had forgotten to set off all of the artillery simulators, half-pound blocks of TNT, they had buried in the sand.

Next came some low-altitude aerial maneuvers. We marched down the beach to two towers with ropes stretched between them. Unlike the slide for life, we would be rope walking from one platform to another. The bottom rope was for your feet, and the other, a couple of feet above your head, you held on to for dear life because below the ropes there was a deep pit full of muddy water. This looked like it was going to be easy until we noticed that there was a third rope that had one end tied to the bottom rope and the other end to the bumper of the instructors' jeep. Most of the class made it halfway across before the bucking bottom rope, being pulled by the jeep, threw them into the muck. It wasn't a long fall at all, but I was pissed that the instructors were laughing so hard that they might have been crying as I fell into that crap. I swam my way out of the hole, and Instructor Blais waved me over to where he was standing at the edge of the pit. The bastard was smiling and saying something. It took me a couple of seconds to get the mud and water out of my ears as he reached down and grabbed my arm, then said one of the sweetest, shortest sentences I ever heard, "Hell Week's over, Keith." I almost could have kissed him, but UDT men don't kiss other UDT men, and now it looked like I was going to be a member of the UDT.

Seventy men started Hell Week, and forty-four finished. We lost another ten before graduation in January of 1964. Ensign Larry Bailey, our class leader, was selected as the honor graduate of Class 30 by our instructors. These thirty-four men had done what we had set out to do, but making it through Hell Week was just the first step down a long, long road.

With Hell Week behind us, the survivors were ready to learn all the advanced skills that would turn us into members of the dangerous, nasty navy UDT. After Hell Week, no matter how tough it might be, any training the navy could throw at us was going to be a cakewalk. All we had to look forward to was three weeks of weapons training at Camp Pickett in Virginia, a couple of months of seven-mile island-to-island swims and demolitions training at the naval base in Puerto Rico, and six weeks in Key West, Florida, for underwater swim school using open-circuit, closed-circuit, and mixed gas rigs. Once we got out of the water, we would spend three boring weeks throwing ourselves out of perfectly operating aircraft at army jump school at Fort Benning, Georgia. It was not a cakewalk, but the thirty-four survivors of UDT replacement training would be ready for graduation on January 4, 1964.

Vice Admiral L. M. Mustin, COMPHIBLANT, was the honored guest speaker at graduation, but in my book the speaker who had earned the honor was one of the men who had gone through UDT training and survived Hell Week with the thirty-four other men graduating that day, Class 30 honor student Ensign Larry Bailey. With the graduation being held at Little Creek, it wasn't too difficult for my mother and father to be there to congratulate me for doing what I had set out to do. That day, and the pride that my parents showed, has always been one of the memories that will never fade until someone is playing taps over my grave. I was now a member of UDT 21 with two weeks of leave before I was to report for duty and deployment.

My two weeks of leave were spent trying to eat enough steaks to gain back the weight that I had lost during Hell Week and chasing those soft, lovely, curvaceous things that make life worth living. I had a wonderful time, but the fourteen days were gone much too fast. I reported for duty for the first of two six-month tours in the Mediterranean, the first aboard an APD high-speed transport and the second aboard a converted destroyer escort. My first experience in battle was in 1965 during the invasion of the Dominican Republic. I had accomplished my goal of becoming a UDT man and had tasted battle, but there was a new group of secretive operators who were looking for trained UDT men. As more and more information filtered down through the teams, I realized that I had a new goal. I was going to become a SEAL.

The war in Vietnam was starting to heat up, and UDTs and SEAL Team 1 from the West Coast had already started deploying. It wouldn't be long before SEAL Team 2 from Little Creek, Virginia, would be sending platoons over to strengthen the navy's ability to wage a strategic guerrilla war in the riverine environment that encompassed most of Vietnam. SEAL

Team 2 had three fourteen-man platoons rotating to Vietnam on six-month deployments. They were looking for volunteers from UDT, and I was lucky again. I volunteered and was transferred to SEAL Team 2. In six months I had completed BUD/S (Basic Underwater Demolition/SEAL) training. In January 1968, I reported to SEAL Team 2 for duty and was assigned to the 10th Platoon. Our fourteen-man platoon was made up of two seven-man squads, six enlisted men and one officer in each squad. Our platoon chief was SEAL Team 2 Command Master Chief Rudy Boesch, our officer in charge (OIC) was Lieutenant AL Quist, and Warrant Officer Dale McCleskey was our assistant officer in charge (AOIC). We were officially a platoon, but we weren't ready for Vietnam just yet. There were a few more things that we needed to learn about guerrilla warfare, and some things to work through together as a team.

4

Gearing Up

One of the most important lessons that every SEAL learns early in his career is that SEALs depend on ourselves first, second, and usually last. Forming up a new platoon for our first deployment to Vietnam wasn't just an exercise in finding the right number of men to fill out the team, signing off on the paperwork, and gearing up. Master Chief Rudy Boesch had earned his rank; he was a master at getting the best of the best. From weapons to the men who would use them, Rudy could scrounge like nobody else in the SEAL Teams. He wasn't going to let anything or anybody get in the way of putting together the best platoon he could build, beg, borrow, coerce, or dig out of the Operations Department.

Rudy found us two SEALs who had already completed one tour of duty and convinced them that they would be a great asset to the 10th Platoon. There was no question that Pierre Birtz and Jim Finley had skills that would be very important to the platoon. In addition to their combat experience, Pierre spoke French, the second language of Vietnam, and Jim spoke Vietnamese. Communicating anywhere in-country would be a lot easier, and, as we learned later, would allow us to listen in on conversations between captured VC who didn't know that we had two people who could understand every word they said. An added bonus was that Jim had been based in My Tho, the city where our platoon would be relieving the platoon that had been stationed there for the past six months. That meant that we would know where to find the best food and drinks and, more importantly, where we could evade the MPs when we were sneaking back to the base after a cordial evening out with the ever-present bar girls, who made us forget that there was a curfew.

At this point in time, SEAL Team 2 had three platoons operating in Vietnam and several advisers running PRU teams of up to eighty men. These Provisional Reconnaissance Units were made up of hardcore Vietnamese commandos who were experienced, tough-as-nails fighters. It was time for the PRU advisers to rotate out for three months of training before rotating back; the 10th Platoon would be their replacements. The SOP was that platoons would be replaced every six months on a staggered calendar. Most of the time, the men rotating back would be transferred to a platoon just starting their three-month predeployment training. This way there were almost always experienced SEALs who could add their direct experience to the knowledge base of the entire team before returning to Vietnam with new platoons. There was no question that as long as you were fit for duty you would continue to deploy to Vietnam until the end of the war. All of us would deploy for six months, return to the United States for three months of training, then redeploy unless we were killed, severely wounded in action, or transferred out of the teams.

Before we could deploy, we would spend a week at the E&E (escape and evasion) course held in the wilderness near the Canadian border just outside of Brunswick, Maine. Because SEALs were deemed to be high-value and high-risk captures, we were all required to take the course. After a week surviving and evading capture in the wilds of Maine, we headed to the Panama Canal Zone for three weeks of the U.S. Army Jungle Warfare School at Fort Sherman on the Atlantic end of the canal. The army was accommodating and clearly understood that SEALs are clandestine, unconventional warriors who just don't fit into a regimented mold. We concentrated our training on river crossings, camouflage, navigation, and living in the jungle. The highlight of this training was when we were asked to be the opposition force against the army platoons going through the course. This allowed us to work together to plan and set up ambushes, and we were encouraged to attack base camps, combat and recon patrols, and anything else that we could dream up. We were really having fun pissing off the poor ground-pounders who just didn't have any experience or skill at counteracting the guerrilla tactics we employed against them. More important, we were becoming a team. Our next stop was back at our home base in Little Creek to clean ourselves up. Then we moved along to Union Camp, North Carolina, for training in riverine operations. We learned how to insert and extract from moving boats and tried to see if our beer consumption could equal the amount of water we sucked down while the boats were dragging us up and down the river. Our last stop would be either Camp Pickett or Fort A. P. Hill in Virginia for a few weeks of advanced small-arms training.

Twelve hours a day, for fourteen days, we honed our skills and became experts with pistols, rifles, shotguns, 40 mm grenade launchers, flares, and grenades; then the heavy weapons: .50 caliber machine guns, 57 mm recoilless rifles, and 60 mm mortars; and last, but far from least, the LAAW (light antiarmor weapon) rockets. Tons of ammunition and explosives were expended, and a very good time was had by every member of the platoon. Then it was time to get back to Little Creek for ten days to begin our load out for deployment to Vietnam.

No matter how you try to forget it or block it from your mind, it is like the eight-hundred-pound gorilla sitting in the corner: There's a good chance that a few of the men, who are now closer to you than most brothers, may not be coming home, and you might not be coming home, either. We all took time to say our long good-bye to wives, girlfriends, and families. We were the best-trained, toughest, and most dedicated fighting men in the history of warfare, but even the toughest of us knew that we were not bulletproof. We might never have the chance to say good-bye again.

With our families, wives, and sweethearts waving to us, we were finally ready for departure. We convoyed our way to Norfolk Naval Air Station and boarded a naval version of the 727 that would fly us across the United States to Coronado, California. For three intense days we were in almost constant meetings with either SEAL Team 1 or Naval Special Warfare Group 1. Their experience in Vietnam would prove to be invaluable, and even though there was some competition between the East Coast and West Coast teams, we were accepted and treated as brother SEALs. There was much to learn and not a lot of time to learn it, but when darkness fell our indoctrination became even more intense. In only three long nights, SEAL Team 1 made sure that we were well indoctrinated in the most interesting nightlife of Coronado, the Miracle Strip, and Tijuana.

At the Coronado Naval Air Station, we said good-bye to newfound girlfriends and wives— I can't prove it, but I'm sure that at least a few of the lovelies that had helped us survive the long nights of tough training were other men's wives. After a final round of kisses, tearful hugs, and lingering good-byes we boarded a four-engine navy cargo plane and headed for our next stop on our way to war, Midway Island. Our layover at Midway was for only one night, so the small local clubs tried their best to take what little cash was left in our pockets after Coronado and Tijuana as quickly as possible. We obliged them as best we could. Early the following morning we headed for Wake Island, another stop on what seemed like an endless journey to Vietnam. After yet another long, enjoyable night of toasting everything we could think of at the base club, we were finally on the last leg of our trip. Bored and listening to the constant drone of the engines, I looked out the window. It seemed to me that one propeller was turning very slowly on the port side of the aircraft. Checking the starboard side, it seemed there was a problem there, too—only one prop was turning at full speed. I figured that I should tell one of the crewmen, and he looked at me like I was a real newbie. It seemed that the navy, to save fuel, had decided to use only two of the engines. I guessed that only SEALs would have been in a hurry to get to Vietnam, and were the only passengers pissed off that it was going to be such a long, slow trip.

The thump of the wheels locking down woke me up just in time to see the coastline of Vietnam pass under the starboard wing; we were already on approach to Saigon and Tan Son Nhut Air Base. As far as I could see, there was nothing but bomb craters; I couldn't see even a small patch of jungle terrain. From the air it reminded me of the photographs I had seen of the surface of the moon, desolate and devoid of anything green or growing. The landing was smooth, and as the aircraft taxied up to a hangar I could see the 7th Platoon waiting to welcome us. We were relieving them, and they would be flying out the next day on the same cargo plane that we had flown in on. We off-loaded our gear, and they loaded theirs. Our gear went onto the 6-by-6 truck that they had just unloaded, and two of their guys volunteered to guard our gear while the rest of the platoon gave us a one-night indoctrination into the wild and wonderful ways of Saigon.

With all of our personal gear and two platoons loaded onto a 4-by-4 and a jeep, we made our way into Saigon and checked in for one night at the President, a beautiful hotel built by the French. After checking in, muster was held on the seventeenth floor, and I learned how wondrous a place the President was. The entire seventeenth floor was an enormous bar, with at least a hundred tables. There was a large dance floor, and on the raised stage there was a band playing Beach Boys surfer music. As our eyes adjusted to the dim candlelight, it became apparent that there were more hookers per square foot here than I had ever seen before, even in Tijuana. These beautiful young ladies of the evening were not wearing enough clothing to hide many of their extraordinary and very attractive assets. I bought myself a drink, then another, and a third while I scouted the room. The band was pretty good, the drinks were only watered down by the melting ice, and the women were lovely, but the music was too loud for my liking, so I picked out one of the most curvaceous young ladies and led her out to the wraparound balcony. Two of my friends, Bill and Jack, were already sitting outside, and we joined them. With a drink in one hand and the other engaged with the beautiful woman who was curled up on my lap and whispering in my ear about new shoes, we were like spectators watching the gladiators in the Coliseum. We were safe, sitting what seemed like a million miles away, as we watched the war on the horizon. Ms. Saigon, sitting on my lap, told me in very good English that this happened almost every night. Flares, streams of tracers, and explosions lit up the night. An uncountable number of aircraft flying without any lights were dropping ordnance out of the black sky. Even in training I had never seen anything like this. Nothing could survive the destruction falling from above. I would soon learn that in Vietnam I could never take anything at face value.

The subject of the cost of new shoes came up again, and just before midnight I decided that further negotiations should be held privately in my room. By sunup I had decided that Ms. Saigon needed two pairs of shoes, and maybe we could negotiate a dress to go with them on my next trip to Saigon. When we mustered back at the truck and jeep, we did a quick inventory. When we added it all up we had bought a couple dozen pairs of shoes, half a dozen hats, four dresses, and three miniskirts, and a good time was had by all. It was decided that returning to the President Hotel and keeping all of the young ladies well dressed was now the responsibility of the 10th Platoon. We would be back whenever we were given the chance.

As all but two of the 7th Platoon boarded the cargo plane that would start the journey back to the States and their families and friends, we exchanged handshakes and a few hugs. Lieutenant Pete Peterson and Petty Officer Mike Boynton had been operating for six months, and there was a lot that we could learn from them. Both of them had chosen to stay behind for a week to show us the ropes and get our platoon well situated in our areas of operation. Our little convoy group had grown to include a 6-by-6, a 4-by-4, and three jeeps. Our designated vehicle procurement men, Jim Finley and Jack Lynch, had come through again and we would be riding in style all the way to My Tho, a substantial city built alongside the My Tho River. This was where the 10th Platoon would be stationed for the next six months.

The sixty-mile trip to My Tho was uneventful, but far from boring. We followed a rough road that was just wide enough to allow two six-by-six trucks to squeeze by one another. Some stretches, where it passed through the small villages, were more or less paved, but soon it turned into rutted dirt, and I guessed that the entire road would be knee-deep mud when the monsoons came. As our little convoy rolled past mile after mile of rice paddies that stretched from one village to the next, the villagers and rice farmers barely looked up. We passed several military convoys headed for Saigon. They waved as we passed and stared curiously at Americans who were not wearing uniforms but who were all armed to the teeth.

The small villages obviously eked out a living by planting and harvesting rice. In the fields, water buffalo pulled ancient wooden plows, and the women planted, weeded, or sorted the chaff from the grain the same way that their great-great-great-great grandmothers had done it. They used a large, round woven mat to throw the rice and chaff gently into the air. The breeze would blow the lighter chaff away, allowing the heavier grains of rice to fall back onto the mat until all the chaff was gone and only rice remained. Then the women would store the rice; some would be sold, but most of the crop would be used to feed their own families. It was almost a pastoral setting, but these Vietnamese farmers were tough people. They had survived constant warfare for over a century. As I thought about the history of Vietnam, I wondered how many of these men and women planted rice all day and joined the VC after darkness fell.

The countryside was primitive and pastoral, but My Tho was a different story. The rivers, streams, and canals of Vietnam are the transportation network of the entire country. The only place where you find roads is where no water transport is possible or where the quantity of material to be transported required a road to be built. Sitting right on the My Tho River, My Tho was both a trading and transshipment hub and a regional city where just about anything you desired could be found, bought, or sold. The streets were crammed with men, women, and children. The putt-putt and whine of scooters, mopeds, and motorcycles blended into the honking of horns and the aggressive hawking of the street vendors. My first priority after we had settled into our new quarters would be a recon in force with the rest of the platoon to discover what recreational pleasures My Tho might have to offer.

In addition to our operational responsibilities, the SEAL platoon and any visitors from neighboring SEAL units had been assigned as the quick reaction force for the entire base. We were not ground-pounders or support and supply troops; if and when the shit hit the fan, we would be first in the line of fire. This was not a responsibility that we took lightly. My Tho might look like a peaceful, easygoing, prosperous city, but SEALs had fought and died in other cities across Vietnam during what was supposed to be a cease-fire. The Vietcong had launched a countrywide guerrilla attack during the Tet holiday, and they had their ass handed to them on a plate. Because our troops were able to respond almost instantly, they held their ground, turned the tide of battle, and killed thousands of VC, but the price of victory had been high. To be always ready to fight and destroy the VC, our small PBR (patrol boat riverine) base was just a few blocks from My Tho and only fifty feet from the Quonset hut that was a secure, multifunctional space for the platoon.

The Quonset hut, actually a big dome of corrugated sheet metal, housed the shower where we cleaned the camouflage paint, sweat, and sometimes blood from our uniforms and ourselves, and washed the mud and crud out of our weapons before we stripped them and threw them into a big tank for a more thorough cleaning. It was also where we would sometimes brief or debrief before or after an op, and it was where we stored most of our equipment and op gear. Our heavy weapons were stored in the Quonset hut, but we kept our basic load out, our personal issue weapons and ammunition, with us at what we nicknamed the "My Tho Hilton," the old French hotel where we had been assigned the entire seventh floor. In my case, either the Stoner light machine gun with several hundred rounds of linked 5.56 mm FMJ (full metal jacket) ammunition or a snub-nosed Colt Cobra revolver went with me everywhere.

The hotel was just about the perfect location for a SEAL platoon. If the VC decided to try to hit My Tho, they would find us well armed and with a commanding field of fire from the seventh floor. If the shit was hitting the fan someplace else, it would take our platoon less than ten minutes to get out of the hotel and be loaded, locked, and aboard either our STAB (SEAL tactical assault boat) or the converted Mike-8 boat (a twin-engine landing craft reconfigured for use on the river) and moving out under power. Across the street from the My Tho Hilton was a navy mess hall where the food was good, hot, and plentiful, so we never missed a meal, and with seven rooms, a rec room, and access to the flat roof we were really well situated. Briefings were usually held in the rec room, and each morning we would hold quarters for muster and do an hour or so of PT on the roof. There were many other sights and pleasures offered by My Tho that I was looking forward to experiencing, and the sooner the better, but first we would start the briefings that would help us stay alive in our ops area. I was sharing one of the comfortable rooms with Big Al Ashton and Mike Boynton. At six feet and change and 220 solid pounds, Big Al had earned his nickname.

It didn't take long for us to settle into our rooms, and by 1700 hours

Lieutenant Pete Peterson and Mike Boynton had completed our first detailed briefing, describing our area of operations, telling us what we could expect based on their experience of the past six months, and outlining how navy men were expected to comport themselves in My Tho. Then we were ready to head toward the center of the small city for a few beers and a taste of the nightlife. I decided that carrying my Stoner and several belts of ammo might put a damper on my evening, so I just stuck the Colt in my pocket and headed downstairs to meet Big Al and Jim Finley. If there was anyone who could get me squared away and introduce me to the right people in the right places in My Tho, it was Jim. Jim was so well respected and popular that he had earned the title "the mayor of My Tho."

All cleaned up and wearing my best outfit, in fact my only outfit, I was ready to start my indoctrination. I was wearing the same clothing that I would wear when operating in the bush, on the boats, or in the water—green Levi's, tiger-striped long-sleeved shirt, and boonie boots. I decided to lose the green and black face paint and green triangle bandage that usually covered my blond hair. That night I didn't want to scare the natives.

It took only two stops at two bars before the platoon had shrunk to just Big Al, Jim, and me. Jim steered us toward one of the better-appointed establishments, the Tan Van Bar and Restaurant. Unlike the hole-in-the-wall joints where we had lost the rest of the platoon, the Tan Van was verging on impressive. There was a pair of Old West–style swinging doors that opened onto a dark, cool bar area where several river rats—brown-water navy guys—were satisfying their well-deserved thirst and working themselves into a state of readiness that would require some lengthy negotiations about the cost of shoes with at least a few of the gaggle of lovely bar-girls. In the bar area there were a half dozen or so tables nicely covered with white tablecloths; each table had a small bouquet of flowers, and dinner cutlery had been placed on the red-and-white-checkered napkin in front of each chair. On my left the Tan Van had only a half-wall that allowed the light to filter in from the small side street. Outside of the half-wall but still under cover of the overhanging roof were five small tables where you could get away from the hustle and bustle of the bar and enjoy your dinner while still being able to appreciate the nonstop ebb and flow of navy personnel, bar-girls, and the waitresses and chefs who served what turned out to be excellent French and Vietnamese food. I couldn't help noticing that there was an incredibly beautiful woman almost hidden in the darkest area of the restaurant. She was dressed in a blue silk sheath dress with a slit that flowed from the floor and exposed most of her left hip. Her black hair had been coiled like several intertwined snakes and was balanced on the top of her head. Her arms were bare, and the only jewelry visible was a silver bracelet and a pair of long silver earrings. As I stared at her like I had never seen a beautiful woman before, she waved. I was hoping that she had noticed me staring at her, but no such luck. She was waving at Jim, the unofficial mayor of My Tho. Jim waved back, and the woman started to glide across the floor to where we were standing. As she floated across the room, she stopped at several tables to make sure that her regular customers were being well cared for.

If I remember it right, Jim introduced us and told me that My Lee owned the Tan Van. After a couple of beers he found that his attention was needed on the other side of the room. My Lee was the daughter of a French father and a Chinese mother, and she was fluent in English, French, and Vietnamese plus she spoke a little Chinese as well. The evening was gone before I noticed it; curfew was coming, and Jim and I needed to round up the rest of the platoon and get back to the My Tho Hilton. As My Lee walked us to the door, I asked if she would join me for dinner when I could make it back to the Tan Van. She accepted, and before I could get any better ideas Jim dragged me through the swinging doors and down the street. This had been one great way to start my first tour. Little did I know how important My Lee would become as our friendship grew.

There was no rest for the weary. Reveille was at 0630 the next morning, followed by quarters and PT at 0700 on the roof. Then a shower, breakfast, and muster at 1000 in our rec room, where Lieutenant Quist gave us our warning orders. Warning orders gave us a handle on the op scheduled for that night, who would be doing what, and what we would need to take with us to accomplish the mission. At 1700 hours we assembled in the Quonset hut for a final detailed pre-op briefing. If anything had changed, this was our last chance to hear about it. At the end of the briefing we had our individual assignments, patrol order of march, primary and secondary insertion and extraction points, E&E plan, objective, and actions on objective. When everyone was clear and every possible detail had been covered, we geared up, checked weapons, and walked over to the helo pad. At 2000 hours Alpha and Bravo squads of the 10th Platoon started climbing into two army Slicks (UH-1 "Hueys"). Mike Boynton and Mingh, our combat interpreter, would be going out with us. We were as prepared as we could be for anything that would come our way.

5

First Op

As our insertion choppers carried us to the LZ (landing zone) two klicks (kilometers) from the Mekong River, I scanned the jungle canopy passing below us. We were flying fast and low, moving too fast to become an easy target for the VC. Unseen, hidden in the dense bush under the triple-canopy jungle, there could be a division of NVA (North Vietnamese Army) regulars waiting for a target. Nobody was relaxing or thinking that we were safe from enemy fire.

The SEAL Teams had been running operations in Vietnam for less than a year, but we had already learned important lessons and had lost some good men. As the jungle flew past and the helo crew raced us to our insertion point, I couldn't stop thinking about Clarence "Ted" Risher. Like me, Risher was a young SEAL and Stoner operator who was fresh to Vietnam and ready to prove himself in combat. He was under the command of Dick Marcinko during the Tet cease-fire festivities in Chau Doc.

Even in the SEAL Teams Dick Marcinko gave new meaning to the expression "hard charger." His eleven-man team was being extracted from an ambush operation under enemy fire by a pair of PBR boats when word came down that Chau Doc was under heavy attack and getting hammered; the city might be overrun. Dick asked the chief who was in command of the PBRs for a ride, and long before first light the PBRs arrived at the besieged city. With no intimate knowledge of the layout of the city, no good intel, and no situation report, there was nothing to do but wait for first light. The eleven SEALs and the PBR crew sat, shivered in the darkness, listened to the gunfire, swatted mosquitoes, and waited for sunrise to reveal the damage and destruction.

Chau Doc was a fairly big city with well-maintained streets, restaurants, bars, and well-appointed private homes reminiscent of the French occupation. The VC had decided to use these buildings and rooftops as their own shooting gallery. No matter where you looked, from the edges of the ornate rooftops to the flowering gardens that separated the streets there was one or more VC or NVA pouring down fire on the ARVN (Army of the Republic of Vietnam) and American troops. Dick decided that he would start sweeping the north side of the city while other SEALs, with a few dozen Nung, Chinese mercenaries, worked the south end of the city. Before they could even get moving, though, a more pressing problem needed their attention. Word came in that an American schoolteacher and two nurses were trapped in their house, and the VC had control of the entire area. It was decided that three of the team would take a jeep with a .50 caliber machine gun mounted and go fetch the ladies. The rest of the team would start fighting street by street in the same direction. The plan was to drive the VC back, save the ladies, and maybe kill enough of the enemy to turn the tide of battle.

Dick split his team into two five-man groups so that each group could provide fire support to the other as they fought. The plan was to pick their way through the buildings and along quaint streets lined with trees, flowers, and what seemed like too many VC with AK-47s. They were taking heavy fire and improvised by returning it with LAAW rockets fired into the buildings, where the VC thought they were safe. While the dust and debris from the explosion of the rocket was still gushing out of the building, Dick would kick the door in and finish any VC still alive. If the VC tried running out of another door when they saw the LAAW launch, Ted Risher would cut them to pieces with his Stoner. As the VC wised up and figured out that a rocket exploding in a closed space wasn't good for their health, they moved out of the confined spaces and up to the rooftops.

After they'd cleared several buildings and three streets and killed too many VC to count, the sound of AK-47 fire had diminished. It seemed that there were at most only fifty VC left in Chau Doc, and the decision was made to keep pushing, to clear as much of the city as possible. To take advantage of all the cover they could find, the teams leapfrogged from doorway to doorway, covering each other's backs, taking out any VC that stuck up their heads to try to get a round off. Anyone who detected noise or movement inside the buildings threw in a grenade, waited for the explosion, then kicked the door open and sprayed the room down with an M-16.

Progress in rooting out the remaining VC had been slow and steady, but the VC were dying and yielding ground. They knew that they were whipped, but someone forgot to tell a couple of VC on a rooftop at the other end of the block. Just when they thought that they had established superior fire control, the team started taking heavy fire. Everyone but Ted Risher dove for cover. Standing tall in the middle of the street, bullets smacking into the dust around his feet and whining away into the distance, Risher kept firing his Stoner on full automatic, trying to sweep the rooftops of Chau Doc free of the VC.

The way I heard the story, Risher was smiling a crazy grin and screaming as the Stoner cut the rooftops to pieces. Dick screamed for the kid to get off the street, to get under cover. Maybe he couldn't hear Dick over the muzzle blast of the Stoner, or maybe he was just dumping every round in the ammo belt before he ran for safety; we will never know. Ted Risher never moved. The Stoner must have run dry, because there was a split second of silence followed by the pop of a gunshot. Risher was killed by a single round through the head.

It didn't make any sense to me. I kept asking myself what really killed him? Did he run out of luck, have too much guts for his own good, or was his death due to an overdose of stupid? Bravery is a good thing, a necessity to any man who is going into battle, but reckless bravery can get you and your team killed. Even though they saved the schoolteacher and nurses, the cost had been high. Dead soldiers can not be brave—or fight. It is one of those questions that has no answer, and I had more important, immediate questions that I hoped would get answered tonight on the banks of the Mekong River.

For the third time I checked my load out. My Stoner light machine gun carried a drum magazine that holds 150 rounds of linked 5.56 mm ammo; there were four more bandoleers strung across my chest and back. When I fired the Stoner on full auto, I could turn the jungle and everything hiding in the bush into a chopped and diced green salad in only a few seconds. Hanging across my back, where it wouldn't get in my way but was easy to get into action, was a 66 mm LAAW rocket, a weapon I would come to rely on when the odds were against us. On my web belt and harness I had attached two fragmentation and two concussion grenades. In addition to my primary weapons I also carried an M-18A1 claymore mine, a red star para flare, two white star para flares, a green star cluster para flare, first aid kit, canteen, compass, poncho liner, flashlight, my booby-trap kit, and my Ka-Bar knife. A good knife was always handy for cutting vines, rope, or netting, for digging a shallow pit where I could brace my feet on a steep incline, or for opening ammunition cases and C-rats. Going out into the bush, my gear and ammo would be almost half my body weight. After a hot firefight, with the ammo, claymore, grenades, and LAAW rocket expended, the weight was reduced to almost nothing.

6

First Blood

The Slicks dropped like rocks into a small clearing, and we cleared the rotor wash almost before the skids had stopped moving. Our weapons were loaded and locked, and we were ready to fight when we hit the ground. Our insertion was fast, and the helos were gone in seconds. As soon as we hit the ground, each of us moved into the bush to take a defensive position on the perimeter of the clearing. Fourteen sets of eyes scanned every inch of the dense bush and listened for anything that would tell us that we were not alone. The VC knew that any clearing in the jungle where the rotor blades wouldn't hit anything could be used as an LZ. Charlie had a widespread network of intel that seemed to have eyes and ears just about everywhere. We were at our most vulnerable at insertion and extraction, so the VC would frequently set up an ambush on the best landing sites if they had any intel that there might be a chopper inserting troops in the area. We were only two klicks from our ambush point and needed to get there and set up our ambush while there was still some light, but the first order of business was making sure that we hadn't been seen, that nobody was hunting us.

When the perimeter had been secured and we were sure that there were no VC waiting for us, Lieutenant Quist, using hand signals, got us up and moving through the bush toward our ambush point. Two klicks isn't a long hump, but we would be moving carefully, cautiously, and slowly as we looked for trip wires and punji pits. It would be over two hours before we reached our ambush positions on the canal.

Long before then, we could hear the lapping of water and the chattering of birds in the trees. The sound of the birds told us that they had not been disturbed, that we were alone in the jungle. Still, we moved like jungle mist up the bank of the canal. In our full camouflage, with green-painted faces and all our gear secured and silent, we didn't bother them as they preened, dried their feathers, or dove from branches to snatch an occasional fish from the brown water.

The last few slanting rays of the sun that penetrated the dense bush threw soft-edged shadows of the leaves and branches almost horizontally across the jungle floor. With moonrise still hours away, darkness would come quickly, and soon. Invisible in the approaching darkness and shadows of the jungle canopy that covers the banks of the Mekong River, fourteen men of the 10th Platoon of SEAL Team 2 slithered through the jungle and slipped silently into our ambush positions. Each man had chosen his own uniform. Tiger-stripe camo, fatigues, jeans, sneakers, tire tread sandals, boonie hats, or an occasional beret were common in the bush. I usually covered my blond hair with an OD (olive drab) green triangle bandage that almost matched the green camouflage paint covering my face.

Daylight was our enemy, darkness was our friend; we moved into our ambush positions like green-faced ghosts. The battle-hardened VC we had come to kill or capture would see nothing but shadows, would hear nothing but the rustling of the bush moving in the breeze that flowed slowly down the channel of the Mekong River. Until we sprang our ambush, nothing but our eyes would move.

Fresh intelligence collected from three different sources told us that there would be one or more heavily loaded sampans carrying weapons, munitions, food, and other supplies moving down the Mekong tonight. If the intel was good and the VC hadn't changed their route in the past twenty-four hours, they would come under our guns long before daybreak.

The SEAL Teams were always operating in new terrain; very rarely, and only when it gave us the advantage of total surprise, did we hit the same target twice. As a small-unit force, we depended on a force multiplier—in our case, complete surprise, overwhelming firepower, and tactical superiority—to give us the edge that allowed us to defeat much larger forces. This really pissed off the VC, and they were not going to just let us run our operations with impunity. The most dangerous part of an ambush is the risk that you will be the one who is ambushed. It wasn't difficult for the VC to let some intel leak to our intel sources that there would be sampans running through a specific area on a specific night. The VC knew that it was very likely that someone would be trying to take those sampans out, and it would probably be the men with the green faces. All the VC needed to do was to place a numerically superior force in a large semicircle, like a bag with one end open, around the area where they expected the SEALs to show up. Then they could just wait, allow us to infiltrate the area, and close the open end of the bag. They would have us inside the sack, surrounded, and we would have to fight our way out against a much larger force. This might have worked on some green or poorly trained troops, but not there and not then.

Sampans are simple shallow-draft vessels that are handmade of wood and bamboo by local people; they are as common in Vietnam as pickup trucks in the States. Sampans, though, can haul a lot more cargo than any pickup; they are more like eighteen-wheel trucks in most of Southeast Asia. Anything that could be crammed into or piled onto them could be floated up or down the many rivers, canals, and deltas that crisscrossed Vietnam. The VC and NVA used sampans to move men, weapons, and supplies to distribution points where they could stash them in tunnels or caches until they needed them. If the intel was as good as we hoped it was, we were going to capture or destroy the sampans and make sure that they never made another delivery. Those of us on our first op had been told that it was always a priority to try to capture as many of the crew alive and capable of being interrogated as possible before we placed our C-4 and destroyed the sampans and their cargo. This was easier said than done; the VC were tough and rarely surrendered without a fight, but gathering intel was possibly the most important aspect of our ops.

SEALs are not like any other forces on earth. We never fought a pitched battle if we could avoid it. Our primary mission was to get intel that could be sent up the chain of command so that the army and marines could plan their offensive or defensive actions, the big battles that the war planners thought would win the war. When we captured intel about troop concentrations, it was sent up the chain of command and may have been used by the air force to plan bombing campaigns. Our secondary mission was to interdict and destroy VC and NVA infrastructure, munitions, and material. All of our ops were guerrilla ops, a small force inflicting the highest possible damage, grabbing up people and intel, and getting out before the VC or NVA could surround us and take us out.

When the ambush area and any prisoners were secured, we would search the sampans, the prisoners, and the bodies looking for paperwork, orders, maps, or manifests. If we were lucky, we would capture at least some of the crew alive. Live prisoners were one of the best sources of fresh intel we could find. Of course, intel gathered from captured VC could just as easily be disinformation that had been purposefully planted to run us around in circles or lead us away from their real area of operation or into an ambush. We never trusted what they told us. Trusting even the best intel could turn what should be a well-planned and well-executed ambush or VC body snatch into the worst kind of nightmare. No matter how good we thought the intel was, we never took anything for granted; we could never afford to lower our guard for even a split second. Our eyes, ears, noses, and that sixth sense that sometimes tells you more than all of the other senses put together were always on full alert even after we had confirmed our intel through other sources.

Any mission, no matter how well you think you know the terrain and the territory, or how much air or artillery support you think you have, can get you killed. There are many ways to die in combat. Even before the first shot is fired you can buy the farm. Your chopper can be shot down or crash at insertion, your parachute can fail to open, your rebreather hiccups, spewing caustic liquid into your mouth thirty feet underwater, or that little lump of what looks like dead leaves turns out to be a land mine or an unexploded 155 mm artillery round that has been booby-trapped. Get even a little bit lazy or start believing that Lady Luck is on your side and, sooner or later, you're going to get your ticket punched.

As I learned later, even the most boring missions, when we hunted the bush for days, feeding the leeches and mosquitoes with our blood and never making contact with the enemy, were dangerous; maybe the most dangerous. Several dry missions in a row could dull the edge that we needed to stay alive when the intel was good and the air was full of shrapnel, bullets, and exploding grenades or satchel charges. The VC had been fighting a guerrilla war long before most of us were born; they had been fighting and ambushing their enemies in this jungle for decades. It would be my first combat operation, my first face-to-face meeting with some of the best guerrilla fighters in the world, and they would want to kill me.

Even there in the jungle I could still hear the droning thrum of the engines and smell the mixture of sweat and oil that permeated the C-117 that had carried me across the Pacific and finally touched down at Tan Son Nhut Air Base. Although I had been in-country for only two days, in some strange way I felt at home in the bush. The grip of the Stoner light machine gun was more than some small comfort. Running on full auto the Stoner is pure hellfire. In a firefight I wanted to be the guy with the biggest, nastiest weapons. One of the many lessons I had learned in studying military history is that the man with the most firepower almost always wins the fight, the battle, and the war. The Stoner gave me that advantage, but it had a couple of drawbacks. The first was that if you didn't practice good fire control, the Stoner would burn through a lot of ammunition. In only a few minutes you could find yourself out of ammo and in deep shit. This meant that you had to hump a lot of ammo up and down hills, through the jungle and swamps, wherever you needed to go to find the VC. Sooner or later the weight of all that ammo was going to slow you down, degrading your ability to fight effectively. On the other hand, when we were outnumbered and fighting our way out of a mess, my Stoner could instantly throw up a wall of FMJ bullets in a heartbeat, shredding the jungle and anyone hunting us. I practiced good fire control, carried as much ammunition as I could, and ignored the weight.

The second negative was that, like the M-60 machine gun, the Stoner was a bullet magnet. As soon as I started laying down a field of fire, the enemy instantly reacted, trying to silence the most powerful, deadliest weapons first. The Stoner and M-60 machine gun operators attracted enemy fire like tall trees attract lightning. Someone told me that in battle the VC concentrated so much fire on the machine gunners that their life expectancy was measured in seconds. That first night in the jungle, I hoped that they were wrong. I would know soon. If I screwed up I would probably be going home in a body bag, and my mistake might take some of these men with me.

Then with almost everyone settled into his ambush position, four of us left our weapons and in teams of two, again moved silently through the shadows thrown by the dense bush. It was our job to set up the claymore mines that would protect our flanks and escape route to the rear.

Positioning a claymore securely is a two-man job that requires four hands. One man positions the claymore, a few feet off of the ground if possible; the second stands guard and checks position and the aiming point. The hundred-foot length of firing wire that attaches the claymore to the clacker and detonator is also well secured. To ensure that the claymores will not be detected, the line is hidden, snaked through the bush, over and under whatever camouflage is available, or buried under the loose dirt, rocks, and fallen leaves found on the jungle floor.

With the claymores in position and the clackers that would fire them under the control of Lieutenant Quist, our ambush site was secure. We had positioned ourselves in the jungle, only a few feet above the mud-brown water of the canal. Like camouflaged statues hidden in the bush, the team was ready, patient.

Under cover of the bush, it was as dark as the inside of the deepest coal mine. Only the reflection of shimmering starlight rippled across the water; little light penetrated the jungle. Soon the three-quarter moon would rise above the horizon. As the moon rose higher, light would leak down through the leaves and our visibility would improve. Anything that moved within a hundred yards of our ambush site would be spotted by one or more of fourteen sets of eyes. The VC manning the sampans would see nothing until the muzzle flash of our weapons and the exploding grenades or claymore mines initiated the ambush.

So that we could focus on the sampans and the river, and not need to cover our flanks and rear, Lieutenant Quist would fire the claymores to initiate the ambush. The claymores had been placed so that they would shred any VC within fifty yards of our right and left flanks. The claymore to our rear would protect the team by clearing away anyone foolish enough to try to sneak in the back door. Lieutenant Quist would blow it just before we withdrew.

The grip of the Stoner filled my hand as naturally as did all of the guns I have used since childhood. When I was twelve years old, my father started teaching me to shoot. Through familiarity and constant practice with rifles, shotguns, revolvers, and automatic pistols, I became an instinctive shooter. The guns I carried on my forays into the woods and wild places almost seemed to aim and fire themselves. By the time I was seventeen, I had become a deadly shot with them all. The Stoner was no exception.

My father taught me the basics of shooting and the importance of keeping my weapons clean and well maintained; he also instilled in me the love of wild places and the desire to master firearms. As I grew older and wandered farther and farther from home, I learned more and more about firearms and used every weapon I could get my hands on. My father's training and my constant practice taught me how to use firearms, but it was the wild lands and the animals I stalked that taught me to be a hunter.

It was from the animals that I learned how to see what was invisible to men who had never challenged themselves in the wilds. Through hard-won experience, hunters learn that climbing high or crawling low will let you see above or below the trees and brush. Leaves turned belly up when all others are belly down signal the passage of an animal. A broken branch with still-wet sap in the break told me the height of the animal that had passed only a few minutes ago and the direction of his travel. Muddy water at the edge of a clear pool told me that an animal had very recently stopped for a drink; the tracks at the edge of the water told me what kind of animal had drunk. The wilderness and animals had taught me more than I had imagined.

Even as a child when I wandered the swamps, forests, and fields, I always had a weapon in my hands or at my side. Rifles, shotguns, pistols, revolvers, bows and arrows, knives, even blowguns, all put food on the family table and taught me the most important skill of a hunter: one shot, one kill. Now, as a member of a SEAL Team, I had become a hunter of men.

I spent most of my youth in the wilds of Tennessee and North Carolina, along the banks of the Mississippi, and in the Atlas Mountains of North Africa. I was only truly at home in the wild places. I hunted, trapped, and camped alone on the trail and learned what most of those not so lucky would never know. I knew, almost instinctively, how to blend into my surroundings, the difference between concealment and cover. There were hundreds of seemingly small things that my father and the wilderness taught me. Before the sun would rise, I would know if I had learned enough to survive, to be a brother SEAL.

Our intel told us that before daybreak there would be one or more sampans loaded to the gunwales with weapons, ammunition, and other supplies coming into the area. The sampans would pole their way up the river, hide during the daylight on one of the many canals, then move back to the river to deliver their load of weapons, munitions, and material somewhere along the Mekong River under the cover of darkness. I had been told to keep a close eye on the Chieu Hoi who was our guide on this operation. Normally our Vietnamese interpreter, Mingh, went out on every operation, but tonight we were led by one of the Chieu Hoi, a captured VC who had decided to join us and fight against the Communist forces. He had replaced Mingh because he knew the area well, and this mission would be the test of his loyalty. As our local guide, he had done an excellent job. He had brought us this far undetected and had shown us where the VC sampans would hide until nightfall.

The moon was now high in the night sky. After hours in almost total darkness, the pupils of my eyes had become completely dilated. With the bright moon above, and my eyes taking in every bit of light, the visibility was better than I expected it to be. As we watched the water and jungle, small, scattered clouds moved across the moon, throwing shadows that added to our invisibility. All of us were constantly sweeping our eyes across the river and jungle, but it was our ears that detected the sampans long before they were within our planned field of fire.

For half an hour before the sampans reached our position, we could hear the tinny sound of music playing from a transistor radio, and the hollow banging of their long poles against the sides of the sampans as they pushed their way up the river. The sampans were smaller than I thought they would be, not more than twelve or fourteen feet long. One VC sat in the bow with a weapon, and one stood aft, pushing the shallow-draft vessel along with a bamboo pole. As I peered out from the shadows, the clouds broke and the moonlight reflecting off the water outlined the darker sampans. The moonlight was so bright that I could see the ripples from the bow of each of the sampans. Silently, using hand signals, I let Lieutenant Quist know what was coming our way.

The only thing between me and the VC in the bow of the first sampan was the muzzle of my Stoner and fifteen yards of the muddy canal. I had been listening to the tinny music that poured from a transistor radio for almost a half hour. With the radio blaring and the long pole splashing and banging against the gunwales, it was obvious that they didn't know that fourteen of the "green-faced devils" were about to make sure that no cargo would be carried past this piece of real estate tonight. *How safe they must feel,* I thought to myself. Out here, smack in the middle of west fucking nowhere, deep in their own territory, they didn't know that hell's fire was going to fall on them hard and fast. Silent and invisible, we waited. There was no more than twenty-five feet between the sampans; all three of them would be within our kill zone when the claymores were fired.

As they moved into our field of fire, the VC in the bow of the first sampan must have sensed something was wrong. Somehow, over the blaring of the radio, I heard the snick of metal sliding on metal as he slipped the safety of his AK-47 to fire. From fifteen yards I watched him as he lowered himself to one knee. His eyes swept the bank, looking for whatever it was that had made the hair on the back of his neck go stiff. In my mud-caked blue jeans, tiger-stripe camouflage shirt, green painted face, and with a OD green bandage covering my blonde hair I knew that I was invisible in the jungle darkness.

Suddenly he stood and raised his hand, a silent signal for the two trailing sampans to stop. The VC in the bow of the second sampan was now on his feet as well. They both had their rifles in their hands, and I heard the charging handles on their AK-47s slam home, loading a round into the chamber, but it was too late. Before the third man could rise or pick up his weapon, before a single round was fired, Lieutenant Quist hit the clackers.

The deafening blast and flash of the claymores detonating was almost swallowed up by the simultaneous firing of two M-60 machine guns, two Stoner machine guns, a pair of 12-gauge shotguns, eight M-16s, and several concussion grenades thrown into the canal. As lines of red tracers and balls of exploding, incandescent gas from the muzzles of our rifles and shotguns streaked through the darkness, the sky lit up with two white star para-flares. Instantaneously the night had been transformed into daylight. The entire ambush took only thirty seconds. Lieutenant Quist called cease-fire; the VC had not gotten off even a single round. We immediately reloaded our weapons, checked that no one had been hit, and covered our assigned field of fire. In the silence the dead VC and sinking sampans bobbed slowly in the current of the canal. In the glare of the para-flares, I watched the blood draining from the VC stain the brown water, then dissipate as it moved downstream in the flow of the current.

A security perimeter was quickly set up, and a five-man search team waded into the canal to retrieve the bodies, the sampans, and their cargo. There was no question that every VC within five miles knew that we were in their backyard. It was time to find anything that would give us more intel, destroy the cargo, and get out of Dodge. There was no elation, no confusion, and no wasted motion. We all knew our jobs. We moved quickly and efficiently.

The search team looked hard for several minutes but found only four VC bodies. The dead were searched thoroughly. Every pocket was turned out, and a single canvas pouch that contained maps and documents was retrieved before it sank. Because we never knew what might yield more actionable intel, we took all of the personal items from the dead VC. Wallets, watches, rings, necklaces, even the money they were carrying might have some intel value. While the search team was retrieving the bodies, the rest of the team was busy dragging the rapidly sinking sampans to shore where we could remove anything with intel value. The cargo was searched to make sure that nothing would be left behind that could be recovered and used against us. Lieutenant Quist took an inventory of everything we found.

From the wreckage we pulled a couple of old M-2 carbines, a full-auto version of the standard .30 caliber carbine used in World War II and Korea, a pair of AK-47 rifles and several magazines of ammo, two Chinese-made SKS rifles, several crates of small-arms ammunition, half a dozen fragmentation grenades, and two cases of 61 mm ChiCom mortar rounds. The most unusual piece of intel we dug out of the mess was four NVA uniforms, complete with caps. They looked as if they had just come from the tailor shop. They were wrapped in watertight plastic and well sealed. The creases in the pant legs were still sharp. They were brand-new. This was valuable intel because there had been no report of any NVA troops in this part of the delta.

With the uniforms and other items we were taking secured in our packs, we prepared to pull out for our extraction point. The demolitions team placed several two-pound blocks of C-4 explosive on top of all of the weapons, ammunition, and supplies that we couldn't take with us and armed it with a double five-minute fuse firing assembly, and the team was ready to haul ass two klicks west to the Mekong River where our Mike 8 boat was waiting for our extraction. It had been less than five minutes since the claymores were fired, but we could now hear voices from three different directions. Lieutenant Quist got a head count and hollered, "Pull," and we moved out.

The moon was no longer our friend. With the dappled light that penetrated the bush, we could see movement. People were coming our way fast through the tree line. The moonlight let us move quickly through the bush, but the downside was that the VC could also see us. We hugged the shadows, the bush, and any defilade, but now we could see people moving along the dikes across the rice paddies. They were trying to cut off our escape route to the Mike 8 boat. It only took a few minutes for the VC to close to within a hundred yards. We saw dozens of muzzle flashes and started taking small-arms fire from across the paddies. The VC were firing single rounds; they didn't know exactly where we were, and only if we returned fire would they know our position.

With rounds from the SKS and AK-47 rifles being randomly scattered through the bush, smacking into trees, and whining off of the ground, we set up a secure position in a coconut grove. Our platoon chief, Master Chief Rudy Boesch, got on the radio to call in fire support from the 81 mm mortar on the Mike 8 boat. Rudy had the coordinates right, but the first rounds overshot and exploded too far behind the dikes the VC were using for cover. Nobody was complaining; better to have the rounds fall behind the VC than falling short, on our position. We broke cover and headed for the river. Boomer, our radioman, stayed right beside Rudy as Rudy adjusted the range on the 81 mm high-explosive rounds that were falling behind us. As we ran through the darkness I could hear Rudy yelling, "Drop a hundred, drop a hundred." The VC now knew where we were, but that creeping curtain of explosions and shrapnel protected our rear and kept us moving at a solid trot toward our extraction point on the river.

With the moonlight and the flash of the exploding 81 mm rounds to our rear, we could now see the river in the distance through the scattered trees. We picked a small chunk of defilade, set up security, took another head count, and caught our breath. Rudy called for 81 mm illumination rounds, and in the glare we could see the VC coming for our position like angry hornets out of a hive. Big Al Ashton was one of our best M-60 operators—he could squirt controlled rounds out of his M-60 the way most men could squirt water out of a garden hose—and as the VC fire intensified and tracers started streaking into our defilade, Al got his M-60 running. My Stoner was already throwing a stream of red tracers into the bush and trees along the rice paddies, making the VC keep their heads down in the dirt. Now that the VC knew where we were, there was no reason to try to stay invisible. We all got ourselves online and laid down withering fire across the rice paddies and into the tree line where the VC patrols were trying to hide.

After breaking one of my own rules and almost running the Stoner dry, I stopped firing long enough to get one of my favorite weapons into the firefight. As green tracers erupted from the tree line and incoming small-arms fire impacted around our team, I fired my 66 mm LAAW rocket into the treetops above the massed VC patrol. Although it had been designed for use against lightly armored vehicles, when a LAAW exploded in the treetops it had an airburst effect that seemed to discourage just about anyone not bent on suicide. I didn't know if my rocket killed or wounded any of the VC, and I wasn't going to go see for myself, but the tracers and small-arms fire stopped long enough for Rudy to take a second head count and get us moving the short distance to our extraction point and the Mike 8 boat. As we scrambled up the lowered bow ramp, both of the .50 caliber machine guns and the 7.62 mm minigun on the Mike 8 opened up on the area we had recently evacuated. Tongues of flame and tracers lit up the murky darkness, leaves and branches fell, and chunks of bush and dirt flew as hundreds of rounds tore up just about every inch of ground between us and the VC. If any of the VC were determined to die for Uncle Ho, this was the perfect time and place, and we were ready, willing, and able to help them along.

All on board, head count complete, bow ramp closing, we reloaded our weapons and took up security positions along the boat's gunwales for our moonlight cruise up the Mekong River to My Tho and our small riverine base. We would be cruising through Indian country, and the VC could set up an ambush anywhere along the river. Nobody would start relaxing until we were back in My Tho. The VC had learned the hard way that we were their worst nightmare. They would take any risk or go to any length to kill us.

In two hours, the sun was breaking over the horizon, and the Mike 8 boat was pulling alongside our dock. Now we had the rest of the morning to clean our weapons and ourselves and to replace gear and replenish ammunition for our next mission. First, we would turn over our captured documents to Mingh, our combat interpreter. He would search through every scrap we had brought back, looking for anything of intelligence value. If we were lucky, he would find some intel we could use to set up our next op.

7

Tools of the Trade

In the history of American military might, nothing like the SEAL Teams had ever existed. Thirty-four Underwater Demolition Teams had fought and been bloodied in combat on the beaches of the Pacific campaign of World War II, but the rapid demobilization at the end of the war almost extinguished the UDTs. From thirty-four teams they were reduced to only four, two on each coast, each team with a complement of seven officers and forty-five enlisted men. The SEAL Teams would carry on the traditions of the UDTs, but we would also continually expand our capability as unconventional warriors and would develop new forms of guerrilla warfare far beyond those ever envisioned by the UDTs.

Even before the SEALs were officially commissioned in 1962, the best UDT operators had been recruited. They were the plank owners (original crew when a ship is commissioned), the first in a long line of the best unconventional warriors in the world. Starting from ground zero, the new requirements of fighting and winning unconventional wars demanded that these new sea, air, and land warriors would be trained as had no other men before them. When we completed specialized training, we were cross-trained until every man was an expert in several operational areas and a well-trained generalist in every operational area. Every aspect of SEAL training was designed to find any weakness in ourselves and in our equipment. As we worked through each stage of our training, we learned what worked and what didn't. It didn't take long for us to figure out that we were capable of performance beyond what most of our issue equipment had been designed to do. We started looking for new and better equipment that would let us push the envelope as far as it would go.

Every piece of our equipment was tested, evaluated, tested again, improved, then issued for real-world testing where it counted: on the field of battle. Rebreathers, scuba tanks, boats, boots, explosives, weapons—everything that could make us more effective, able to do what no other warriors had ever done before—were tested to success or destruction. If your boat gets shot out from under you, you can swim; if your infiltration helo goes down, you can walk or run; but when people are shooting at you, superior weapons made the difference between life and death. On some missions we had air cover, and we could call in artillery support when we were close enough to a firebase or a ship, but we didn't like to bet our lives on anybody but the men who were right there on the ground, covering our back. Coming home in one piece after completing our mission depended on the weapons we carried, so our weapons got most of our attention.

Unlike the other services, the SEAL Teams always ran lean and mean. We had little infrastructure and, in the early years, damn little experience in fighting a guerrilla war. In Vietnam we would be fighting people with decades of experience in waging a small-unit guerrilla war. Out in the bush, with people who knew every inch of the ground trying to find and kill you, staying alive and killing or capturing the enemy is the only way you find out if your tactics and weapons are good enough. We didn't delude ourselves; we knew that the learning curve was going to be steep—and bloody.

In the end we always played a zero-sum game—with our lives and dead or captured VC the only way to keep score. As long as we came home with zero casualties and left the field with zero VC still operating, we were sure that we were winning. As tough and well trained as we were, it didn't always work out the way we planned it. We suffered injuries and lost good friends. We toasted our lost and sometimes wept when good men left us. Ours was a very personal war and we fought it our own way: face-to-face with our enemy.

No two operations were the same; every mission required different tactics, manpower, and weapons, sometimes very specialized weapons. Using the best intel we could get, our OIC and AOIC made sure that every op was as carefully and meticulously planned as possible. That planning started with debriefing after every operation while every aspect of the op was still fresh. The SEAL Teams were fighting a very different kind of war. We didn't hump the bush hoping to find the VC, plan mass troop movements, or measure our success by ground captured. We were the devils with green faces, surgeons who cut out the heart of the VC infrastructure, and debriefing was one of our scalpels. We used it to share every minute piece of information that might help us kill or capture more VC with less risk to ourselves.

Everything that could affect the mission was dug out and planned for, and at least one backup contingency plan was put in place. Planning was never completed until just before the mission was going to kick off. Right up to the last minute, new information was coming in from our intel sources, and nothing was ever ignored or left to chance. Our pre-op warning orders gave us a good idea of the mission, how the op was going to be run, and the weapons we might need to get in, accomplish the mission, and get out unscathed. However, the best intel we could get was never as good as we wanted it to be, so we were always trying to make sure that no matter what went wrong we would have decisively superior firepower.

There were two kinds of weapons that we needed to fight and win a guerrilla war: the weapons that Uncle Sam gave us and the weapons that we adapted, changed, or invented. SEALs are expected to be always looking for a better way to accomplish their mission, the most effective way to get the job done. No SEAL will ever fight fair if he can avoid it. We were always looking for better equipment, weapons, and tactics, force multipliers that would give us the biggest advantage we could get. Tactics and weapons are two edges of the same sword. Our weapons, and especially the weapons modifications made by the SEALs, let us develop and employ guerrilla tactics that would have been impossible with "off the shelf" weapons.

One example of a very specialized weapon was the "Belgium Blue" kit developed when we found out that the VC were using our own captured munitions against us. As reports came in from the field about our own unexploded or captured munitions being used in booby traps or being stripped for the powder and bullets, it became obvious that something needed to be done, and the sooner the better. When we decided that it would be a good idea to leave behind some little surprises that would make the VC think twice about using anything they captured against us, the CIA came up with a unique approach to take the enemy out even after we were long gone.

Working with several different special ops technical advisers, the CIA took the lead in the development of a suitcase-sized 903 kit, code-named "Belgium Blue." It was a small suitcase, only slightly bigger than a briefcase, but it was chock-full of nasty surprises that we could leave behind for our Vietcong friends in the north. There was a canteen that held a quarter pound of C-4 that blew its top, and most of the VC, into a large ball of fine red mist when the cap was opened a quarter turn. The case also held boxes of modified AK-47 ammo that would detonate in the chamber of the rifle, nicely removing the face or head of the shooter. The CIA did an excellent job in copying the AK ammunition. If you mixed the 903 ammunition with a few rounds of captured AK-47 ammunition, it was impossible to tell them apart. Even the head stamps on the bottoms of the cases (indicating which arsenal had manufactured the rounds) and the sealant on the primers and bullets were perfect; this made it close to impossible for the VC to segregate captured ammunition by manufacturing lots. Although this ammunition killed and maimed the enemy, it had another, even more important, effect. After a couple dozen of their AK-47 or SKS rifles mysteriously exploded, killing or maiming the VC firing the weapons, word traveled through the ranks fast. In a day or two the rest of his cadre would be wondering what had happened, and if it was going to happen to them. Why had the rifle exploded, blowing the shooter's face all over the bush? Was it a bad rifle, bad ammunition, a plugged bore, or just bad luck? Because the weapon and ammo had been destroyed, there wasn't much qualitative analysis that could be done to pinpoint the cause, but one thing was sure: For a long time nobody wanted to put his face next to the receiver of an AK-47 or SKS and squeeze the trigger. They were so afraid of the weapon exploding that they would hold the rifle as far away from themselves as possible and fire it full auto. The resulting reduction in accuracy and increased use of ammunition put the VC at a disadvantage, another disadvantage that we could and would exploit.

Along with the exploding ammunition, the 903 kit contained a couple of thirty-round magazines for the AK-47 rifle that detonated after the first two rounds were fired. If we couldn't kill them with the 903 ammo, we would kill them with the 903 magazines. The exploding magazines and most of the ammunition were distributed to all the SEAL platoons. It was our job to leave the exploding ammo and magazines where the VC would scarf them up and use them.

The 903 kit also held a few nonmilitary devices that might get the job done when the VC had become too afraid of any ammo or magazines found in the bush. There was a flashlight that detonated when it was turned on and one of the Kodak Instamatic cameras that just about everyone used. The Instamatic would explode when the shutter was pressed or the film compartment was opened. Although the "Belgium Blue" 903 kits kept the VC off guard and let them know that we would use any method or munitions to kill them, our small arms were where we concentrated our efforts.

Every operation was another chance to become a better warrior, to discover new and better ways to stay alive and capture or kill our enemies. Give a SEAL a knife, three sticks, a length of rope, a couple of bungee cords, and a handful of smooth rocks and he will make you a pretty good weapon. We knew how to improvise when necessary, but when we had a choice our weapons were always the best that we could buy, find, steal, borrow, or invent.

Our platoon Quonset hut was our armory; weapons and ammunition took up almost half of the entire building. Everything we might need for any op was cleaned, oiled, stockpiled, and always ready for use. Standard-issue weapons like the M-16 rifle, the M-60 machine gun, the Stoner machine gun, the .50 caliber Browning machine gun, grenades, claymore mines, and other munitions were always available, but to fight a guerrilla war we needed a few specialized weapons.

The weapons that we needed were dictated by the mission and the way that we fought. If we needed a weapon to accomplish our mission, even if it didn't exist, we'd figure out a way to get it. After too many delays, getting the wrong weapons, or being told that there were no weapons that could do what we needed them to do, we did what SEALs always did—we improvised.

Getting SEALs to work directly with the manufacturers to help them understand the special circumstances that SEALs faced in battle wasn't too difficult. After years of dealing with bureaucrats from Washington, many of them civilian armchair experts who let other civilians decide how to build weapons that men would use to stay alive in battle, most of the manufacturers didn't know what we needed or how to improve the weapons they were already making. It has been a long sad story, but the gun companies pay the bills by meeting minimum specs and underbidding every other manufacturer to meet a low-ball price set by some REMF (rear echelon motherfucker) at DoD who has never even heard a weapon fired in anger. It was our job to help the manufacturers see the light, so we rolled up our sleeves and ignored all orders to the contrary. We didn't care if the gun companies learned something from us and used it to make their civilian guns better. We needed specialized weapons, and helping the guys running the lathes, milling machines, and rifling machines understand what we needed and how we would be using the weapons got the job done cheaper, faster, and better! From silenced weapons to full-auto shotguns firing hundreds of fléchettes or buckshot when the trigger was slammed to the rear, when we needed special weapons we got them. As far back as I could remember I had always liked small arms, and although some people didn't like the Stoner, I bet my life, and the lives of my platoon, on my Stoner on a daily basis. That you are reading this right now is proof positive that the Stoner never let me down in a firefight. As much as I liked the Stoner, though, I did, at least in one very specific case, become almost religiously devoted to another wonderful weapon.

In addition to my Stoner, the weapon that I carried on almost every op, and that saved our ass on more than one occasion, was the 66mm LAAW rocket. The standard-issue LAAW had been developed as a lightweight, powerful, shoulder-fired rocket designed to be used against lightly armored vehicles at ranges up to 375 meters. It was a great weapon for taking out vehicles, but we didn't run into many armored vehicles when we were hunting the VC in the bush. For us, the LAAW was close to being the perfect weapon when we needed to destroy a bunker, a hooch, a pagoda, or any other fixed target that the VC thought would provide cover while they shot us to pieces. A 66 mm high-explosive round also, as I proved on too many occasions for there to be any doubt, had just about perfect terminal effect on anyone who thought that the dense bush would protect him. When the high-explosive round was used as an area suppression weapon, it made mincemeat of VC hiding in the bush.

Ironically, had I listened to the people who told us how to use the rockets, we would never have discovered how effective they could be when used to fight a guerrilla war. The folks who taught us the manual of arms told us that it had a maximum range of only 375 meters, just over a thousand feet. Being able to reach out farther than three football fields end to end might sound like a long way, but I didn't want to get any closer to people who were shooting rifles, machine guns, RPGs (rocket-propelled grenades), and mortars at me than was absolutely necessary. Most people believe what they are told, but I've always been a hardheaded type. I ignored the specifications because I really wanted to be able to reach out and touch Victor Charlie from as far away from our position as possible. I thought that there were probably very few VC shooters or snipers who could hit a target at 500 yards, so, just to be on the safe side, I doubled that range and started my own R&D project. Being able to accurately place a rocket on top of an enemy position at 1,000 yards was actually a lot easier than I thought it would be. After thinking about the easiest way to modify the LAAW, it became obvious that I could make a very simple modification that would give us the range and accuracy we wanted.

The first rule for any weapon that you are going to bet your life on is KISS: Keep it simple, stupid. If you modify any weapon, it's a good idea to make the most robust, simple, reliable, and easy modifications to use in a shitstorm when you don't have time to think and your life depends on overwhelming the enemy. Don't get cute, don't get fancy, and never build a weapon that has so many moving parts or such fragile technology that it is prone to malfunction or failure. If you do, it will fail when you need it most, you will be dead, and your team will have to carry your body out of the bush.

Following the KISS principle, I removed the bottom plate from a thirty-round M-16 magazine, painted a white stripe every quarter inch so that I could use them as aiming points for different ranges, and fitted it into the rear sight slot of the LAAW. With the standard-issue sights, I could easily hit a fifty-five-gallon drum at 375 yards every time I fired the weapon. My long-range sights were a little crude and not as accurate as the issue sight, but I could still hit fifty-five-gallon drums at 375 yards and put almost every rocket into an area the size of a basketball court at 1,000 yards. The LAAW was a great weapon as designed, but when I used it against fixed targets, or as an airburst weapon out at 1,000 yards, it shut down the incoming fire with great authority. It may not have been as good as artillery, but it was always right there, right now. When we needed to reach out and destroy structures or kill concentrations of VC at long range, a rocket that could reach out 1,000 yards was far better than anything else we could carry on an op. After a little experimentation with ranging the distances and experience using the white stripes on the new rear sight, I had come as close as I could to the perfect long-range area suppression weapon.

Being able to reach out over a half mile with a powerful weapon was a great added capability for any SEAL platoon, but most of our ops put us very up close and personal to the enemy, so most of our weapons tended to be those that would be employed at ranges counted in feet and yards.

Intelligence gathering was very important, so important that it was our first priority on most ops. The best way to gather good, fresh intel was to capture the local or regional VC commanders, tax collectors, and other high-value members of the VC government infrastructure. Unfortunately, the VC we wanted to capture were frequently guarded by well-armed people who took their orders to protect their superiors seriously. They had to be neutralized before we could gain access to our main target. For these ops we developed weapons that got the job done, and a few that seemed like a good idea at the time but didn't prove to work all that well when put into practice.

Possibly our worst failure was a weapon that was totally silent. We had several different silenced weapons in the Quonset hut, but not even our best were really silent. The correct term for a very quiet weapon designed to be used in covert operations is "suppressed." To reduce the report of any gun, even a .22 rimfire, you must use specially loaded ammunition that does not reach or exceed the speed of sound. The next step is to add a "can," or silencer, to the muzzle end of the barrel that captures the hot, expanding, exploding gasses that propel the bullet down the barrel and out of the muzzle. If you know what you are doing, you can make a very quiet weapon. If you build a single-shot weapon with no moving parts other than the firing pin, it can be very close to silent, but any firearm capable of being fired multiple times makes noise. The movement of the slide or bolt, the slapping of the slide or bolt as it strikes the ammunition and pushes it into the chamber, the ejection of the spent brass, even the brass clatter as it hits the ground—all of these make noise, and we wanted a truly silent weapon.

I am sure that it was late one night after many, many hours trying to deplete the entire supply of potable alcohol in Vietnam that it was decided by someone who will forever remain anonymous that a crossbow was what we needed. This made sense to everyone because it could be truly silent, would have no muzzle flash that would be visible to the enemy when used at night, and could be fired multiple times without detection. To ensure that this weapon would have the required penetration to kill sentries or guards, the damn thing was designed to use ten-inch-long steel arrows (called bolts in a crossbow). Each bolt was tipped with a razor-sharp broad-headed point. They were like flying scalpels. It took almost six months to get all of the bugs ironed out and to eliminate even the smallest squeaks and slap of the string. A couple of us practiced with the new weapon, and it really did work. It was silent, powerful, accurate out to forty yards, and, for anyone who knew how to use iron sights on a rifle, relatively easy to use. Fortunately, before we actually used it on a mission, somebody asked what would happen if our target was wearing a helmet and we couldn't make a head shot. He wondered how long it would take for a couple of guards with razor-sharp bolts fired into their chests to die and how loud they would scream until they were dead. The crossbow was, as far as I know, never deployed on a mission, and our attention was soon turned to modifications of issue weapons and the development of more specialized weapons that could give us an edge on every op.

With the LAAW now giving us a long-range capability, we started looking for a short-range weapon that could put out more firepower and could be used either in an antipersonnel (AP) capacity or with high-explosive (HE) rounds for blasting big targets like bunkers or sampans. As an added bonus we thought that it would be just great if this weapon could be carried by anyone in the team. The SEAL Teams were the first to use the 40 mm XM-148 grenade launcher that attached to the underside of the M-16. It was light, easy to use, and very powerful at close range. When the AP rounds using buckshot went off, it was like triggering a hailstorm of destruction that shredded everything in its path. Although the trajectory of the HE rounds was arched like a rainbow, it was a very powerful weapon for use against big targets out to a couple of hundred yards. With several improvements, it became the standard 40 mm M-203 grenade launcher that is still in use today.

As much as we liked the XM-148 grenade launcher, it had one drawback in a close-range firefight: It was a single-shot weapon. No matter how fast we reloaded, it took too long when tracers were streaking past your head, and being able to load and fire rapidly was the best way to kill the VC and bring hostilities to a rapid end. The platform we decided to use for our next weapons development was the simple, ubiquitous 12-gauge shotgun. Shotguns are cheap, easy to use, fast to load and fire, and easily available from several different manufacturers in pump, semiauto, and double-barrel configuration right off the shelf. Shotguns are also a well developed, thoroughly tested, simple weapons platform that is easily adapted to firing different and interesting projectiles.

The 12-gauge shotgun had been used by police forces and had even been employed for short-range antipersonnel use in the trenches of World War I. There was little question that the buckshot loads, nicknamed "Blue Whistlers," were devastating at close range. In a 12-gauge shotgun round, the standard load of #4 buckshot was twenty-seven lead balls that were each .24 caliber. Every time the trigger was pulled, we could fire twenty-seven projectiles that made a bigger hole than the standard 5.56 mm bullet fired from the M-16. Effective range was only thirty to forty yards, but the closer we got to the enemy in a firefight, the more important it was to be able to dominate the field of fire instantly. The more deadly projectiles we could put in the air, and the faster we could get them flying downrange, the better. Shotguns, however, are not ammunition sensitive. Just about anything you can fit into the standard-sized 12-gauge shell will fit in the magazine and feed into the chamber and can be fired down the barrel.

With a weapons platform capable of firing multiple types of ammunition, and excellent pump and semiautomatic shotguns available from several different companies, we thought only a little weapons development and fine-tuning might be required. It didn't take long to decide that we needed three different weapons. First, though, before we started modifying the guns, we developed some specialized ammunition that would make the shotgun just about perfect for several close-range combat applications.

The first special cartridge developed was a fléchette round that contained dozens of small steel fléchettes, basically nothing more than nails with a point on one end and metal fins on the other end that turned them into little high-speed arrows. The biggest advantage of the fléchette round was superior penetration when compared to the round steel or lead balls fired from conventional shotgun cartridges. Those little steel arrows would slip right through leaves that would deflect buckshot, and they penetrated human flesh deeper, while the metal fins cut a big wound channel like little flying scalpels. They didn't kill quickly, but they did give us extended range and penetrating capability.

Even so, we decided that they were not the answer to the question we had asked. We needed to have the ability to shoot through the bush and stop the VC with a single, devastating blow at longer range. To increase range, we needed to increase the penetration of the buckshot that could almost tear a man in half, so we came up with the Mk-5 load that replaced the standard soft lead buckshot pellets with hardened pellets. Because they were harder and didn't deform on the foliage like soft lead pellets, they flew faster and straighter and penetrated better.

Last, but probably one of the most effective experimental weapons we tested in the jungle, was the pump-action grenade launcher developed by the China Lake Naval Weapons Center. With three grenades in the tubular magazine and one in the chamber, it was almost like having mini artillery on call. After a little practice, we could get four rounds headed downrange and be reloading before the first round landed on the target. Even though the 40 mm grenade couldn't carry as much high explosive as the single-shot, M-16 mounted M-203, it was effective out to 375 meters and could be reloaded in half the time.

With new ammunition coming online and more still in R&D, we switched gears to figure out how we could improve the shotguns themselves. We started off using a standard Remington four-shot-capacity pump-action shotgun to fire the new Mk-5 loads. It worked flawlessly, and we often found ourselves covering both sides of a canal by lacing the jungle with buckshot from aboard our exfiltration boats. Next we decided that we needed to figure out how to make a shotgun more effective in the bush. The answer to that question was finding some way to increase the pattern size horizontally and reduce the spread vertically when we were firing antipersonnel rounds. We knew what we wanted to do, but we found out that getting a shotgun to fire a pattern that would keep most of the projectiles, whether pellets or fléchettes, inside a maximum kill zone was easier said than done.

After long discussion, we decided that a standard shotgun just wasted too many projectiles by spreading the pattern too high and too low. Damn few VC were hiding in the treetops or crawling in the dirt. We wanted to keep as many pellets in the kill zone as possible out to twenty-five yards. Our specification for the new shotgun was to be able to cover a wider field of fire with the special Mk-5 loads and, when necessary, with standard buckshot or fléchette loads. Working with the engineers at Remington, we soon got an answer, but the shotgun the engineers handed over for testing looked a little strange. It was a standard Remington pump but had a long, seven-round magazine hanging under the barrel and a duck-bill choke at the end of the barrel. It might have looked strange, but a good man using that duck-bill Remington could put out a wall of hardened lead buckshot that patterned in a kill zone three feet high and nine feet wide at twenty-five yards in less than ten seconds. Reloading the magazine was just as fast.

The idea of an even larger magazine didn't slip past us. If a seven-round pump shotgun was good, we asked ourselves, wouldn't a full-auto shotgun with a fifty-round magazine and a range of seventy-five yards be a handy weapon? It turned out to be a terrific weapon, but the gun and ammo were so heavy that it was too much of a load to hump in the bush. It could only be used effectively from aboard a boat or helo.

If there was a better weapon, we wanted it, but new weapons took too long to get through the R&D pipeline, so our issue weapons were always our first priority. They didn't go unmodified for long. With all of the gear we carried, excess weight and bulk didn't make our issue weapons any easier to use. Our M-60 gunner, Big Al Ashton, was 6'4" and strong as a couple of oxen put together, but even he wanted to lose any weight that didn't make him more effective in a firefight. His standard load out was the M-60, seven hundred rounds of ammunition, an H-harness with a couple of pop flares, a Ka-Bar knife, a canteen, a first aid kit, a flashlight, a poncho, a UDT life jacket, and a couple of grenades. Even though Al was a strong swimmer and wore a life vest, he sank like a stone in any body of water. When we had to cross water on patrol, Al just walked across on the bottom. Al decided that the M-60 was too heavy and needed a few other modifications to make it better meet the needs of our missions. The first thing that went over the side was the heavy butt stock. Al figured that he would never need to fire the M-60 from the shoulder, so the butt stock was replaced with the small rubber boot that the door gunners on the helos used. The next modification was removing the bipod and chopping five inches from the muzzle of the barrel. The bipod was useless in the bush. If you dropped into prone position to fire the M-60, all you would see was jungle and more jungle. The front and rear sights were not really necessary, either. Most of the time we were fighting at close range and at night. Sights in that type of firefight are as useless as teats on a bull. If you were firing at longer ranges, you just used tracers and adjusted your fire based on the impact of the red glowing line of bullets. When Al got done chopping off all of the unnecessary parts, the weight of the M-60 had been reduced by over a third, and that let him carry even more ammunition or grenades when we were going out hunting for a fight.

When we were running a snatch-and-grab op, looking to bring home some VC prisoners who might provide us with information that could help us plan more and more productive ops, we had some more specialized weapons that let us get in and out as silently as possible. Our snatch and grab ops usually required us to slip past a few sentries, get into a hooch or pagoda, and secure the target before anyone inside knew what was happening.

The M-16 rifle had been used as a platform for a silenced rifle, but it was at best a lousy, second-rate silenced weapon that was most often used for quieting yapping stray dogs that were not too close to your target area. The silenced M-16 had several problems that made it unsuited for our type of operations. The first problem was that the oversized silencer added fourteen inches to an already long rifle, and if we didn't have any of the special subsonic ammunition it wasn't even close to being silent. If we did, the M-16 was still too damn big, and the ammunition wouldn't operate the action of the rifle, even on semiauto. I can't remember even one operation when we used the "silenced" M-16.

When we were running a silent op, we were working so close to the target that a much smaller silenced pistol was more than powerful and accurate enough, and as lousy as the silenced M-16 was, we had two silenced weapons that more than made up for all of its shortcomings. Our standard Smith & Wesson 9mm "hush puppy" was a very quiet pistol, utterly reliable, and deadly at any range out to twenty-five yards. Our second silenced weapon, the .45 ACP "grease gun," was a real winner. No special ammunition was needed, the silencer was less than a foot long, it carried a thirty-round magazine, and it was as close to silent as you can get. Even when fired full auto, the only sound the grease gun made was the click-clunk of the bolt feeding the rounds into the chamber and the ejected cartridge cases hitting the ground. As good as the grease gun was, it had one major flaw. It was just too damn heavy to lug along on most operations. Fully loaded, the grease gun weighed over ten pounds. Throw in a couple more loaded magazines and you were dragging around twenty pounds.

Fortunately, our silenced Smith & Wesson pistols were compact and fully loaded weighed less than two pounds. Even at the subsonic velocity of 1,040 feet per second the FMJ bullet would punch right through the VC helmets at short range. If you could shoot a pistol with good accuracy, the smaller pistol worked perfectly for silently taking out sentries from as far away as twenty-five yards. Inside of a hooch, a tunnel, or a pagoda, the smaller and more maneuverable your weapons were, the better. The compact three-inch-long silencer attached to the muzzle made the entire weapon less than sixteen inches long and easy to maneuver in close quarters. There were only two drawbacks to the Smith & Wesson hush puppy. The first was that after six or seven rounds were fired the inserts in the silencer had to be replaced, but that was never required in the field. The second drawback was the low rate of fire; the reduced-velocity, downloaded, subsonic ammunition used in the pistol wouldn't cycle the slide.

To fire a round, the slide had to be manually cycled, then locked closed. As long as the chamber was loaded and the slide was locked closed, the pistol was ready to fire. When the cartridge in the chamber had been fired, the slide was manually unlocked and cycled by hand. This ejected the spent cartridge case and allowed the slide to push a loaded cartridge into the chamber. Then the slide was locked closed, and the pistol was ready to fire again. A rate of fire of one round of aimed fire about every four or five seconds was as fast as we could get—even with plenty of practice.

As we ran more ops and gained experience, the search for new, specialized weapons that gave us an edge or fulfilled a specific operational purpose never stopped. Even when we were using our issue weapons, more often than not, we adapted them or the tactics used to maximize their effectiveness and lethality to fulfill the specific operational need. Of course, the tools are not worth much without the men who took them into harm's way.

Everything we learned as we stalked the bush became a part of what we used to hone our strategy and tactics to a deadly cutting edge. In the first few months after the Tet offensive, the VC had more experience than we did in the bush. They might have had a head start, but we learned fast, were far better trained, and learned more, faster, on every operation.

As good as they were in the bush, the VC could never use the same tricks twice. We learned, adapted, and used their own tactics and strategic planning against them. Everything that we learned helped us to turn the tables on them, and more and more VC surrendered or ended up facedown in the mud. Experience shared in every debriefing honed our skills, and our confidence kept growing. It was in the jungle and on the rivers that the SEALs became "the men with green faces," the stalkers of the night, and the most feared warriors any enemy had ever faced.

8

The Death Tax

As far back in time as we can find records of warfare, and probably long before records were kept, gathering good, actionable intelligence has been the bottom line, the life's blood of putting together successful military operations. Lousy intelligence or the lack of enough intel has probably been responsible for more lives and battles lost than any other single cause. There are many examples of good and bad intelligence leading to victory or defeat. One of the most often studied and well known took place in 480 B.C. at a mountain pass in central Greece.

The enormous, well-trained, and well-equipped Persian army under the command of Xerxes was completely stalemated for four days at Thermopylae by an infinitely smaller Greek force led by the legendary three hundred Spartans. The Spartans, professional, lifelong warriors, used their intelligence-gathering skills to choose the ground where the Persian army could not bring their superior numbers to bear. Had a local shepherd not told Xerxes of a pass that allowed the Persians to encircle the Greek army, the Spartan warrior king, Leonidas, would certainly have held fast and might have defeated the army of Xerxes through attrition.

Battles and wars can be won with weapons, technology, and blood spilled on the battlefield, but that is an expensive, wasteful way to fight.

Good intelligence, acted on quickly, fully exploited, and used to develop more and better intel, wins battles, saves lives, and wins wars. Intel is the most powerful force multiplier in warfare. It wasn't unusual for us to get reports back after a firefight that the VC had been attacked and had their ass handed to them by a force that numbered in the hundreds of men. The reality was that the VC usually outnumbered us by more than three or four to one when we dropped the hammer on an ambush. Somehow they never figured out that it was good intelligence, acted upon hard and fast by rarely more than twenty SEALs, that was kicking their ass. The good intel that we managed to dig out multiplied our force by a factor of fifty, maybe more.

For the SEAL Teams, intelligence gathering was a 24/7 priority. Like breathing, intel gathering, checking, and double-checking never stopped. Jim Finely and Mingh, our combat interpreter, probably worked at least twice as hard as most of the team. They were both operators who went out on missions, but they were also responsible for checking everything that we found on the dead or captured VC, and for building a network of reliable intelligence contacts throughout the province. Because My Tho was both a port and a center of economic activity, it became a hotbed of good and bad intel.

The VC had become experts at misdirection. The more dead-end missions they got us to swallow, the fewer hot, productive missions we could run. We learned to hate the dead-end missions when either the intel was wrong or the enemy changed their plans and never showed hide nor hair. As good as our intel sources were, we spent too many long nights hiding deep in the bush with the mosquitoes and snakes. When the intel was wrong, the high point of the long wait was a local farmer staggering home just before the sunrise so he wouldn't get caught cheating on his wife.

Bad intel, or intel that we had to act on without the time to double-check the information, was the most dangerous. The VC never passed up an opportunity to use disinformation to get us to waste our resources on a dry hole or to pull us into an ambush. Both Jim Finley and Mingh were experts at sniffing out the dangerous intel that was designed to draw us into a blind alley where the VC could do to us what we did to them. When the target was just too juicy, too easy to reach, too high up the chain of command, or would only be in the province for one day at a specific time and place, it didn't pass the sniff test. When intel smelled bad it usually was bad, and we avoided taking any action or risks based on it. Even so, there were times when the target was just too important to pass up. We almost always jumped at the smallest opportunity to grab up any mid- or high-level VC official. It was risky, but with rumors of Americans being held hostage in jungle POW camps, we hoped that the intel would make the risk worth the reward.

Jim and Mingh had gotten word through their network of informants in My Tho that a certain tax collector, not a small fish local tax collector but a bigwig VC district tax collector, would be visiting the small village of An Boc that night. The job of these big-time tax collectors was to intimidate the residents of the small village and to assure them that if their taxes were paid in full, on time, every time, their friendly local VC cadre wouldn't show up in the middle of the night. On the other hand, unpaid taxes would soon lead to a visit by the local VC, who would make sure that the taxes would never be late again. To help the poor farmers remember to pay their taxes, the VC would take away their sons as volunteers in the glorious people's army of Ho Chi Minh, burn down their hooches, commandeer most of their rice supply, and maybe slaughter their buffalo and ducks.

This attitude pissed us off a little, and we wanted to help the hardworking farmers keep their sons at home, their hooches unburned, their rice in the village storehouse, and their livestock alive. In fact, we would have liked nothing more than killing that tax-collecting VC bastard as dead as a nickel beer, but we didn't have that option. What he knew, the names he could give us, and all of the other intel we might persuade him to provide meant that he was to be captured and brought back to base, alive and kicking if possible. Tonight the village of An Boc would be visited by the men with green faces. By completing our mission we would send a loud, clear message to the local VC and the VC province command structure: If you fuck with the people in our province, we will come and get your sorry ass, we will drag you off to someplace you really don't want to be, and you will tell us everything you know; end of discussion. Your days and nights will never be safe. No matter what you do, or how hard you try to hide, we will hunt you down, dig you out, and make you wish that you had never been born.

The SEAL Teams were created and trained to operate in any terrain, in any weather, and with any mission objective. In the bush we specialized in only two different types of ops. One was the interdiction and destruction of weapons, munitions, food, or other material that could be used to sustain the fighting. The other was intelligence gathering. Intelligence was the lifeblood of the brass who were in charge of planning the war, and everything that we could dig out and pass up the chain of command was valuable. If the air force knew where the VC would be concentrating their forces, they could destroy them from the air. When the VC moved in force, or small groups all headed in the same direction, it tipped off the marines and army that a major offensive on a base or bases was in the works. Our ops were designed to give the war planners the best intel we could find.

Our operational briefing by Mike Boynton was short and sweet. Tonight we would be running a snatch and grab mission—the tax collector would be taken alive, and unwounded if possible. His bodyguards were expendable. Mike walked us through the mission plan and gave us all of the information we needed to get ourselves and our gear ready for another night in the bush. That night we would also be breaking in and evaluating one of the new STABs (SEAL Tactical Assault Boats) for the first time. The STAB had been designed and developed to carry a crew of eight men. The driver would insert the team and remain on board. It was his job to find a safe place to stash the boat while the mission was under way and then return to pick us up when we had completed the op. One of our guys would double as the gunner in the bow until we inserted, so that of the eight men on the STAB, seven would go out on the mission.

Smaller and faster than the Mike 8, the STAB was supposed to give us a lower profile and higher speed in the riverine environment. At twenty-one feet long and eight feet wide, it didn't carry as much firepower, but the twin 110 horsepower Mercury engines turned it into a real river rocket. In a couple of hours we would know how well the new boat would work.

At the last minute Mike Boynton decided that he was going to drive the boat to get himself familiar with how it would perform; Mike Bailey, our dog handler, was given the task of boat gunner for the night. With the last rays of the sun illuminating the rippling water, we loaded onto the STAB at the dock. Boynton was in the rear of the boat at the helm, and Bailey was in the bow manning a 7.62 mm machine gun. Three of the team were on each side of the STAB with our radioman in the middle. Mingh, our combat interpreter, the ninth man on this op, was up front in the gun tub with Bailey.

The first thing I noticed about the STAB was how low it sat in the water. Fully loaded it had a very sleek, low profile that would make it a difficult target for the VC to hit at full speed. As we picked up speed and got "on step," I really started to appreciate how well it protected us. Running on step means that the boat crew is able to get up enough speed so that the entire bow and most of the hull is above the waterline, planing with only the stern skimming on the water, which means that the boat can really move out. The driver and gunner were the most exposed, and they were only slightly higher than the rest of the team. The second thing that made the STAB a terrific boat was the sheer speed those twin Mercury engines produced. These were not just off-the-shelf motors. Even wide open, shaking and baking down the river at full speed, the engines were quiet, spooky quiet. I found out later that Mercury had made it a priority for all of their best designers to muffle the engine sound. I never got to thank any of those engineers, but they did an exceptional job.

Barring any problems, we would be at our insertion point just after full darkness fell, forty-five minutes give or take a couple. With the STAB whistling down the river, we were early by five minutes. Mike slowed the STAB in the middle of the mile-wide river and turned the bow toward the dark riverbank on our port side. He cut one engine and, with the underwater exhaust of the single engine barely audible, moved slowly and almost silently to the mouth of a small canal that was our insertion point.

Barely touching the overhanging brush, Mike nosed the STAB into the canal. As the bow gently kissed the bank, we all eased ourselves and our gear over the side and into waist-deep water. We pushed the STAB back toward the mouth of the canal, and Mike quietly backed out into the darkness of the river. He would run the STAB out into the widest part of the river and find himself a safe place to wait for our signal for extraction.

If the operation went to hell in a handcart and we needed gunfire support from the navy Seawolf helos, or needed to relay a message to TOC (the Tactical Operations Center) for any reason, Mike was the man who would get the call from our short-range PRC-25 radio and relay the message.

We moved silently out of the water, up the bank, and into the protection of the bush and set up a security perimeter. As we moved into position the only sound was the dripping of the canal water from our camouflage and the squish of the water as it drained from our shoes. With our muzzles pointed out, into the bush, we covered our fields of fire, waiting, watching, and listening for twenty minutes for anything that might tell us that our mission had been compromised. When it was clear that the VC hadn't drawn us into an ambush and we were alone on this particular chunk of real estate, Lieutenant Quist got a head count, and we silently moved out toward the village of An Boc. It always made me uneasy when we used the well-worn paths along the canals, but the chance that the VC would put booby traps along trails that they used themselves was slim to none. I guess I knew that this was what made it worth the risk of running into a cadre of VC coming the other way, but it still made me more than a little jumpy anytime we were on a trail. I didn't question Lieutenant Quist because he had been in-country a lot longer than I had been, but even after my second tour, walking a trail instantly put me into condition red.

There are, according to military psychologists, three stages of readiness that soldiers experience. In rear echelon areas where they are safe, soldiers allow themselves to enter condition green, alert but relaxed. On a normal patrol where enemy contact may happen but is not expected immediately, soldiers enter a state of readiness called condition yellow, fully alert and looking for anything that could indicate the presence of the enemy. When the shit could hit the fan any second, we go into condition red—we're ready to instantly respond to any threat with full-tilt boogie kill-or-be-killed action. They tell me that it is impossible to stay in condition red for an extended period of time. I can't speak for other SEALs, but when we walked a trail I was always in condition red. Tonight was no exception. With every silent step my eyes and ears were searching the bush, looking and listening for anything that might give away the presence of the VC.

Jim Finley and Mingh were on point, Lieutenant Quist was behind them, and I dogged his heels by about fifteen yards. We were moving cautiously and were about twenty minutes and several hundred yards into the mission when a hand signal passed back through the team stopped us in our tracks. I melted into low bush on the side of the trail, lowered myself to one knee, and covered my assigned field of fire with the muzzle of my Stoner. Ahead of me I could see the faint glow of a lantern. Mingh and Jim were gathering more intel from a local farmer they had grabbed up as he headed home after a long day in the paddies. He hadn't even seen us until he walked right into the muzzle of Mingh's rifle.

Word was quietly passed back that the farmer was on his way to An Boc and that a negotiation was being held that would convince him to lead us to the rear entrance of the village and to point out the hooch where the village chief lived. We never knew if the locals were VC or not, but it didn't matter a whole lot; we didn't really need to trust them. If there were any trip cords or booby traps along the trail, the locals knew exactly where they were and how to avoid them. If they led us into an ambush, they could be dead sure that they would be an early casualty. Not much trust was needed when we explained the situation.

These types of negotiations always took longer than we would have liked, but sometimes the wait was worth more than we could have guessed. While they negotiated for his help as our guide, the farmer mentioned to Mingh that he had seen the man that he believed we were looking for walk past his house at dusk. He had two bodyguards with him, and he was spending the night with the village chief. Mingh made sure that it was the tax collector and that there was no other hooch where he and his bodyguards could have been billeted for the night. With all the palaver, it was almost a half hour before we moved out toward An Boc. Our newfound friend leading the way, we moved quickly down the trail and were soon close enough to hear transistor radios playing. Vietnamese music filtered through the bush, and through the bamboo walls we could see that there were lanterns burning in a few of the small huts.

The hooch where the tax collector and his bodyguards were staying was at the entrance of the village, and it was even better than we had hoped. Most hooches don't have a back door, but this hooch was big enough that it did, and that fit our planning perfectly, with one small exception. We hadn't brought any silenced weapons along. If we'd had a hush puppy or two with us, we could have just burst in the door, killed everyone with a gun who didn't look like a tax collector, snatched up our target, and boogied out of Dodge. Without a silenced weapon it would be more dangerous, but if the VC inside the hooch reacted as we hoped they would when we set up a ruckus in the front yard, we could pull it off like clockwork.

Jack Lynch and I took up covering fire positions on opposite corners of the hooch. Quist, Rudy, Pierre, and Mingh ghosted silently into position along the rear wall, next to the door where we figured the tax collector would exit when the firing started. Boomer, our radio man, Big Al, and Jim, concealing themselves in the shadows, worked their way around to the front of the hooch. The op would kick off in ten minutes with Boomer, Big Al, and Jim trying to draw the bodyguards out of the front door where they could be neutralized. My head was only a few inches from the wall of the hooch, and as I waited in the darkness I could hear people talking and what sounded like one angry voice coming through the bamboo walls. From just the tone of his voice I already didn't like this guy, and I was fairly sure that the poor farmers of An Boc wouldn't miss his sorry ass much, either. I had to remind myself that we were supposed to try to take him alive. I wouldn't go out of my way to take him out, but if he even thought about pointing a weapon in our direction I was going to toast him in his tracks.

As the seconds ticked past, I covered my half of the field of fire and watched as everyone moved into position. The trap was set, and right on time the sound of a pack of dogs barking and a herd of ducks going apeshit broke the stillness. There were a couple of loud shouts and four rifle shots, and a squirrelly little guy carrying what looked like a briefcase stuffed with paperwork came tearing out of the back door of the hooch. He was running in sheer terror, and his eyes hadn't had time to adjust to the darkness; the chickenshit couldn't see a damn thing. Running as fast as he could, the little bastard slammed head-on into Pierre Birtz. At 5'10" and only 175 pounds Birtz wasn't the biggest guy in the platoon, but he was all muscle, built as solid as a brick from head to toe. It was like the tax collector had run headfirst into the door of an old, solid steel Kelvinator refrigerator. There was a thud from the impact, and the little guy was on the ground. Pierre didn't even have enough time to grab him before he dropped like a sack of cement. "That was neat and easy!" was the first thing that came to mind.

Mingh immediately took control of the briefcase and all the paperwork; Jim searched the tax man for weapons and tied his elbows together behind his back. On the other side of the hooch, both bodyguards were lying in the dirt where they fell. Their blood, leaking from several entrance and exit wounds, spread out in a ragged pool and soaked into the earth. They had paid the death tax. Their unfired AK-47 rifles, chambers empty and still on safety, were where they had fallen from their dead hands.

Our M-16 rifle fire had compromised our position; every VC for a mile or more would know that something bad was going down in An Boc. We didn't know how many bad guys would be moving on our position, but we did know that it was time to leave An Boc behind and get the tax collector someplace safe so that Mingh would be able to question him in comfort before he was passed up the chain of command for further interrogation. Our friendly farmer sort of volunteered to lead us back, and in the pitch black of a moonless night, we followed him to his small hooch on the bank of the canal. In the distance we heard several different voices calling out, and several shots as they tried some recon by fire. It was an old trick, the VC firing a few rounds into the air in the vain hope of getting us to return fire and reveal our position. We held our fire, crossed the canal, and said good night to our farmer friend. I'm sure that he was about to crap his pants and more than happy to head home after an eventful evening entertaining the men who appeared out of nowhere, killed two armed bodyguards, captured the VC tax man, then disappeared in the night.

With our extraction point a half mile away, we followed our own back trail and moved as fast as we could. Knowing that there were no booby traps on our line of march, we could really move quickly and quietly. We wanted to put as much real estate between us and those voices in the darkness as possible. At the extraction point, Lieutenant Quist took a head count and set up a security perimeter, and Boomer radioed the STAB boat to identify our signal and home in on it. If the sound of our gunfire or the VC firing into the surrounding bush had reached him, Mike would be ready and waiting for our signal. We didn't have to wait long before the quiet, almost silent rumble of the Mercury engine rolled across the river and the nose of the STAB touched the bank of the canal just a few feet from our red-lens flashlight signal. With the team all accounted for, no casualties, and the gagged and bound tax collector and his briefcase chock-full of information secured, Mike got us out into the main channel of the Mekong River and rocketing back to My Tho.

9

Good Ops, Bad Ops, and
Grand Theft Auto

An Boc was the kind of operation that we always tried to put together and pull off flawlessly. It was based on good intel, almost everything had worked as planned, and we had even gotten lucky by grabbing up a more or less cooperative local who gave us an even bigger advantage. We had taken no casualties, killed two VC bodyguards and snatched their weapons, captured the tax collector, who turned out to be a big fish in the VC infrastructure, and brought back a couple hundred pages of hard information that might lead to another, maybe bigger VC fish we could target on a future mission. All in all it was a good night's work, a solid operation, maybe even a great operation. That didn't mean that we couldn't learn from our own mistakes and make it even tougher on the VC. We all knew that the instant that you started thinking you were the king of the jungle there would be some skinny VC in black pajamas with an SKS rifle who would be ready to prove you wrong. An Boc was the kind of operation that could make you start thinking you had it all down pat. It was a good op, but I had never been on an operation that was perfect.

Immediately after every mission, before we cleaned up, ate, or put our prisoners in the lockup, while every detail of the op was still fresh in our minds, we held a debriefing session to evaluate every aspect of the mission from start to finish. Every man in the squad could report on what he or the squad could have done better, what we might add or subtract, alter or eliminate to keep ourselves alive and become more effective at destroying the VC and NVA. These weren't bitching sessions or dick-measuring contests, no egos got ruffled, nobody was pissing on somebody's back and telling him it was raining. The more we learned from one another, the better we could fight and the harder we would make it for our enemy. Military historians will tell you that the best way to win a fight, a battle, or a war is by studying your enemy, but we didn't believe that letting our enemies train us was such a great idea. If you accept that you are going to learn lessons from your enemy in battle, you will pay the price of those lessons. Usually the tab is paid in lives lost. To stay alive in battle, you can't afford to let the enemy teach you very much. Hell, if they're dead and you're alive when the smoke clears, it is easy to figure out that the VC and NVA couldn't teach you very much. We screwed up, paid the price, picked apart every op like it was a slow-motion surgical procedure, learned from one another, and bet our lives on the men covering our six (six o'clock or rear). The more we learned about guerrilla warfare, and the more we twisted, turned, and made new rules that kept the VC off guard and guessing, the more effective our ops would become, and the longer we would stay alive.

We dumped our wet, muddy gear in our washdown tub. The mud and dirt was almost half buffalo dung that was used to fertilize the rice paddies. It was sticky, gooey and smelled almost as bad as we did; letting it soak for a half hour or so made the scrubbing go a lot faster and washed out most of the stink. Our weapons, still loaded and ready for use, were stashed next to the Quonset hut. As soon as we had debriefed we would unload, strip, clean, reassemble, and oil them. Then we replenished our supply of fresh ammunition. The tax collector, still bound and gagged, was turned over to one of the base guards who would keep an eye on him until we finished up and it was time to turn him over for interrogation.

The biggest screwup on the op was that we forgot to bring a hush puppy. We always wanted to travel as light as we could, carrying as little equipment as possible so that we could carry more ammunition, but the right tool always makes the mission run better and gives you less chance of screwing yourself headfirst into the dirt. If we had remembered to bring the 9 mm Smith & Wesson hush puppy, we could have burst through the door of the hooch, whacked the bodyguards, grabbed up the tax collector, and left the little village in complete silence. With no hush puppy we had to improvise. The worst part of forgetting our silenced weapons was that two of the team had to be unnecessarily exposed when they started the ruckus in front of the hooch. We also made trouble for ourselves because we had no choice but to take the bodyguards out with our M-16s. The sound of even four M-16 rounds being fired in the village at night was almost as good as sending out an engraved invitation to the local VC saying that the green-faced devils were in the neighborhood and that they should grab their guns and come running. It was easy to tell the difference between the report of the AK-47 and the M-16, even for green troops. We didn't have much choice if we were going to complete our operation, but those four rounds were all it took to get the VC on our ass.

Another point that was always high on Lieutenant Quist's list was clinking of metal. There is almost nothing that can give you away in the bush faster than the sound of metal clinking on metal. One reason the Stoner was a great weapon was that the ammunition didn't bang around on a belt; it was contained in a nice tight drum magazine. The spare ammunition belts I carried wrapped around my shoulders and chest could slop around and make noise when I was reloading the Stoner, but that was usually after the festivities had started, the shit was hitting the fan, and more noise was the least of our problems.

The M-60 belts were another story. They were big, heavy, and clunky, and they were not held in a secure, quiet box magazine. It always seemed to me that they had a mind of their own. Those belts could find a tree, a stick, a vine, or something to wrap themselves around just when you didn't need them to be fucking with you. If we were moving fast and they started swinging around, they slapped on the side of the weapon and made enough noise to drown out a small brass band. The M-60 gunners did their best to keep the belts secured, but that wasn't an easy job in the bush. Dull black demolition tape was usually wrapped around anything that made noise. Stealth and absolute silence might have been our best weapons. In the bush, silence is better than golden. Everything in my load out from my LAAW rocket to my grenades, flares, knives, and any other ops gear that could make noise, was always secured with tape to keep it quiet.

While we were riding the STAB back to My Tho, I had been thinking about the debriefing, scrubbing down, cleaning my weapons, and then getting ready for a night out on the town. I had been planning to spend some serious quality time with My Lee, the owner of the Tan Van Bar and Restaurant. As the debriefing was winding down I was thinking more about My Lee and the long, luxurious night I hoped we would spend together. I was almost ready to head for the door when our AOIC, Warrant Officer Dale McCleskey, let us know that Bravo squad would be running a target of opportunity canal ambush op that night. There was no hard intel, but the VC had been moving a lot of men and material down this particular canal on sampans, so there was a good chance that we would be at the right time and place to interrupt the flow, destroy a few sampans and their cargo, and capture or kill more than a couple of VC.

Everyone in the platoon was a qualified gunner, but there were only five men qualified to drive the STAB: Big Al, Rudy, Pierre, Boomer, and Finley. Tonight Pierre Birtz would be driving the boat. I thought to myself, *The poor bastard just got back and he's going out again. He'll be sitting somewhere in the STAB while the bugs chew on every exposed piece of fresh meat and sweat runs into his eyes, and I'll be in a nice, clean, soft bed with a beautiful woman.* Like the old song says, "It ain't necessarily so." It had been decided by someone way above my pay grade that the boat driver got to pick his gunner. I was told to stick up my hand to make it official; I had volunteered to go out as gunner. Rat shit!

I wouldn't have minded even a little if we'd had some good intel. Shit, if we had *any* intel I would have been first in line to get back to the boonies, but giving up a long night in a soft bed and the companionship of My Lee for an op with no confirmed VC in the area seemed like a really lousy idea. I reminded myself that this was why I had joined the SEALs and that every op was another chance to stick it to Uncle Ho and his boys. I might not be spending the night with My Lee, but the briefing for the new op wouldn't take place until 1800 hours. Even allowing for cleanup, weapons maintenance, and mission prep, we had several hours before we needed to be back in the Quonset hut and geared up. Pierre, Doc Pecuric, our platoon corpsman, and I decided that an early dinner would be an excellent idea, so we hustled through our after-op duties, cleaned and reloaded our weapons, loaded up our grenades and flares, changed into clean clothes, and headed to the Tan Van for some good food. I would have to break My Lee's heart for tonight, but tomorrow night would be a different story. Come hell or high water, in twenty-four hours I would be stretched out in a nice soft bed next to a beautiful woman or somebody would be in a full body cast.

At 1800 hours we were back at the hut. We had shucked our civilian clothes and dressed for the op, our gear was ready, and the briefing was short and simple. Bravo would be setting up the ambush on the Chuc Lo canal. Bravo would position themselves close to the water and a trail that ran along the bank. We would be setting up our ambush in a designated free-fire zone. All the local farmers and fishermen knew that after darkness fell they were not allowed to be roaming around the bush. If anyone came through that area it would be the VC, and Bravo would take them under fire. As dusk fell at 1930 hours, Pierre and I had the STAB alongside the dock. The boat was fully fueled, and ammunition for the .50 caliber machine gun and the twin M-60s had been loaded. The engines murmured, and the deck thrummed. The STAB sank lower in the water as Bravo came aboard and got situated for the hour ride to Chuc Lo. With Jerry Hammerly and Terry Sullivan manning the M-60s, and me behind the .50 caliber Browning, Pierre got the STAB under way and headed into the middle of the river where he could crack open the throttles and pick up speed.

The .50 caliber was at half cock, the M-60s were loaded and locked, and Pierre had the STAB rocking down the river as the last glow of light disappeared from the sky and total darkness made the river and bush disappear. The average VC or NVA soldier, like most soldiers, didn't like the darkness, but every SEAL had been trained to fight underwater, where little light penetrated. We had learned to use the darkness to our advantage. The darker the night, the better we liked it.

About ten minutes into the op a light mist was falling, then a drizzling rain, then sheets of rain. The weather was now perfect for the op Bravo would be running tonight. Rain was smacking down on the bush and the water was noisy, so noisy that it would muffle even the sound of our boots sucking out of the gooey mud. In a heavy rain, it was easier to move quickly into and out of an ambush position without being detected. Unfortunately, the VC were usually more concerned with getting out of the rain, staying dry, and under cover. This meant that this op, like too many others, might end up being just another long night in the bush with no contact and nothing to show for our efforts.

With the rain cutting our visibility to about six inches down the barrels of our rifles, Pierre was having a bitch of a time even finding the mouth of the Chuc Lo canal. We knew that we were close, but close only counts in horseshoes and hand grenades, so Pierre cut one engine, slowed the STAB, and pulled it in close enough to shore to pick out landmarks. In a couple of minutes we were pulling the STAB into the mouth of the canal. The rain was now falling so hard that all I could hear was the raindrops smacking into my poncho. We used the sound of the torrential rain to cover our movement, but now that we were running slow along the canal with very little engine noise, I didn't have a choice. With this much noise I wouldn't be able to hear anything, even if Pierre was screaming out orders to repel boarders. If I wanted to be able to hear anything, I had to take off my poncho. What the hell, I had been wet before and I'd be wet again. The few little dry spots that had been protected by the poncho were soaking wet before I could fold the damn thing up and stuff it into my pack.

Pierre got the STAB so close to the left bank of the canal that the mangrove roots thumped the hull as we moved closer to the insertion point. In the downpour even our starlight night vision gear was worthless. I don't know how he did it—that he could even see the bank of the canal was almost a miracle—but he put the bow right where it was supposed to be. Bravo slipped over the side and immediately disappeared into the bush to set up a security perimeter. Pierre swung the STAB back into the canal and moved us back into the river, where we would wait for the call from Bravo for extraction.

It was literally PDL, pure dumb luck, that we heard the bow bump into a set of fish traps that were attached to long poles driven into the mud at the bottom of the shallow river. We tied up the STAB to the poles, away from the bush and the bugs, and waited for the signal from Bravo. The rain started to slack off and was now no more than a miserable, spitting drizzle. McCleskey had scheduled extraction for 0500 at their primary extraction point, so Pierre and I had a long night of waiting ahead of us unless Bravo got lucky and hit pay dirt sooner. Sure enough, the VC stayed inside where they would be dry and warm while Bravo, soaked, cold, and muddy, wasted their time on one of too many hit-or-miss operations. Intel was the key to good ops, and good intel took weeks, sometimes months to develop. We knew that for every good op we would run we would run three, four, and sometimes a lot more dry missions where all we got was dirty, wet, cold, tired, and pissed off that the VC wouldn't come out and fight.

At 0400 hours McCleskey called for extraction. With Pierre at the wheel, I untied the STAB, and we moved back to the Chuc Lo canal and started looking for Bravo's extraction point. As we approached the area where Bravo should be waiting for extraction, the blinking of the red lens of a flashlight gave us an exact location where Pierre could slip the bow of the STAB through the morass of mangrove roots and into contact with the bush.

Insertion and extraction, no matter how quiet we had been, were always the most dangerous few minutes of the op. While the platoon climbed aboard, we were dead in the water for a couple of minutes. If the VC had spotted the ambush and set up one of their own, we would be sitting ducks. Until the squad was aboard manning the M-60s and the STAB was under way, I would be the only man who could return fire.

We all knew how fast a boring night could turn into a shitstorm, and Bravo came aboard and manned the guns as fast as the mud, the water, and their soaking wet, heavy gear would let them. Pierre backed the STAB away from the shallow bank, swung the boat hard left, centered the canal, and slapped the throttle of the STAB full forward. With both Mercury engines running flat out, we got up on plane in only a few seconds. Dawn was breaking, the rain had stopped, and we were all in one piece and headed back to My Tho. It would be daylight before we reached our base, and another couple of hours would be spent cleaning our gear and weapons, but there would be no debriefing, and no op was scheduled for that night. It looked like I might just be able to keep my promise to My Lee.

All of my plans for a good dinner and a better breakfast with My Lee almost went in the shitter when I heard that Finley had gotten sick and tired of never having enough vehicles for our use. Nobody had bothered to tell the people in charge of handing out equipment that the SEALs, a new bunch of special ops guerrilla-style warriors, might actually need jeeps and trucks. Maybe they thought that we would enjoy carrying all of our gear, ammo, and spare parts on our backs since we were such hard-ass bastards, but Finley wasn't waiting any longer for the requisitions to get found and run through channels and for us to get some transport. Like all good SEALs, we were going to improvise and overcome.

In the brilliant planning of the vehicle acquisition system, probably done by some former car thief turned Pentagon paper pusher, it had been decided that using ignition keys would be too expensive and inconvenient for the poor, dumb troops. It had been dictated that military vehicles, at least in Vietnam, didn't need keys. Vehicles were equipped with a neat little toggle switch, on-off, and a starter switch. It didn't take long for the rightful users of these vehicles to learn the hard way that if they didn't figure out how to secure their ride, it would be stolen like everything else in Vietnam. I don't know who coined the saying, but in Vietnam it was said, "They could steal your radio and leave you the music." So, as soldiers have done since the Roman legions, an "expedient locking device/ key" was found: A hunk of chain was looped through the steering wheel and secured through the floor or any other place where the chain would deter steering until removed by the member of Uncle Sam's best and brightest who had the legal and lawful right to use that vehicle—and the key to the lock that secured the chain.

We may have been Uncle Sam's best, but the guy who thought that a hunk of chain was a good idea for securing a vehicle sure wasn't the brightest star on the top of the Christmas tree. Finley took five guys and three sets of bolt cutters that he had requisitioned and went to Saigon for some R&R and grand theft auto. Finley was the All-Navy heavyweight boxing champion, and one of the nicest guys anyone ever knew. Always a law-abiding type, he believed in God and America, and he would never, ever do anything that might besmirch the reputation of the SEAL Teams, but when he decided that we damn well needed our own vehicles, there was nothing that was going to stop him from getting them. His first step in the plan was to requisition the bolt cutters, and they had shown up in less than a week. The jeeps and trucks he had requisitioned hadn't shown up in five months. Clearly this was a message that God or the folks who had so quickly sent the bolt cutters had decided that we were supposed to make use of the bolt cutters to get our vehicles. We started to see it as our duty as red-blooded Americans to free those poor captive vehicles from their chains of bondage whenever possible. We doggie-robbed so many vehicles from Saigon that we came up with a new name for bolt cutters; we called them master keys.

When the newly freed jeeps, 4-by-4s, and 6-by-6s got back to My Tho, they all seemed to have suffered under their previous owners' poor upkeep—each and every one needed a new coat of paint. Problem was, everybody thought that somebody else had written down the serial numbers before we painted over them, and since we were just dumb SEALs who didn't deserve our own jeeps and trucks, we couldn't remember what the serial numbers had been. Happily, Finley never failed to come up with new numbers and paperwork that matched. After all, we didn't want any of Uncle Sam's property to go missing, especially when we needed it for our own nefarious and necessary purposes.

Luckily, I was not asked to go along on the great jeep heist. For the past five months we had been running pretty hard on ops, both good and bad, and my first tour would be ending soon. Because we were deployed to Vietnam on TAD (temporary additional duty) orders, we were limited to six-month deployments. Six months was the longest time period we could be away from our command. After our six-month tour was completed, we would report back to SEAL Team 2 and liquidate our TAD orders; then we could go back for another tour. Since I wasn't going to be stealing jeeps and trucks, I had an entire week off. All I had to keep me busy was regular weapons maintenance, experimentation with my own improvements to our ordnance, showing up for morning muster, PT, and afternoon muster. I was almost as free as a bird to spend as much time as I could with My Lee at the Tan Van or at the beautiful home that she had made for herself only a couple of blocks from her business. My Lee was the major reason that I couldn't wait to get squared away and back to My Tho.

10

Reason to Celebrate

Seven days and nights in Vietnam sometimes seemed to last close to forever. For the past five months we had been burning the candle at both ends—planning ops, checking and double-checking intel, linking up with the navy Seawolf helos, the army artillery, the fast flyers that could smoke the jungle with rockets, napalm, or machine-gun fire, and everyone and anyone who might be needed for artillery support, air cover, or emergency evac. Added to the schedule were briefing and debriefing, cleaning weapons, gear, and ourselves, and running ops almost every night. Sooner or later the constant stress started taking its toll. No matter how well trained we were or how many ops we had gone on, we had to remind ourselves that the biggest danger we faced wasn't the VC or NVA, and it wasn't mortars or machine guns. The most dangerous enemy that we faced was routine.

If our mission planning, our intel gathering, the way we inserted and extracted, or any other part of our ops became routine or predictable, or we started getting sloppy, the VC would be able to do to us what we did to them. When your ops start to become routine, the enemy starts getting smart.

No matter how much we wanted to be out in the bush running ops, digging out fresh intel, and capturing or taking out the VC, everyone had a limit where he would become a liability. Even the best of us reached a point where we were fried crisp around the edges and it was tempting to just start putting one foot in front of the other. As soon as we started doing what we had done before or became predictable, the VC would be able to turn the tables on us. If we got too burned out, started running on empty, or allowed ourselves to adopt a routine, they would catch us in an ambush and shoot us down. After ninety operations in five months, most of it in the bush, our adrenaline had been running wide open for too long. Still, none of us wanted to admit it. SEALs never quit; it was our job and our choice. We were the people who always took advantage of our enemy's routine. We didn't want soft beds and silk pajamas; we lived to be out in the bush where we could outwit and outfight anybody. Nevertheless, when day-after-day operational routine started to reduce our combat effectiveness, something had to change.

Our officers knew that not even SEALs could run op after op without a break. Officers who valued their men's lives looked the other way when we bent the regs or bailed us out when we got caught red-handed after curfew. A few of them even came along when it was time to blow off some steam and do what comes naturally with the local ladies. Sooner or later, though, no matter how hard we worked to keep ourselves at full combat effectiveness, all of us needed to drain the adrenaline tank and kick back— or risk becoming a liability to ourselves and our team in the bush.

Many, maybe most, of the SEALs that I knew took advantage of the opportunity to decompress with female companions, but there were some guys that never went over the line and cheated on their wives. They might be well lubricated, even as drunk as a skunk, but when we headed for our rented rooms with the ladies they headed back to base alone. Maybe I could have learned something from these guys, but that just wasn't in the cards I was holding.

Master Chief Rudy Boesch informed me that I needed a break and that there were no promising ops on the schedule. He figured that the platoon could handle whatever came our way without me for a whole week. Whether I liked it or not I had been ordered to take seven full days to unwind and enjoy myself. I didn't argue.

My first order of business was being clean—really clean. I took a very long soak in the huge bathtub we shared at the My Tho Hilton and scrubbed away every trace of mud, gun oil, and buffalo crap. I had forgotten that my feet didn't always smell like my boonie boots, a mixture of sweat, rubber, dirt, and mold. Cleaner than I had been since I landed at Tan Son Nhut, I relaxed, daydreamed, and started planning how I was going to spend the next seven days. When the water became too cold for comfortable relaxation, I toweled off, got into my best off-duty outfit, dropped my Colt revolver into the pocket of my jacket, hung the Stoner over my shoulder, and headed across the street to the navy mess hall for a very late breakfast. It wasn't raining, the sun was shining, and it was unlikely that anybody was going to be shooting at me for at least the next couple of hours. This was luxury beyond anything I could remember. I had been ordered to stand down. I had seven glorious days all to myself, and I planned to spend as much time as I could sleeping, eating, enjoying life at the Tan Van, and rolling around in the hay with My Lee at her beautiful home in the center of My Tho.

If there is a heaven, it must be a whole lot like that first long day and night that My Lee and I spent relaxing together at the Tan Van, in her big, comfortable bed, or sitting sipping coffee and eating fresh croissants on the second-story balcony that overlooked the gardens surrounding her home. We had spent most of the previous evening at the restaurant and the rest of the night trying to exhaust one another exploring new and wonderful ways that the human body could be turned into a pleasure machine. There hadn't been much talking, and there hadn't been much need for any. Exhausted and satiated, we finally slept, but first light wouldn't be long in coming.

The morning dawned clear. The humidity wouldn't turn My Tho into a steam bath until the sun heated the river, canals, and paddies. The sky was blue and cloudless. Even the birds were flitting through the trees and flowering bushes. It was so peaceful, beautiful, and perfect that I wasn't sure that I was still in Vietnam. My Lee hadn't wasted any time getting dressed. Her gleaming black hair was wrapped into a neat pile and held in place with long red and black lacquered hairpins that looked a little like fancy chopsticks. She had wrapped a long, flowing, hand-embroidered silk robe around her and tied it at the waist. Covered with an intricate design against a dark blue background, it clung to her every curve like a silken skin and concealed her naked body underneath, but that made her even more beautiful and alluring. She smelled like wildflowers and the ocean wind before a storm.

Like My Lee, I hadn't taken long to dress, but I was in total comfort. While My Lee was finishing her morning shower, I had found and commandeered what would amount to a skirt, a piece of cotton cloth that I wrapped around my waist and tied off as best I could. I was as close to naked as I could get and still not be subject to arrest for being seen out on the balcony. Even my feet were bare; I hadn't bothered to put on my boonie boots. Just a few yards away, my Stoner rested against the dressing table. My Colt revolver was lying on the table next to the bed, where it was in easy reach while I slept.

Two white wrought-iron chairs and a large white wrought-iron table dominated the small half-round stone balcony. The table was covered with a heavy ivory-colored tablecloth; matching napkins were folded and held in place against the gusting breeze that rustled the flowers below by what looked to be real silverware. What was obviously an expensive, handmade white porcelain carafe of steaming coffee and a matching but smaller carafe of heavy cream had been delivered on an old-fashioned silver serving tray. Our breakfast had been brought silently by a young woman who I guessed was one of My Lee's servants or one of her ladies in training, who would someday take her place providing one of the services offered at the Tan Van. She was no older than twelve and almost as beautiful as My Lee. Nestled in another napkin, inside a basket made of woven palm leaves, were half a dozen hot croissants. Breakfast at the navy mess was really good, but this was a breakfast that made me feel like the luckiest SEAL who had ever lived. I told myself to remember to thank Rudy. I had a beautiful woman, great food, perfect weather, and six more days before I needed to show up for muster, or anything else.

The carafe of coffee was almost empty, I was sitting in the sun with a full stomach, and My Lee was telling me more about her family, and how she had become the owner of the Tan Van, when I heard a familiar and unwelcome sound. I moved instinctively. The heavy wrought-iron chair went flying, falling over backward. I grabbed My Lee, knocking her chair out of the way, and pulled her under me, with my body protecting hers, we hit the floor of the bedroom still rolling. I knew that My Lee was shocked that I had grabbed her so roughly and buried her under my body, but the cracking boom of the mortar round exploding in the street just outside of the stone wall that surrounded most of her garden was all the explanation she needed. Doing a quick check, I was relieved that the only damage immediately apparent was a broken coffee cup and the almost invisible stain on her robe where the coffee had splashed as I dragged her away from the table. Neither of us had been hurt, but the double doors that closed off the balcony from the bedroom were missing three panes of glass. Three pieces of shrapnel going as fast as an AK-47 round had pierced the glass. Inside the bedroom I found that two had buried themselves in the ceiling and one was still smoking, stuck deep into the carved wood of the night table where I had put my Colt revolver. I was glad that both of us were unhurt and that the week hadn't come to a sad end in a split second.

The rest of the week was even more relaxing than the first night had been, and my respect for My Lee increased every day. Unlike most of the women in Vietnam, My Lee turned out to be independent and very resourceful. The day of the shooting, while we were relaxing together at the Tan Van, then having a late dinner that evening, someone had come to do a little improvement to her home. When we returned, new steel shutters had been installed on the bedroom side of the double doors that led to the balcony. They had obviously been custom made. They swung open or closed easily on heavy steel hinges and had louvers that were open at the top to allow the breeze to flow through the bedroom but were solid steel along the bottom to stop shrapnel or anything less powerful than .50 caliber fire. Anyone who could get that kind of work done in less than a week, let alone in a single day, was well wired into the system. This was my first hint that My Lee was a part of a network that might become useful someday soon. For the time being I was glad that we could sleep, play, and shower without worrying about the VC dropping another mortar round in our bedroom, but I was still pissed that the VC mortar crew had almost ruined my week. I made a mental note to send my own personal message to the VC crews that were terrorizing My Tho by lobbing mortar rounds indiscriminately into the city every chance they got.

Morning muster, after a week of long nights with My Lee, breakfast on the balcony, and detailed, interesting lessons in her personal history, was not as welcome as it might have been. The ops that had been run while I was off base had produced little of value, there was no promising intel, and nothing that was going to need my full attention in the near future was even in the planning stages. I decided that it was time to ask Lieutenant Quist if I could do a little experimentation that might pay off in dead VC mortar crews. I got the go-ahead, and in a couple of days we had an operational plan in place and were, with Mingh, Finley, and Quist adding their two cents' worth, putting together a big surprise for any VC that thought they could continue to drop mortar rounds into My Tho with impunity.

A mortar was an almost perfect weapon for poorly trained troops like the VC. Just about anybody with a few simple hand tools can put together, from scrap metal if necessary, a working mortar. In addition to being simple and cheap to build, a mortar is easy to operate with fifteen minutes of training. To make an effective mortar, all you need is a hunk of steel tube, a couple of steel legs, and a steel plate welded onto the bottom of the tube. Inside the tube is a fixed steel firing pin that smacks the primer on the mortar round when it is dropped down the tube. The primer ignites the propellant; the round goes up the tube, is stabilized by the fins on the round, and falls someplace close to where the tube is aimed. The detonator in the nose of the round fires the explosive inside the round, and hundreds of pieces of shredded steel—shrapnel—goes screaming away faster than the speed of sound. If you are within a twenty-yard radius, or just unlucky when a mortar round lands, odds are that you are going to be dead or really torn up.

Since the Tet offensive, when they had been slaughtered by the thousands, the VC had wised up and decided that taking us on face-to-face in a pitched battle, or even in urban warfare, was going to earn them a lot of funerals that would discourage new recruits. They had limited access to Chinese mortar tubes, but one of their new tactics was to build dozens of homemade mortar tubes and send three- to six-man teams out into the bush to drop a couple of rounds into My Tho or other cities, villages, and towns every week. They couldn't pick out a specific target to hit, but the mortar rounds had a range of fifteen hundred yards, and when a mortar round carrying a pound and a half of TNT fell out of the sky, it would blow a hole a foot and a half deep in the street and throw shards of shrapnel for fifty or more yards, shredding or severely injuring anybody close to the impact point. If they got lucky and hit a building, the explosion would flatten a wall or roof. I had decided, after digging the shrapnel out of My Lee's bedroom, that this was getting personal, and if I had anything to say about it this particular shit was going to stop.

The problem was that there was no way for us to figure out where the VC were and reach their firing position before they were long gone. Even trying to interdict them on their way back to My Tho wouldn't work because the mortar tube and ammunition would be stashed away somewhere safe where they could easily retrieve it and use it in their next attack. Without catching them red-handed, or at least carrying the mortar tube or ammunition, we couldn't just blow away anyone we captured in the area where the mortar fire had originated. We pushed hard on our intel sources, and even some of My Lee's contacts were asked to make discreet inquiries, but we never got any names, or even the names of the villages that were hiding the mortar teams and allowing them to operate. It was time for the SEALs to do our thing, to get creative and innovate, figure out how to kill those mortar teams before they could drop another round on My Tho or another local village.

One thing that set us apart from most operators was the fact that we never wasted anything that we might be able to use against the enemy. When we captured anything that might be useful, from sampans to enemy weapons, we dragged it back and stashed it away for use when we needed it. Over the past five months, we had accumulated a big pile of VC equipment, including several sampans, dozens of AK-47 and SKS rifles, crates of ammunition, and other assorted VC gear. It was a case of ChiCom 61 mm mortar rounds that gave me a great idea. As a trained explosives man I wondered what would happen if I drilled a little hole right next to one of the stabilizing fins, right where the cast TNT charge would be, and then inserted a sensitized, nonelectric blasting cap with a two-inch length of det cord crimped into it? I figured that the instant the mortar round was dropped down the tube and the primer hit the firing pin, the det cord would fire the blasting cap, the blasting cap would fire the TNT, the mortar round and tube would turn into a ball of incandescent gas and flying metal, and the VC mortar team would be turned into a red mist or bloody chunks of human remains in a microsecond. I was pretty sure that this would work, but we tried a jury-rigged test just to make sure. It worked like a charm. Now all I had to do was fit out the rest of the captured mortar rounds and figure out how to get these rounds to the VC so that they would use them.

The solution to that problem was stashed away behind our Quonset hut. Usually when we captured a sampan we gave it to one of our sources of good intel or sold it to one of our friendly contacts and added the cash to our platoon party fund. For some reason this one had been forgotten until we needed it to serve a higher calling. Mingh and I dragged the sampan out from behind the Quonset hut and down to our firing range at the other end of the camp. We shot it full of holes with an M-60 until all that was left of it looked like a typical sampan that had been caught in a firefight. Then we shot up the receivers of a couple of captured VC rifles to make sure that they could never be used against us, dumped in some captured VC gear—an ammo vest, web belt, a canteen, packets of rice that the VC used as their version of C-rats—tossed in the case of "Uncle Tom's Special Mortar Rounds," covered the whole thing with fresh chicken blood, and waited for muster at 1900 hours at the Quonset hut.

After dinner at the navy mess, the platoon assembled to decide how we were going to deliver our little gift to the VC. At 2200 hours we boarded two of the riverine force PBR boats and, with the sampan tied alongside, headed for a point about four miles upriver from My Tho. When we were at the designated dumping point, and in the middle of the My Tho River, Boomer, Jack Lynch, and I climbed aboard the sampan and slipped into the swim fins that we had stashed in the bottom of the boat. Wearing nothing more than the fins, swimming suits, black pajama tops, and web belts, and carrying our Ka-Bar knives as our only weapons, we paddled the barely floating sampan about a half mile on a moonless night. As we approached the riverbank, the water became so shallow that we couldn't float the sampan onto the bank; we had to get out, strip off our fins, and drag the shot-up hulk the rest of the way through the mud.

With the sampan on the bank, we put on our swim fins and started swimming back out to the middle of the river, where we would be picked up by the PBRs. We hadn't gotten very far, maybe fifty yards, when we got separated in the darkness and, almost too late to avoid it, I heard what sounded like someone poling a sampan. I was dead in the water, all of my senses reaching out for more information, when a sampan appeared. The man pushing the pole hadn't seen me, but he was going to hit me between the eyes with the bow if I didn't get out of the way. In my peripheral vision I could now see Jack—and he was ten feet closer to the sampan and also dead in the water. We both pulled our only weapons, our Ka-Bar knives, and waited. We couldn't see a weapon, and the Vietnamese man in the sampan seemed to be looking for something; he kept turning his head as if he had heard something and was trying to identify it. Jack and I, with only our noses, our eyes and the tops of our heads above water, had been very slowly stroking ourselves away from the angle his sampan was taking up the river. I am almost certain that he saw at least one of us, but the river was crawling with crocodiles, and he probably thought that we were just another small croc out looking for dinner or a girlfriend. Boomer, as big as a full-grown croc, gave us a few quick heartbeats when he popped up from nowhere in the middle of the river. Taking on an eight- or ten-foot long croc with a Ka-Bar would have been a new experience, and more excitement than either Jack or I had planned for or wanted right about then.

The sampan disappeared in the darkness, the PBR responded to my signal with the red-lens flashlight, and we had pickup in less than a minute. Then the fireworks began. Both PBRs ran in line up and down the river popping flares that lit up the riverbank; their gunners swept the shoreline and bush with their twin mounted .50 caliber machine guns. As they raked the bush with machine-gun fire, they were careful not to hit the sampan that we had placed on the bank; it already had enough holes in it. After a fifteen-minute fake firefight we turned for home. At our after-op debriefing it was decided that Doc and I would hook up with a navy Seawolf gunship and do a quick flyover in daylight to see if the rat had taken the cheese from our trap.

At 0800 hours the next morning, two Seawolf helos landed at the base helo pad, and I explained what we would like to do. With Doc on one helo and me on the other, we headed upriver to the site of the huge firefight we had faked last night. Even from several hundred yards out, I could see that the sampan had been dragged completely out of the water and up the bank until it was sitting high and dry. As we circled, it was clear that there was nothing left in the boat; everything we had placed in it was long gone, including the case of my special mortar rounds. I took a handful of Polaroids of the empty sampan and the area around it. Even in the Polaroids it was easy to see that the area around the sampan was covered with the footprints of whoever had grabbed up the gear and munitions. We headed for home, flying fast and high above the mud and jungle. Now all we could do was hope that the mortar rounds would be distributed to the VC mortar teams. We didn't like it because we always liked to be the aggressor, but we had to play a waiting game.

For the next two weeks we planned our canal ambush ops with no intel. We inserted where there were rumors that the VC were moving supplies and equipment at night, but the only enemy movement we saw was a few piles of several-day-old human crap a few yards from the canal. It had been almost two weeks since we planted the sampan, and no mortar rounds had fallen on My Tho, but we were all starting to wonder if we had worked up that op for nothing. Maybe the mortar rounds had never even gotten to the VC. Then Mingh got word from one of his reliable intel sources in a village not far from My Tho.

From the report that came back it was almost a lock that the mortar crew had been standing in a circle around the tube. Maybe they were training a new crew, but in the long run it didn't matter. According to the intel six pairs of feet, a couple of legs, three heads, and other assorted body parts that had belonged to a VC mortar team, along with the remnants of a mortar tube that had obviously exploded, had been found in a bloody circle about twelve hundred yards from My Tho. We marked that day on the calendar, and I bought the first three rounds at the Tan Van that night.

11

Fishy Intel

Following the op we had run with rigged mortar rounds, it had been a lousy couple of weeks. After the VC mortar teams got themselves shredded, everything went into slow motion, and good intel seemed to dry up completely. What little intel we had managed to drag out of the locals was pure bullshit, they wanted to keep us coming back for more, so we'd keep handing out rewards, but it was total crap. It didn't make much sense to me. They were the victims. It was their businesses, huts, and houses that the VC were blowing to kingdom come. With a little more good intel, we could do even more to keep My Tho safe. We were running around all night chasing bad guys who were almost never where the intel said they were. In less than a month I would be rotating home for more training, and it might be months before I would be back in Vietnam. It was time to change our tactics, get some good intel, and break the chain of bone-dry ops that was becoming SOP. Mingh was the guy we depended upon to get it done.

I was never really sure how Mingh had ended up as our combat interpreter. He had already been working with the platoon we had relieved, and long before American ground forces became involved in the war he had proven to be a valuable asset and a fierce enemy of the VC. The rumor was that he had been recruited for the SEALs by the CIA. Word was that before he became our translator Mingh had gotten himself into and out of a few close scrapes. The scar that remained from a bullet wound on his left hand made it obvious that he had been through some dangerous operations and survived. He was deadly serious when planning or running an op, but when the shooting stopped Mingh was really a friendly guy. He had an infectious smile and laughed easily, even at himself, a rare quality that let him fit right into our platoon.

At only a couple of inches over five feet tall and maybe a hundred pounds soaking wet, he didn't appear to be the guy that could look you in the eye, bury the blade of his knife in your liver, tear your eyes out one at a time with his bare hands, and smile while he was doing it. In a firefight, though, or interrogating prisoners who thought that they would be uncooperative and keep their mouths shut, Mingh was pure, undiluted hardcore mean and aggressive. His wife and child lived in My Tho, and he wasn't about to sit on his ass and let the VC destroy their lives or his beautiful hometown.

Mingh suggested that we might get some intel that was worth chasing if he and Jim spent a few hours buying beers and talking to some of the new recruits at the regional Chieu Hoi center in Can Tho. The Chieu Hoi program, which loosely translated means Open Arms, had been kicked off in 1963 to recruit VC or NVA soldiers to return to their homes and villages and to fight against the Communist forces. Some people have said that the Chieu Hoi program wasn't effective, or was even a total waste of time and resources, but the U.S. Marine victory at Khe Sanh over the NVA General Vo Nguyen Giap was at least partly due to information provided by Lieutenant La Thanh Tonc, an NVA officer who defected through the Chieu Hoi program. Some estimates of Chieu Hoi defections during the war run as high as two hundred thousand. For every Chieu Hoi, there was one less VC fighting against us and one more experienced soldier fighting for his country. More would have been better.

Mingh was sure that some fresh intel could be dug out at Can Tho. A new group of a couple of dozen Chieu Hoi had just arrived, and he hoped that the latest VC to join the program might have fresh intel that hadn't been compromised. If it was there to be found, Mingh and Jim were the guys that could dig it out, bring it back, make sure that it wasn't going to lead us into an ambush, and help put together the operation that would put it to good use. When I found out where we would be running the op, I almost wished that they had come back with nothing more than more vague rumors. No such luck. They had gotten the same story from three different sources, and Mingh, using other sources outside the Chieu Hoi camp, made sure that the intel checked out. We had actionable intel for the first time in weeks, but if we were going to use it before the VC knew that we were coming, we had to get the op planned and executed fast.

I had never thought that I would prefer to miss out on an op, but when Mingh told me that there was a VC VIP running propaganda tours during the day and hiding at night in the *nuoc mam* factory, which we passed on almost a daily basis on our way out and back from operations, I wished that the Chieu Hoi had kept their mouths shut. *Nuoc mam* is a fish-based sauce that it seemed was used by just about everyone in Vietnam, almost like Americans use ketchup or mustard. I had never tried the stuff because it smelled so bad that it almost made me gag. I could smell even a little tiny bit of it from, say, fifty yards away. To me *nuoc mam* smelled like a large dead fish had been rolled up in the old socks worn by a rugby team and left to sit in direct sunlight until it got moldy, the mold had turned purple and green, the fish guts had bloated and blown the belly open, and even a maggot wouldn't get near it. The factory where they made thousands of gallons of that reeking slop had to be at least a thousand feet away when we sped up or down the river on the STAB, but even with the wind at our back there was no way to avoid the stench of that rotting fish sauce.

Still, stink or no stink, it was good intel, and we were itching to get the op planning done and get in position to grab up this VC, who was supposed to be a part of the high-level infrastructure in the My Tho area. The whole platoon would be going in with full load outs. I would be carrying plenty of ammo, grenades, and at least one LAAW rocket. Big Al would be carrying even more ammo and several claymore mines in case we decided to leave behind a few booby traps. On most ops Big Al carried so much ammo and other gear that he just held his breath and walked across the bottom of the canals because his flotation vest couldn't keep him above water. I asked him once what he would do if he ran out of air before he got across the canal. He got a serious look on his face, thought about it for a minute, and told me that he might just have to get to the other bank with a little less ammo.

With the entire platoon geared up and ready for the operation, the briefing was held at 1600 hours. Because the *nuoc mam* plant was so close to the river, we would lose the element of surprise if we inserted from the water. Tonight we would be inserting by helo, but the navy Seawolf pilots were already scheduled for other operations, so we contacted the army helo group, and they were more than happy to give us a ride. Artillery and other support that might be needed was also called, given the fire coordinates, and put on alert. If the op went as planned, we would get in, snatch the VIP, and get out before anyone could react, but if we ran into overwhelming enemy opposition, the artillery needed to have our coordinates plotted and be ready to react—fast. The plan was for us to use the tactic called the stay-behind.

We would insert using four army helos four klicks inland from the *nuoc mam* plant. With our load outs of ammunition, grenades, radio, and other gear almost outweighing us, we saddled up and headed for the helo pad. Alpha and Bravo squads would be in the lead helos; a dozen or so volunteers from the base would ride the other two. We had planned to insert in a rice paddy two hours before sundown, a time when we were sure that we would be seen by at least half the VC near the *nuoc mam* plant and all of the local villagers. As the sun dropped toward the horizon, the four helos skimmed the treetops, then flared, shedding forward momentum, and briefly touched down. We unloaded quickly and moved into the surrounding trees and bush where we could lie low. A tight security perimeter was set up, and everyone waited for last light.

In the last few minutes of fading sunlight the four helos repeated their performance, and the volunteers, yelling out to one another and generally making enough noise to wake the dead, rushed the doors and jumped aboard. Keeping the rotors whipping up dust and making as much noise as they could, then, rotors whining, flying high where they could be seen for at least a couple of dozen klicks, the army pilots did their best to let everyone within My Tho province know that we had headed back to base.

In the bush Alpha and Bravo, left behind in the noise and confusion, kept our heads down and waited. In minutes the word would go out that the devils with green faces had gone home and that everything was safe. On this type of op we would normally have stayed hidden in the bush until the horizon was as black as the inside of a coffin buried in a coal mine, but tonight we had a couple of problems. There was going to be a full moon, and we had several canals to cross before we would reach the target. We had planned to reach the factory just before daybreak, so we didn't have time to waste. We had to stay behind or under whatever cover we could find, blend into the shadows, and start moving out. It was going to be a long night.

With the moon now rising, we broke our 360-degree security circle and headed out toward the *nuoc mam* factory. Even this far away I was sure that I could follow my nose and find the place in the dark, but it wouldn't be a quick trip. We had six or seven canals to cross, and each canal would slow us down. When we crossed even a small canal, we always set up security and waited until the point man crossed first to reconnoiter the other side. When he finished scouting the area to make sure that there were no booby traps, and no VC waiting to spring an ambush, he signaled that it was safe to cross. The next two men in the patrol column would cross and set up security to cover our right and left flanks, and the rest of the platoon would cross two men at a time. When we were all on the other side, we'd take a head count, hump to the next canal, and do it all over again.

We had crossed only one canal and had just reached the second when the unmistakable sound of a pole whacking against the side of a sampan stopped us cold. It only took a couple of seconds for Alpha squad to move into position for an ambush, and, like fog blown by a steady breeze, Bravo disappeared into the dark shadows of the bush. I was down on one knee with the muzzle of my Stoner pointing toward the middle of the canal; kneeling beside me was Lieutenant Quist. We didn't want to start shooting because it would alert the VC VIP and his guests at the factory that there was something bad going down too close to where they thought they would be safe and secure. The last thing that we wanted was for somebody to decide that it might be a good idea for him and his friends to spend the night running or hiding someplace that wasn't where we wanted him to be. Lieutenant Quist would make the call.

In the moonlight I could see two people poling the sampan, but I didn't see any weapons. It was probably just a sampan full of black market goods that these two people were smuggling past the VC tax collectors. I was hoping that if they spotted us Mingh, dressed in his black pajamas and looking like any other late traveler, would just call them over where we could take them prisoner, tie them up and gag them, and leave them while we continued with our patrol. The steady rhythm of their poles never hiccupped as they passed within ten feet of our position. We listened as the sound of the poles slapping on the water and banging against the sides of the sampan grew faint and then stopped as the sampan disappeared around a turn in the canal. Now we needed to make up some time. Pierre Birtz was on point, Lieutenant Quist was next in line, and I was third man. We were moving as quickly as silence and stealth would allow. In the light of the now full moon, I could see almost our entire platoon strung out behind me. It was about 0200 hours, and we had made up some of the time lost at the second canal, when Pierre signaled to halt. Everyone immediately dropped to one knee and moved as much as possible out of the moonlight and into the shadows or available cover.

Most of the time we waited for word to be passed back as to why we had stopped. Tonight nobody needed to tell us what was going on; we could hear laughing, talking, and even the sound of footsteps coming in our direction. In the moonlight I could now see movement coming toward us along a dike that ran through the rice paddy, parallel to the path we were following. The dike was only thirty or forty yards away, and it was crawling with well-armed VC. I was really surprised at how lax their security was. Only a few of the VC carried their rifles at port arms; most of them had their weapons slung over their shoulders or across their backs. There was no way for them to be able to get to their weapons before we cut them all down where they stood. It looked like there was no security covering their flanks, and nobody was even watching for a potential enemy, and to top it all off they made enough noise to wake the dead. I couldn't help but think that tonight our stay-behind tactics had worked exactly as planned. If there had been even a hint of the men with green faces being in the neighborhood, the VC would have been running away or out hunting for us, not walking down the middle of a dike in full moonlight like it was Fifth Avenue in New York City and this was St, Patrick's Day.

We were all down on one knee, waiting for the VC to see us and start the festivities. I couldn't believe that they hadn't seen us; all we had to break up our silhouette was our camouflage, face paint, and the thin screen of scraggly bush that surely wouldn't stop any incoming that they threw at us. We could run, but we couldn't hide behind anything because there wasn't anything to hide behind. I kept wondering how many of them I could take out before they took me out. I kept thinking about how best to sweep the dike with the Stoner, what would be the most effective use of my firepower to protect the platoon, how long it would be before the drum magazine was empty—and if I lived long enough to empty the drum, would I live long enough to get a belt of fresh ammo into the gun?

The VC just kept coming. More and more of them stumbled along the dike until I was sure that this was a whole freaking battalion out for a midnight stroll. The legendary Doc Rio—I would meet him on my second tour—told me that there is a psychological term for what happens when things slow down to something like a slow-motion movie, but I never remembered what it was. He said that this slow-motion effect isn't uncommon in battle or a car wreck, and I know that he was right because it seemed to take a couple of years for the VC to finally disappear into the distance and for me to start thinking about all the time we lost and how hard we were going to hump to make it up.

After a half hour of waiting to make sure that there were no more VC headed our way, and with a head count complete, Lieutenant Quist got us up and moving. Now we were way behind schedule, and we were moving as quickly as we could. If the VC had spotted us, the mission would have been compromised, but I was almost disappointed that we hadn't been able to take out as many of the enemy as we could. If we had even a small amount of cover, trees, a dike, or other defilade, we could have taken most of them out all by ourselves. With some support from artillery and maybe a couple of Seawolf helos we would have chopped them all into pieces and ended in one firefight the careers of more VC than we had seen for months, but our primary mission was to capture a high-level VC and drain him of every bit of intel we could get. Cut off the head of the snake and the snake can't bite; it just thrashes around until it dies. If we could capture this guy alive and squeeze some good intel out of him, it might lead us to several more important members of the VC infrastructure, and that might lead us to even more high-level VC. If we could cut off the heads of enough big snakes, sooner or later, all of the lesser snakes would die.

In the moonlight it was easy to see where I was going, and to keep my night vision focused far enough ahead of our line of march to see Pierre on point and Lieutenant Quist following in his footsteps behind him. I would be able to see any threat long before we were in danger. Thinking back to the lifetime or two that it took for the VC to pass us by while we were frozen out in the scraggly bush like rocks, I wondered why I never felt any fear when death was so close at hand. In a firefight there isn't time to think. Everything goes on autopilot. When the shit hits the fan and 7.62 ball and tracers are tearing up the trees, bush, and dirt, the explosion of the claymores is blasting your eardrums and keeping the VC from over-running your position, and grenades are flying high on their way to an invisible enemy, there isn't time to be scared. When we were back at our base and I was washing the mud and blood off of myself and my gear, I would realize just how close it had been and try to figure out how to do it better, how to keep myself and my platoon safe when all any sane man would want to do was dig a hole and keep his head down.

The briefing called for us to be in position behind the *nuoc mam* factory before first light. We crossed two more canals and walked another half mile or so before we could see light coming from several lanterns hung somewhere inside the factory. Following a well-traveled dirt road that led right up to the back of the factory, we were so close that we could hear voices and noise from inside. Quist moved the platoon into the bush, set up a security perimeter, and waited for the sun to rise. As the horizon grew lighter, we could hear more voices and could see people moving along the road along the canal that led to the front of the factory. Mingh listened to the chatter and reported that they were the workers coming in from nearby villages to start their day before the heat and humidity became unbearable. We didn't have long to wait, and at 0800 hours Boomer radioed the Seawolf detachment at Dong Tam and our Mike 8 boat that was already in position. It was time to put our ops plan into motion, to let the games begin.

In less than three minutes the Seawolf helos were circling the factory only a few dozen meters from the ground with rotors flying, dust and stink being blown everywhere. The Mike 8 boat roared up to the bank of the canal right in front of the factory and lowered the bow ramp. We got exactly the reaction we had hoped for. The workers stood stock-still, staring bug-eyed at all the unwelcome, unnerving activity. Everyone who had something to hide or worry about headed out the back of the factory and down the dirt road. Alpha squad had positioned ourselves alongside the rail gate leading into the factory so that we could stop and question anyone who came out the back. Bravo squad had set up as security to our rear just in case anyone heard the commotion and came to investigate. Several people in black pajamas were headed in our direction, and they were in a hurry. If we spotted anyone carrying a weapon, that individual would be taken out on the spot. They couldn't see us, and before they could even think about how they might avoid us, Mingh, carrying his M-16, stepped out of the bush where we had concealed ourselves and called over two men and four mama-sans. He told them to sit down on the side of the road and put their hands on top of their heads. In a minute or two, a couple more sets of black pajamas showed up, and it looked like we had grabbed all of the people who had tried to escape to the bush. Boomer got on the radio and let the Seawolf crews know that their service had been much appreciated and that they could depart. The Mike 8 boat was asked to stand by for extraction with prisoners.

Mingh and Jim started questioning the people that we had sitting along the side of the road. We asked nicely about the VC official that we were looking for, and there was no response. We decided that it was time to let the women loose and to tie the elbows of the four men behind them and gag them while we searched the factory to see if anyone of interest was still hanging back or hiding. Bravo squad took over the prisoners, and I tried to figure out what I could use to stuff up my nose to keep that stench out of my nostrils. I considered cutting a piece from my shirt or even cutting a pocket off of my jeans but didn't want to destroy the half of my wardrobe that had survived so far. With nothing else I could use at hand, I tried to breathe through my nose as little as possible. We moved cautiously into the factory.

The owner of the factory was a rotund little guy that was in our face almost before we got inside. He wanted to know who we were, what we were doing, and who we thought we were to be keeping his workers from doing their jobs. Mingh, with his face only an inch or two from the owner's, spoke to him softly and asked him where the VC official was hiding. I couldn't hear what Mingh said, but it did get a reaction. The eyes of the owner of the *nuoc mam* factory went as wide as hubcaps on a VW Bug; he tried to speak but only stuttered, pissed his pants, shut his mouth, and never said another word.

There were several people standing around the factory who were trying to do their work as if nothing had happened and it was just another day at the stink factory. Mingh was sure that if we hadn't already grabbed the VC target in the first batch of prisoners that were now tied and gagged, we would find him hiding somewhere in or around the factory. We split into two-man search teams and started looking. Nothing unusual was found in the factory, so we moved on to the hooches where the fish were processed before being sent to the factory for bottling. Most of the hooches had nets full of fish guts, fish heads, and fish parts, hanging over open steel troughs. As the stuff in the nets fermented or rotted, it dripped into the troughs and flowed down into big steel vats. I was almost certain that I would have to burn my gear to get rid of the stink.

There were a few kids and mama-sans still working in the hooches, but Mingh hit the jackpot when he searched the storage hooch where the largest vat of fermenting fish parts was kept. Three men were hiding in the vat, and the *nuoc mam* was up to their necks. I couldn't believe anyone could stand that stench, let alone sit neck-deep in rotting fish.

With seven prisoners bound and gagged, we mustered everyone up, got a head count, and loaded aboard the Mike 8 boat for a short cruise to My Tho, where we would implement the second part of our plan for getting better intel from people who didn't want to give it to us.

Back at our base in My Tho, the prisoners were off-loaded and taken over to our Quonset hut. Mingh sat them down in a row against the wall and one at a time, so they wouldn't be talking to one another, removed their gags and asked which one of them was the VC bigwig that we were looking for. As we expected, nobody said a word. We got no response, not even lies or bullshit. Mingh started his interrogation quietly, with an even voice, but with each refusal to speak his voice went up another notch. While Mingh was slowly interrogating the prisoners, Part B of our plan was coming together.

Part of the training that all medics get is as real as it can be before they actually see what can happen to the human body in battle. Somebody at the Pentagon, bless his REMF ass, had decided that it would be a good idea if medics could be trained using real battle wounds. Since that was impossible, the Pentagon spent a bunch of tax dollars to develop the most realistic fake wounds anybody has ever seen. These things can even bleed. They are made out of a rubberlike stuff called moulage so that they look like real flesh, bone, and tissue and can be used over and over again in training. These things were just what the doctor ordered, so we had requisitioned two or three dozen when nobody was looking.

It took about half an hour before Mingh had completed his interrogation, but not a word had leaked out of the prisoners. In a fit of fake rage, Mingh grabbed up one of the prisoners that he was sure wasn't the VC we were looking for and dragged him away from the others and around the back of the Quonset hut. Once there he was stripped of his black pajamas, and a Chieu Hoi volunteer almost the same size as the prisoner slipped into them. While the fake stomach wounds and a horrific head wound were carefully put in place and fake blood was liberally poured where it would do the most good to hide the true identity of the volunteer, we slapped half-empty sandbags with rifle butts. Mingh continued to scream questions, and, as the fake torture went on and on, another volunteer screamed out in artificial agony. When the fake wounds were ready and Boomer and I could keep ourselves from laughing, Al slowly fired three rounds from his M-16 into the ground. Then we picked up the stretcher with the now unrecognizable Chieu Hoi aboard and, with the fake entrails hanging out of the fake belly wound that was dripping blood and the head wound gushing more blood, we paraded the stretcher past the line of prisoners sitting on the ground next to the Quonset hut. Mingh, his pants and boots covered in fake blood, stepped around the end of the hut, wiping fake blood from his hands onto his green camouflage shirt. He removed the prisoners' gags and asked again who was the VC official. Nobody said a word. Mingh pointed to the last man in line and said, "Next." Even before Jack started to pick the guy up, their eyes were open like saucers and they were all staring at one guy in the middle of the lineup. They were all trying to outshout one another and were calling him by name. Our ruse had worked and the VC official was turned over to two interrogators who we guessed were CIA field agents. The rest of the prisoners were set free to make their way back to their villages as best they could.

Next was the debriefing, cleaning up all of the fake blood and mud, and then an afternoon nap. At 1800 hours I would head down to the Tan Van for a couple of cold Ba Me Ba beers and a good meal. If my luck held, beautiful My Lee would ask me to spend the night at her home, where we could indulge in some extracurricular activities.

12

First Tour—Last Dance

The sheath of my Ka-Bar knife was looking like it had been used as a toothpick by a middling-sized tiger shark. As I carved another of the small notches I used to keep track of our ops, I realized that if we ran another op before our turnover to the next platoon I sure as hell couldn't use this sheath or I would lose the knife. With other, more important things than counting to occupy my mind, like not getting killed, working out some new tricks that would help us operate even better in the bush, developing ways to get hold of more intel, and figuring out how to avoid being grabbed by the shore patrol getting from My Lee's house to base, I had decided to use the sheath to keep track of our missions. In only six months, the sheath had accumulated over ninety slices. It was hard for me to believe that I had been out on more than ninety operations. With both edges cut up and the stitching sliced to shreds, the sheath was close to falling apart; the only thing holding it together was the rivets. Looking closely at every square inch, there was no more room, or time, to add another op to the count. I figured that it wasn't a problem. I would be going home soon, and I could retire my first sheath and find myself a new sheath for my next tour. How wrong a humble young SEAL can be.

I was only five days and a wake-up away from turnover to a new platoon and the trip home to Virginia Beach. Given any choice in the matter, I would have liked to stay another couple of weeks so that I could help to brief the new platoon, take them out on their first ops, and get them settled in before the long, slow journey home. However, being only a miserable, lowly E-4, I was far down the list of volunteers that would get to stay and play hide-and-seek, live-or-die in the bush with the VC. Besides, as much as I would have liked to stay, I knew that most of what needed to be done was paperwork and administrative details, like hooking the new guys up with all of the support assets available, and that surely wasn't my strong point. Rudy Boesch or Jim Finley would get one of those slots, and another officer would get the second. Still, there was at least a little method to my madness. If I could have arranged to stay I could spend another couple of weeks with My Lee, and for reasons other than just the long, passionate nights.

As the owner of a prosperous business, My Lee had developed a network of people who, although they were not VC, knew more about what the VC were planning than almost anyone else in the entire My Tho area. Some of these people had daughters and sons who worked for My Lee, some were old friends My Lee had helped out in the past, and many of them were the farmers and fishermen who sold her the meat, fish, and vegetables that her cooks turned into wonderful, exotic meals that would melt in your mouth. The one thing that they all had in common was their trust of My Lee and their distrust of anyone wearing a uniform.

Trust was the only currency that we had to try to get the freshest intel we could find. "Mayor" Jim Finley, who was so well liked that half of the people on any street in My Tho waved to him when they saw him coming, had set up a loose intelligence network. Money got us some intel, but money alone rarely got us any *good* intel. If we did get good intel and hurt the VC they would find out where we had gotten the information sooner or later, then simply assassinate anyone that they suspected of handing it over. To overcome this problem, Jim used the only currency that worked: He proved that he could be trusted. He protected his sources and made sure that when we pulled a good op the intel couldn't be traced back and get the source killed. That My Lee trusted me, and her friends trusted her, made intel gathering at the Tan Van a lot easier. Neither Jim nor I ever got the intel directly. My Lee was always the cutout, the person who passed on the information, but there was no way for anyone to know where the information came from. She would get some intel, then try to see if the same intel came from another source. If she could confirm it, she passed it along directly to Jim, and he made sure that there was no way for the VC to track it back to My Lee or any of her contacts. Because Jim worked directly with My Lee I never knew for sure, but I think that My Lee's wide network of trusted friends and contacts gave Jim some of the best intel he got in My Tho. I hoped that My Lee would keep supplying Jim, or whoever took his place, with good intel after our tour in My Tho came to an end.

Everything that we did, at least everything that our officers told us to do, was classified. I didn't like it much, but I couldn't tell My Lee when I was leaving. I sure wasn't looking forward to breaking the news, or ending our growing friendship. If everything went as planned, the op last night at the *nuoc mam* factory would be my last for this tour. If Mingh had dug up some good intel from the high-level VC that we found sitting in the vat of *nuoc mam* we would have been planning the op while the information was still smoking hot. But Mingh and the CIA interrogations people took their time and squeezed the VC prisoners slowly and completely dry. We might not like it, but there was no reason to screw around with interrogation methods that had proven to be successful so many times before. I was starting to feel sorry for myself—no new ops, no My Lee, no getting to stay for an extra week or two—so I put the Ka-Bar in its ratty sheath, stuck it into my rear pocket, and headed toward the door of the Quonset hut. I was headed out to the conex box where we stashed our ammunition to finish an inventory for turnover; but I never made it out the door. Our master chief, Rudy Boesch, blocked the doorway and told me to forget the inventory. It looked like we would be running another op tomorrow night with the PRU team.

The Provisional Reconnaissance Units had been recruited by the CIA, and most of them were mercenaries: Montagnards, Chinese Nung, Muslim Chams, Cambodians, or former VC. The one thing they had in common was that they liked getting paid for killed or captured VC and captured weapons and documents. The CIA kept them from becoming nothing more than an assassination squad by paying them a lot more for live VC than dead VC. Dead VC couldn't talk, and intel from live VC was what the CIA wanted more than anything else. The PRUs worked in teams of sixty-five to seventy-five men. They were highly specialized units led by experienced officers and a PRU chief that was, more or less, their OIC, a job that nobody in his right mind would want.

As tough as they were, the PRU teams had one big problem: They didn't get paid to fight. They only got paid for whatever they could steal, blow up, kill, or bring back for the interrogation and intel teams. The CIA paid them, and the CIA had a lot of money flowing to the PRU teams, so, they more or less reported to the CIA; they didn't report to anyone in the military chain of command. To increase their combat ability and effectiveness, each PRU team was assigned a U.S. adviser, most often a SEAL or Green Beret. With a SEAL or Green Beret along, the PRU teams had access to all of our support assets. Everything from artillery to naval gunfire, medevac helos, and air cover could be called up if the op went to hell in a handbasket.

The most valuable assets were the helos used for insertion and extraction. Trying to extract a seventy-man PRU team, six, eight, ten, or more prisoners, captured documents and weapons, and anything else of value that wasn't nailed down was almost impossible without the use of the helos. It was the adviser who laid on all of the available assets needed for the operations, and the PRU teams made good use of everything we could supply.

We helped the PRU teams out and they helped us; it was a two-way street. SEAL Team 1 had an adviser named Dave attached to the PRU team that operated out of My Tho. Dave would give us a call whenever he needed some serious firepower or on-the-ground support for an important op; part of our job was to make sure that the prisoners stayed alive and were brought back for the CIA intel boys to do their thing. We looked forward to going out with Dave and his PRU team because they rarely had a dry op. They had the best intel network in the whole area. It looked like I had better find a new sheath for the Ka-Bar, because PRU intel was rarely wrong. We would be needed, and this would be our last dance before getting on the big, slow bird for home.

With the planning just getting started, we had the night off, so the platoon decided to hit all of our favorite hangouts for one last blast. Just before curfew some of the platoon headed back to our home bar in the My Tho Hilton, and the rest of us stayed in town to enjoy the rest of the night as best we could. I drifted over to the Tan Van and waited until it closed for the night. Even though I couldn't tell My Lee that I was leaving in four days, this might be the last time I would ever see her, if only for a few hours. Quarters were early and I never liked leaving My Lee all alone, but I guessed that this morning we might be getting orders for that one last operation. So, as much as I would have liked to spend the night with her, in the wee hours I took myself back to the My Tho Hilton. In fact, I almost couldn't wait to get there.

The orders were short and simple: Tonight we would be going out with Dave's PRU team; briefing would be held at 1800 hours in our Quonset hut. Following an hour of PT on the roof, most of us grabbed some sack time to catch up on the sleep we hadn't gotten last night. Dinner was at 1700 hours, and at 1800 hours we were all assembled for the briefing. Dave had already briefed Quist, Rudy, and McCleskey and was standing by to answer questions. Our squads, along with Dave and his twenty-five-man PRU team, would be inserted using our Mike 8 boat and two PBRs from the riverine base around 2100 hours.

Our main target was a VC commander, who, as it turned out, was leading the long line of VC that had almost busted our raid on the *nuoc mam* factory. The PRU intel was that this commander was running a very big training program not far from where we had watched them stream past us on the dike two nights ago. It was just our luck to stumble into them when he was collecting all of the local VC and moving them to the training area. I hadn't counted, but I remembered thinking to myself that there were more VC concentrated on that dike than I had ever seen before all put together. After the Tet offensive, when we had killed and captured hundreds of VC and captured and destroyed tons of weapons and munitions, the VC just didn't have enough local recruits; they had been forced to operate in small units. Now it looked like they were recruiting more people and building their strength. It was our job to grab the commander so that he could be interrogated and to reduce as needed the number of VC in the My Tho area.

Dave had brought along some aerial photos of an area that we were familiar with from previous operations. We had named it the coconut grove. We would insert via the river and patrol to within sight of that area where the VC were training. Dave marked our fire support positions on the map. Only six of the PRU team were going to penetrate the VC encampment. Somehow they thought that six men could get in, capture the VC commander, and get out while the rest of the team and our squads stayed back to cover their retreat with the prisoner. It didn't make much sense to me, but that was the plan.

We would never split our force, especially at night, and leaving thirty men to provide cover fire with moonlight the only illumination, when you could never be sure where your guys would grab up the prisoner, or where they would be coming out of the VC encampment, seemed like a suicide mission. I just hoped that the six guys going into the camp could infiltrate the area, snatch the VC commander, and get out before anybody knew that they were there. I also hoped that if somebody started shooting, the PRUs that stayed behind would be able to spot their guys before somebody thought they were VC and lit them up. It was their op and their lives. We would do our best and hope that the op went as fast and quiet as possible.

Dave and his PRU team climbed aboard the Mike 8 boat, and our two squads clambered aboard the twin PBRs. As we headed upriver, the moon was rising high in the sky. Though we normally didn't like to operate when the moon was up, tonight it might give us a real advantage. The SEALs and the PRU had more than a little experience in operating in total darkness. In fact, that was the way we liked it. We were well-trained night fighters who could see well in the dark; in bright moonlight we would be able to see even better, all the way across the paddies and dikes. If the shit hit the fan, the odds were pretty good that we would be able to tell the good guys from the bad guys.

The engines of the boats slowed, and the Mike 8 stayed put in the middle of the river while the PBRs eased up to the riverbank and inserted both of our squads. We set up a security perimeter, listened, watched, and waited for fifteen minutes to make sure that nothing had leaked to the VC, and they hadn't set up an ambush for us. When we were sure that we were alone, we flashed a signal with a red-lens flashlight for the Mike 8 to move in and the PRUs to slip into the bush. With two SEAL squads and the PRU unit ashore, Dave sent his two point men ahead while we drifted behind them by fifty yards, far enough to be out of the line of fire if they walked into an ambush, but close enough to lay down a shitstorm of cover if they needed it. Our fourteen-man platoon was in the middle of the patrol with Mingh and a couple of PRU troops. Dave and his twenty-five PRU were strung out ahead of and behind us. Our total head count was forty-one, and with ten-foot intervals between each two men we were stretched out over a hundred yards.

There had been a lot of scuttlebutt about the PRU teams, most of it bad. Some said that they were nothing more than cold-blooded assassins who collected ears from the dead VC, or anybody else that they found dead, after a battle or firefight to prove how many people they had killed and to increase the flow of American dollars from their CIA paymasters. Some people said that they were just mercenaries who would switch sides in the middle of a firefight if it looked like the VC were winning. Some of the rumors might have been true, but there was no question that the PRU were among the most feared fighters in Vietnam. In many ways they were similar to SEALs. They all carried good weapons and as much ammunition as they could get their hands on and still hump through the boonies. Like us, they knew that a malfunctioning weapon would probably get them killed, so they maintained their weapons well. The PRU were all tough, and most were as mean as a snake, and they had the advantage of the best training possible; they had grown up in the bush, fighting and surviving when the odds were stacked against them. The PRU teams were the only people except the SEALs who carried LAAW rockets, grenades, clay-mores, and white para-flares. Just like us, when they opened fire they wanted the VC to think that they had run into a vastly superior force. The more firepower you can throw downrange, the bigger the enemy thinks you are. In a firefight bigger is always better.

The brightness and angle of the moonlight was an advantage tonight. Being able to see where we were putting our feet let us move fast along the darkness of the tree line; if there were any trip wires or booby traps, we would see them easily and avoid them. As we got close to our objective, the patrol stopped and set up a security perimeter, and Dave sent out a couple of his PRU scouts to check the lay of the land. From my position I never saw the scouts leave or return, but word was passed back that the area was clear and we would be moving forward and setting up our perimeter behind a dike that faced the coconut grove.

Paddy dikes are mostly made of hardened mud mixed with straw, rotting vegetation, and a dollop or two of cow or buffalo dung added to hold the whole thing together. In the rainy season they could become as slippery as ice, and in the dry season they were almost as hard as concrete. They didn't smell too good, but the smell never bothered us very much. When we were using them for cover, hunkered down on the right side, the side away from the bullets coming our way, they would stop just about any small-arms fire very effectively. From our secure vantage point behind the dikes, we could clearly see the line of coconut trees two hundred yards in front of our position. The moonlight was so bright that we could pick out individual leaves on trees and even small hummocks of grass between the trees. Through the trees we could see that there were a few oil-burning lanterns still sputtering, throwing a small pool of light in the dark shadows under the trees. The wicks of several lanterns that had run out of oil were still sending up a plume of smoke from where they had been hung in the coconut trees. It wasn't hard to figure out that the VC training activities hadn't ended too long ago.

On the far right end, between us and the line of coconut trees, was a large hooch. In the bright moonlight we could see that there were two windows and a single door on the front and one smaller window on the left wall. It was very quiet, and we had settled in to wait for the PRUs to grab up the VC commander when somebody must have kicked a dog or stepped on the tail of one of the sleeping VC. In a split second the peaceful coconut grove erupted. Gunfire came from inside and outside the hooch, and in half a heartbeat several people came flying out of the door and windows, running for the cover and safety of the coconut grove.

The PRU team opened up, and we followed suit. In a second or two, hundreds of red tracers went streaking across the clearing from our position behind the dike toward the people running through the paddy and diving behind coconut trees. So far the op was going according to plan. We had taken them by complete surprise, and the VC, confused and under fire, had been cornered in the hooch. They were scared, scattered into the night, and on the defensive. I hoped that the PRU team had captured the VC target before the shooting started.

We were on the offensive, and we had the advantage of good cover. We also had fire superiority, but not for long. Before I was less than half-way through the first drum magazine on my Stoner, the VC had a steady stream of green tracers coming back at us. It looked like there was twice as much incoming as we had outgoing. Hundreds of rounds went sailing over our heads, and hundreds more smacked into the dike. I could even hear the rounds ripping their way through the waist-high elephant grass behind us. The tree line was blazing with muzzle flashes, giving us small targets, but the VC could also see the flash from our muzzles. I was in for a hot time because they always focused their fire on the M-60 and Stoner operators first.

Somebody was turning the coconut trees, where the VC were hiding, into kindling with a couple of 40 mm grenade launchers. The VC thought that the tree line would provide good cover, but when the grenades started exploding on the tree trunks only a few feet above their heads the splintered wood became just more high-speed shrapnel. The fire coming from the tree line slowed to sporadic pops and bursts as the VC who wanted to stay alive started hugging the dirt.

Boomer, as cool and collected as anybody could be when a couple of hundred well-armed people were doing their best to kill him, was on the radio. He was calmly giving the Mike 8 boat the range and fire coordinates and telling them to call in the Seawolf choppers for support. With the choppers in the air, we couldn't use the 81 mm mortar fire from the Mike 8 boat until they had cleared the airspace through which the mortars would come falling. Boomer made sure that they would be ready, cocked, locked on the target, and ready to drop rounds down the tube when he called for mortar support.

As I pulled my LAAW from my back and snapped it open I heard something I had never heard before, the sound of a heavy .50 caliber machine gun being fired in my direction. The .50 caliber machine gun bullet is fourteen times bigger than the 5.56 mm ammo I used in my Stoner. Bullets that big can shoot through brick walls, concrete block bunkers, and lightly armored vehicles. Even a grazing hit or a flesh wound from a bullet with the kinetic energy of the .50 caliber bullet can tear off an arm or leg—and we were on the receiving end.

It was just the luck of the draw that whoever was in those trees running that gun wasn't much of a gunner; most of the rounds were flying harmlessly a couple of feet above our heads. The Mike 8 boat called Boomer to report that the .50 caliber rounds were falling close to the boat, and they were three miles away.

There was no question in my mind that the machine-gun fire was coming from a captured .50 caliber Browning. The VC used green tracers in their weapons, and we used red tracers. The muzzle blast sounded like a .50, and the red tracers coming our way from their position were positive proof that it was a captured Browning machine gun. I was hoping that somebody had a clear shot at the gunner running the .50 caliber Browning and would silence that gun before the gunner figured out how to use the elevating mechanism to lower the barrel and put fire on the dike where we were hiding and returning fire. When the line of red tracers from the machine gun started moving down toward our position behind the dike, I figured that if the job was going to get done before the dike started getting chopped apart, I didn't have time to wait for someone else to put a round into the machine gunner. I had better silence the .50 caliber right then.

With the rocket ready to launch, I poked my head up over the edge of the dike and took a good look. The muzzle flash from the Browning was only 250 yards away, an easy shot with the LAAW. I aimed at the tree line about ten feet above the position where the Browning was chattering away, squeezed the trigger, and let the rocket loose. I watched as the LAAW streaked through the sky and detonated over the position. The airburst effect was devastating. For a split second it lit up the trees like a huge flashbulb. I don't know if they were all KIA or just shitting their black pajamas, but I was pretty sure that the Browning and its crew were not going to be sending any more heavy machine-gun fire in our direction any time soon.

In the distance, over the sound of explosions and rifle fire, I could hear the sound of the Seawolf choppers. Boomer was on the radio telling them to put all their fire on the tree line. Making three runs along the tree line, it didn't take long for the 2.75-inch rockets and the door gunners with their M-60 machine guns to turn that coconut grove into a permanent memorial to the VC dead and dying. With almost no fire coming from the tree line and the Seawolf choppers headed back to base, Boomer called for illumination rounds from the 81 mm mortars. The incoming illumination rounds lit up the coconut grove like it was high noon while we formed up and headed back to the river as quickly as we could. Rudy got on the radio and called for HE rounds from the 81 mm mortar to be fired for maximum range, he would adjust the range as we hauled our ass back out to the river. As we pulled out, the HE rounds went sailing over our heads and fell all over the tree line and rice paddies. I don't know if it was because we had destroyed those VC so thoroughly or because they thought that our force was just too big for them to take on, but we got back to the river with no further contact with the VC and no need for HE rounds to cover our ass.

As we set up a security perimeter to watch our backs, the Mike 8 was called in to extract the PRU force. Then, one at a time, the PBRs came in to extract our two squads. On the way back to My Tho, we transferred our corpsman, Doc Pecuric, to the Mike 8 to treat three PRUs who had been wounded and carried back to the river by their team. At the debriefing it was brought to light that things hadn't gone as planned. Surprise, surprise! Our setup along the dike had worked just fine, but the six-man PRU team that was supposed to infiltrate the base had decided they had a better idea than just doing the job we had come to do. Thinking that they might find a couple more VC that they could drag back for a bigger reward, they made an executive decision to go investigate the hooch. Inside the hooch was a bunch of well-armed VC, and the shit went downhill from there.

Greed got all six of the PRUs that decided to ignore their orders KIA, no VC commander was even seen, let alone captured, and all of a sudden there was one hell of a lot of fire shredding the rice paddies and coming our way. So we did what SEALs always do, we improvised. We changed our objective to remaining alive, killed everything that moved, and got our ass back to the boats ASAP. I would have liked to be in on the capture of a high-level VC, but all in all it wasn't a bad last op for my first tour. We used up all of our ammo, so I didn't need to do an inventory, and none of the SEALs had as much as a scratch.

13

Good Night, Saigon

With almost all of our remaining ammunition spread across a couple of rice paddies and through what was now left of a hooch, there wasn't much that we would be turning over to the incoming platoon. The inventory of maps, ordnance, and vehicles, including the vehicles that we had liberated in Saigon and brought back to My Tho, was now complete except for the signature of the incoming OIC of our replacements. There wasn't much, other than the gear that we had brought with us, that we would be taking home, but, as required by some thoughtful bureaucrat, each of us had registered our war trophies so that they wouldn't get lost in some red-tape hell or doggie-robbed by some REMF clerk. Most of the captured weapons being sent home were ChiCom SKS rifles, CKC rifles, AK-47s, Russian Mosin-Nagants, and even a couple of bolt-action Mauser rifles. Some of the SEALs had helmets, flags, and other captured battlefield gear, but the only thing I was bringing home was my first captured enemy weapon, a relic of our own military history—a genuine U.S. M-1 carbine.

The handy little rifle was well worn, and there was no question that it had seen heavy use, but it was still in working order. The only obvious damage was a small hole through the fore end and some rust where blood had splashed across the barrel. The VC had been pussyfooting down the trail carrying the carbine across his body; he never knew that I had the sights of my Stoner resting on the middle of his chest. When we sprang the ambush, I tapped the trigger of the Stoner and a short three-round burst struck dead center of his chest, shattered his sternum, and knocked him to the ground.

After the cease-fire was called, we started searching the bodies, looking for documents or other intel. As I rummaged through my guy's pockets and pack for documents or maps, I had the time to take a closer look at the damage the three rounds had caused. Judging by the three entry wounds in his chest and the exit wounds in his back, one of the bullets from my Stoner must have tumbled as it tore through the wooden stock of the M-1 carbine. When a bullet tumbles, it starts spinning like the blade of a sawmill and tears the hell out of everything in its path. We had noticed that when we were shooting through even light foliage or through the sides of a hooch and nailed a VC with the lighter, faster bullets fired by the Stoner and the M-16 rifle, the VC dropped almost instantly—but it wasn't unusual for a VC out in the open to get hit with two or three rounds and hardly react at all. Sometimes they kept on fighting until they lost enough blood to black out, so the more of those little holes we could put in them the better. There were a lot of lessons that we all learned after running over ninety operations. If that VC soldier had been carrying the carbine over his shoulder, or in one hand at his side, my bullets might have slipped right through, wounding him but missing his heart and lungs. It hadn't worked out that way. I had decided that everything else that I had brought back from the bush could stay there in Vietnam. The only thing I would be taking home was that little carbine. It would be hung on the wall to remind me that luck is often the only difference between life and death.

With the inventory complete and no new ops even close to being planned, I could slow down and enjoy the three days I had left before heading back to friends and family, but this time there would no longer be a faithful wife waiting for her sailor to return home. Like more than a few SEALs, I had screwed up my marriage. I wished that I could blame it on somebody else, or find some fault that would ease my conscience, but that would have been pure horse crap. The destruction of my marriage was all my fault, I had nobody else to blame, and I knew that this was one of the biggest mistakes I had made in my life. I had screwed up big-time and that was that; there was no patching it up or making it all OK. It was only three days and nights from wheels up and the long ride home; in three days I would be leaving My Lee behind. We had only three days left before I had to say good-bye, and for those three days and nights I would treat her as I always had, as a friend and lover.

Those three days getting ready to ship out and three nights with My Lee went too fast, much faster than I thought they could. On Friday night I told My Lee that my orders had been cut, that I would be leaving in the morning. We both knew that my tour wouldn't last forever, and I was sure that there were more than a couple of men who would be ready, willing, and able to take my place. I knew that I would never be able to come back to My Tho, or to share her bed again. In one tour of duty I had lost two beautiful women, but I had been lucky—I hadn't lost a single brother SEAL.

We loaded up a 6-by-6 and a 4-by-4 with all of the gear we would be taking back home, said our good-byes to all of the people that had become a part of our lives. We didn't neglect to thank the men who had bailed our ass out (more than once): the army artillery, the air force fast fliers, and the navy Seawolf pilots. We also thanked the brown-water navy boat crews and the army Slick drivers that had taken us into harm's way and brought us back. We headed out to Saigon at 1300 hours to meet the new platoon. We still had to unload our gear, load their gear, and be ready for takeoff the following morning. As the platoon came down the ramp, I was a little surprised that I knew all of them. Only five of them had a tour already under their belt, but each of those five men was a veteran of the guerrilla warfare used by the VC. They would make sure that all of their experience was passed along to the entire platoon ASAP.

Nobody was dragging his feet, but it took so long to unload and load up the transport trucks that Lieutenant Quist and Finley couldn't convoy the new platoon back to My Tho that night without breaking regulations. We were all stuck in Saigon, and with nothing else to do, we volunteered to join the new platoon on a WWS recon in force. Wine, women, and song could be found just about anywhere in Saigon, but if you wanted to live high on the hog there wasn't any other establishment that could approach the decadence of the President Hotel. A few of the new guys decided to sack out in the barracks on the air base, and the rest of us decided that we were going to check in and then muster at 2200 hours on the top floor of the hotel. When the elevator doors unfolded, the eyes of the new guys opened up to the size of saucers. They hadn't expected this would be their first taste of war.

We had reserved a long table on the balcony that ran the entire length of the hotel. From this vantage point we could see a very long way into the darkness that was periodically lit up by illumination flares as they floated toward the bush. Streams of tracers swept out of the sky at several different points of the compass as air strikes turned the ground into plowed fields or burning rubble. As the night wore on, more air strikes rained down on remote battlefields while we caught up on the recent news from IV Corps (the Mekong Delta). A steady stream of cocktails was adding up to a bill that none of us wanted to see, and with the hostesses doing their best to get us, and our wallets, to join them in our rooms, the night was soon going to be morning. Wisdom, as it rarely does, won out over sin and debauchery. All of us needed some rack time.

The following morning Lieutenant Quist, Finley, and our replacements boarded the trucks and headed to My Tho. An hour later it was wheels up and we were on the first leg of our journey home. We would be stuck inside a tin can with roaring engines for what seemed sometimes to be an eternity. In reality, even with refueling and rest layovers at Wake Island, Midway Island, and San Diego, it would take only five days to get home to Norfolk Air Station. Flying half way around the world on another of the navy's four-engine transports wasn't easy duty, but we were not getting shot at, we were wearing the cleanest clothes we had seen in six months, we didn't smell too bad, and we wouldn't be spending the night in a swamp hoping that only a few leeches got past the tape that held the legs of our pants to our boots. Nobody was complaining.

As the drone of the engines became nothing more than a dull whine, I thought about my first tour and what had been accomplished. We had run operations every night, Alpha squad one night and Bravo the next. Shoot and scoot ops, ambush ops, going out with no intel at all and just hunting the VC, even using booby-trapped munitions that were left behind as a terminal surprise for the VC—everything had made us better warriors. With just one tour of duty under my belt, I knew that I still had a lot to learn. I had spent over ninety long nights hiding and waiting in the bush, sitting in the muck, or up to my waist or neck in a canal or swamp. I had humped too many klicks to count hunting for the VC high and low. A few of the ops had been heavy contact, but most of our successful ops, with a new wrinkle added here and there, had been well-planned and well-executed ambush ops where the outcome was almost preordained: The VC died, and we went home safe and sound. When I started to add up all the good ops and lousy ops, it was crystal clear that at least a third of the ops turned out to be nothing more than a lesson in leech removal and how much blood a couple thousand mosquitoes could suck out of your hide. We had done a good job. We had learned how to outfight men who were supposed to be some of the best guerrilla fighters on earth, and there were a lot fewer VC still on top of the dirt.

While we had been taking the war to the VC in their own backyard, the army, navy, and marines had been fighting their own kind of war. I had arrived at Tan Son Nhut in March of 1968, just a little too late to get into the fighting that had swept Vietnam when the Tet offensive was launched on January 30–31. There were thousands of battles and firefights across Vietnam, and one battle in particular had proven again that it isn't the size of the dog in the fight, it is the size of the fight in the dog that matters.

The marines had established a forward firebase at Khe Sanh in Quang Tri province. There were no roads into the firebase, and it could be resupplied only by airdrop. The VC thought that it looked like an easy target. They had destroyed the French forces at Dien Bien Phu, and they figured that they would use the same tactics to destroy the fifty-six hundred marines at Khe Sanh. Forty thousand VC and NVA regulars surrounded the base. For seventy-seven days, under constant artillery, mortar, and small-arms fire, the hard-ass marines at Khe Sanh dug in and fought on. With food and ammunition being parachuted in to them, the marines lived in sandbagged bunkers, ate C-rats when they could, and killed everything that moved on the battlefield. Despite desperate VC attacks that had marine rifle barrels glowing red hot, Khe Sanh would not become another Dien Bien Phu.

Since Tet, we had learned some tough lessons, and we were paying for those lessons with American blood and lives, but I would be coming back and bringing everything I had learned, and would learn, with me.

My first night back at Norfolk, I celebrated hard. Coming home alive and all in one piece called for a barn burner of a celebration, and I lit up more than a few barns that night. For the following three days, we crossed all the t's, dotted all the i's, turned in weapons and equipment, and were debriefed several times. I had put in for two weeks' leave and couldn't wait to be heading south in my 1966 GTO. My parents lived in Palatka, Florida, and owned and operated a marina, Brown's Landing, on the St. Johns River. They were doing well and, like parents everywhere, couldn't wait to see their son after a long absence. I didn't back off the gas pedal all the way home.

Mom and Dad were doing great business at the marina. They were both healthy, happy, and busy with repairs, docking, gassing up boats, and selling bait and bag lunches. I offered to lend a hand, but Dad reminded me that squirrel season had just opened. He offered the use of his Browning shotgun and a canoe; he knew that I wouldn't pass up a chance to get a couple or three delicious squirrels for the pot and a few skins for the fur buyer that passed through Palatka every couple of weeks. It was still zero-dark-thirty hours when I slipped the Browning and some ammunition into the canoe and headed for one of my favorite wild places to hunt, Murphy Island. This was just the kind of R&R I needed, an easy, peaceful day of fishing and drifting the river and canoeing four miles upriver to Murphy Island to hunt the abundant fox squirrels.

The paddle, as it always had, fit my hand like it was custom-made for me, and the canoe slipped through the water easily. Moving silently, dipping and sweeping the paddle effortlessly from bow to stern, was just what the doctor ordered. It was graceful, calming, almost hypnotic. For the first time in over half a year, I didn't need to cover the banks of the river with the muzzle of my Stoner or listen for the sound of the first rounds of an AK-47 that initiated a VC ambush. There were no booby traps on the St. Johns River; no sampans with a load of ammunition, food, or well-armed VC would turn this beautiful place into a killing field. The miles passed in absolute serenity, and before I realized how quickly I had paddled four miles I was pulling the canoe up on the bank and dragging it into the bush where it would be invisible to prying eyes; some habits learned in the bush die hard. With the canoe well hidden, I pulled the Browning 12-gauge from its case and loaded five rounds of #6 shot. Walking under the branches of ancient oaks, maple, and cypress trees, I didn't need any light from the moon or a flashlight to find my way. I had spent enough time on Murphy Island to know every inch of the place. I knew it better than any piece of dirt anywhere else in the world; it felt as if I had returned to spend some time with an old friend.

The quiet of the island was welcome, as was the sound of the breeze rustling in the treetops. I moved as quietly as I would have in the bush and found the open clearing where I would wait. This was exactly the place where I knew the squirrels would be coming out as the sun rose and warmed them in their nests. The stars of the Milky Way faded in the sky as the darkness disappeared in the rose color that came before daylight. I could now see the wide expanse of branches stretching overhead, in a few minutes I could see individual leaves. As I waited for sunrise, when the squirrels would start their acrobatics in the trees, I thought about where my life had taken me, where I had been, what I had done, where I was right now, and where I would be going in a couple of weeks.

Even here I could not ignore the lessons I had learned in the bush. They remained an integral part of my consciousness. I could hear the squirrels chattering and leaping from branch to branch long before I could see them. I could hear the shells of fresh acorns falling from the canopy above me and could smell the dead leaves that had fallen here for centuries before this morning. As daylight penetrated the thick leaves, I could see the squirrels running the branches like sure-footed acrobats, moving as quickly and carelessly as if they were running down the yellow line in the middle of a six-lane highway with no traffic. They were perfectly adapted to life in the treetops, above the ground where predators waited. I slowly got to my feet and raised the Browning to my shoulder. I aimed the shotgun carefully at an opening in the branches and emptied all five rounds into thin air. I would never again kill an innocent critter. My hunting days were over. For another week I would fish, pull crab traps, spend some of my hard-earned pay at the Cow Catcher Lounge, and lend a hand at the marina when my mom and dad would let me. I loved my parents, and the peace and quiet of the river and Murphy Island, but I had changed in ways that I had not realized or understood until I fired five rounds into the air. I learned something in that week that never left me. This was no longer my life. I needed to be back with my teammates, back in action, back doing what I knew best, back home. I couldn't wait to get back to Little Creek.

After a long drive to our base at Little Creek and a few hours at the Casino, one of our favorite local bars, I reported to quarters the next morning and found that there were only five members of the 10th Platoon still in the 10th. SOP was for returning platoons to be broken up and assigned to other platoons. The 10th, or what was left of it, would be filled out with new team members or other recent-returning members from other platoons. Landing on my feet, finding another platoon that was going to deploy to Vietnam, wasn't going to be a problem. As a veteran I would be grabbed up by the first platoon headed into combat. Figuring that my future would go a lot smoother if I did the planning, I had already gotten some leads on the next platoons that were going to be deployed. I made it a point to talk to several members of the 3rd Platoon that I knew well and put in a request to Operations to be assigned.

My request was approved, orders were cut, and I learned that I would be the only member of the new platoon who had combat experience in Vietnam. No wonder my request had gone so easily. The 3rd Platoon would be deploying to a town called Nha Be in two months, but first there were a few new tricks that we were going to learn and one "school" we would be attending. The entire platoon would be going through the navy's SERE (Survival, Evasion, Resistance, and Escape) School.

Each branch of the service has its own version of survival school, and all "high-risk capture personnel"—pilots, air crews, SEALs, Rangers, and Special Forces—are required to go through the course before being deployed to combat zones. The navy SERE School I attended is located in beautiful Brunswick, Maine. We spent only two days in the classroom before we were loaded up and bused to some godforsaken area a hop, skip, and short jump south of the Canadian border. This was where the real training started, and none of the instructors was going to make it easy on us. We were given the coordinates of a spot that was supposed to be about five miles away, but we didn't really know. We were issued no maps and no gear except for the green utilities and combat boots we were wearing and were told to haul our ass to these coordinates, time was a-wasting. Before we headed into the boonies though, we got one last piece of the puzzle. While we were trying to find the coordinates, "the Army of the North America People's Republic," a group of navy instructors, would be hunting us down. All we knew was that there was a log cabin out there somewhere and that we were now on our own in extremely hostile territory. Luckily our instructors were kind to us; they gave us a whole day to get there.

I paired up with Bob Moore because it is always better to have four eyes, four ears, four legs, and four arms working as a team than to go it alone. There are people who like going out in the wilderness, and I've always been one of them, but with no food or water, not even a knife or canteen, and very serious people looking to capture me, this wasn't going to be much fun. Of the seventy-five men that headed out into the wilderness, only twelve managed to evade capture and make it to that little cabin on time. Half were from the 3rd Platoon. While we waited for any stragglers to show up, we wolfed down as many sandwiches as we could hold and washed them down with hot coffee. It was a real celebration of evading capture, finding the cabin, and getting to the end of a very tough exercise.

Once we reached our objective we thought the exercise was over; we let our guard down, and forgot that "The Army of the North America People's Republic" didn't play by some rule book. While we were drinking coffee and trying to get back some of the calories we had burned evading capture, the "bad guys" were surrounding the cabin. All twelve of us were "taken prisoner," a mistake that would have gotten all of us killed in Vietnam.

We were now POWs and, as such, could be interrogated by our captors until we spilled the beans or died of lack of food and water. We didn't know how far our interrogators could go, but having survived Hell Week gave us a good idea. This part of the exercise could not be graded by a pass-fail measurement, we just endured everything they tried to get us to start talking, helped one another as much as we could to keep our morale above our boot tops, and got through it. Like Hell Week, it was another valuable experience that let you know just how much you could take. I guarantee that anybody who has experienced it will never forget it.

Having survived the SERE School, we were bused back to Little Creek and told to get ready for our next exercise. With a full load out of gear and weapons, we headed to Camp Pickett on the Virginia-North Carolina border for a week of patrolling as a platoon and in squads. Camp Pickett was also where we could run live-fire exercises with grenades, claymore mines, 40 mm grenade launchers, LAAW rockets, and small arms—all of the weapons that we would be using in combat. After a solid week of this, we headed back to Little Creek.

Next on the schedule was a trip to the wonderful Caribbean, where we would be run through the three-week-long U.S. Army Jungle Warfare School at Fort Sherman in the Panama Canal Zone. I kept my mouth shut and didn't tell the rest of the platoon how much I was looking forward to the rain, stifling heat, bugs, leeches, and tropical diseases that could eat your feet in a week or two. Jungle Warfare School was good preparation for the rest of the platoon, and I figured that there might be some new wrinkle that I could pick up. This would be the third time I had gone through this school, and with one tour in Vietnam under my belt I was able to distance myself from the day-to-day humping through the dense bush and see that the platoon was really working together as a smoothly operating fighting unit.

Unless you count the incident when the stewardess who was sunbathing topless objected to having a navy soft cap full of cold water dumped onto her back and, in a completely unladylike fashion, slugged one of our guys right in the eye, we all made it through Jungle Warfare School and back to base without any injuries or major mishaps. The next morning at quarters, wearing an obvious shiner where that well-endowed stewardess had landed her fist while I was busy staring, I was informed that I had received what we nicknamed a Ho Chi Minh. Due to my combat tour I had been elevated to the pay grade of E-5. Now my pay would be, maybe, enough to buy two rounds of beer for the platoon when we celebrated my elevation to such a high status. If I was lucky, there might be enough left over to fill up the gas tank of my GTO and buy a new pair of laces for my sneakers. The platoon that had started out as a group of individuals had become a team. There was only a single phase of predeployment left before we loaded up for the long, slow trip to Vietnam.

Union Camp, North Carolina, was our next stop. Now we would be spending all day, every day in the water. One of the important lessons that we had learned during my first tour in Vietnam was that inserting and extracting from the water was the safest and most effective way to get in, take the enemy by surprise, and get out before they could mount a reaction force to run us down and force a fight that we would rather avoid.

Inserting from the water almost always seemed to take the VC by surprise. Helos were big and noisy and could be seen and heard for a long way off, so we inserted or extracted by helo only when we wanted the VC to know that we were there or when we had no other choice. The SEALs operated in the water anytime that it gave us an edge, an advantage that we could exploit. As with any other skill that may make the difference between life and death, we all needed to develop our ability to get in and out of all of the SEAL boats and any other riverine craft that might be put into service so that it was second nature. Under fire there is no time for second-guessing or another swing past to snatch you if you missed pickup.

With only a week left before wheels up, the platoon was packed and ready to load up for our trip to Norfolk Naval Air Station. I decided to make the best use of the last five days of liberty I would see on this trip. I was certain that the local beach bunnies that spent every day on the beach right behind my rented house would enjoy a few days and nights of my most ardent attention. Lucky for me, they did.

14

The Rung Sat
Secret Zone

At midnight my new platoon left the Casino Bar to spend the last few hours we could with soft, curvy, round-eyed women, an ample supply of booze, and, later, a good night's sleep without keeping one eye open watching for Charlie and listening for incoming mortar fire. After quarters at 0800 hours the next morning, civilian life as we had been enjoying it all night would stop for the foreseeable future. Bleary eyed, knowing that we all needed at least some sleep, we drank a final toast to those who might not be coming home and headed for our own beds a few hours before sunrise.

In five days I would be back in Vietnam with a new platoon and new officers. The Rung Sat Secret Zone would be one of the areas where we would focus our attention. It was reported that the entire area was crawling with VC who operated without much interference on the ground. Soon there were going to be two SEAL platoons based in Nha Be, and it would be our responsibility to let the VC know that they would no longer rule this particular piece of real estate. If we could establish a solid intel network, the VC would lose their iron grip on what had become a refuge and training ground for their troops. After we started taking the fight to them in the Rung Sat, the VC would be looking over their shoulders night and day.

Staring out the window as we approached Tan Son Nhut Air Base on the outskirts of Saigon, I could see the war-torn landscape all the way to the horizon; it hadn't changed much, if at all. For mile after mile there was nothing but crater-covered, desolate brown earth that had been defoliated with Agent Orange. Everything that might allow the VC to hide while they mounted an attack had been destroyed; not much green had survived. We touched down and rolled across the tarmac to a hangar where the platoon we were replacing was already waiting for us. Their gear had been unloaded, and the trucks that would transport us to our new digs were ready to roll as soon as we were loaded. Traveling in a convoy at night was not allowed. We were all starting to get itchy to see our new base and our quarters and to make all of the connections that we would need for air and artillery support, so we worked fast. With the springs of the trucks groaning under the weight of our gear, we headed south to our new base.

Nha Be had been a bustling, prosperous fishing village before it was converted into the base responsible for navy small-boat operations from the southern perimeter of Saigon to the mouth of the Mekong Delta. Situated on the Long Tau River, we had easy access to all of the canals and rivers that crisscrossed the Mekong Delta. We could operate from the South China Sea all the way to Saigon. Nha Be was at least five or six times bigger than My Tho. Inside the main gate the base was almost like any navy base anywhere in the world: paved roads, a large mess hall, a gymnasium, troop barracks, a library, and even a post office. Nha Be had most of the comforts of home. I couldn't help but notice that there were also more than a few bars and restaurants. Our barracks were set up in two-man rooms, and there was even a shower, no more washing off our gear in a used shipping container or showering under a hose spitting water from the Mekong River. Next to our barracks was a small building where we could hold briefings and a bunker where we would store our weapons, ordnance, and equipment. With all of these comforts and conveniences, it would be easy for a SEAL to get spoiled.

The platoon would be commanded by two officers that I hadn't known before, Lieutenant JG A. Y. Bryson and Lieutenant JG J. C. Brewton, better known as A-Y and Bubba. They were the kind of officers who inspire confidence in their men. Both had the two most valuable traits that a

SEAL officer can have, courage and common sense. A-Y and Bubba might have been officers, but they also knew that there were at least a few people on this earth that might know more than they did. They asked questions, and they listened to the answers from their men. Officers like A-Y and Bubba were the real deal, tough, decisive leaders who never hesitated to lead or follow their men when they knew that their men had a better way to solve a problem. Both of the new platoons were operating without a chief petty officer so Hospital Corpsman First Class Bob Clark would be senior enlisted man, leading petty officer, and, our "Doc."

While A-Y, Bubba, and Doc Clark were getting squared away with the support assets we would have available and getting the latest intel on our operational areas, I looked up one of my mentors from SEAL Team 2. Master Chief Tom Blais had been one of my instructors when I went through UDT training as a member of Class 30, six or eight lifetimes ago in 1963. Tom was now a master chief in the other SEAL platoon operating out of Nha Be. If there was anyone who could help get my new platoon off on the right foot, I was sure that it would be Master Chief Blais. It didn't take long for Tom to get me squared away and for us to decide that it had been far too long since an official inventory of the bars and hostesses of Nha Be had been done.

After a quick but thorough inventory of the delights that awaited us, I got back to base at 1800 hours for our first scheduled briefing. There wasn't much that Tom hadn't told me, but I listened closely to everything Bubba, A-Y, and Doc had to say. If you want to stay alive, do your job, and keep the other members of your squad or platoon alive, you never daydream or let your attention slip during a briefing. I took every briefing seriously. One piece of missed information was one piece too many. My life, and the lives of my platoon, depended on all of us working like dancers in a beautifully choreographed ballet. Every move had been rehearsed, then rehearsed again and again, until it was a flawless, deadly dance that we could perform in total darkness with tracers screaming past our ears, grenades bouncing off of the trees, and mortar rounds falling a few yards away. The good news was that we would be running our first op tomorrow night. Training time was over for the new men.

I'm in the middle, between Jerry Hammerle (right), another member of SEAL Team 2, and Bah, a Vietnamese SEAL (LDNN), who was assigned to our platoon. We were headed out of My Tho on a patrol boat for another ambush operation. We would insert after dark in a mangrove swamp and set up where the intel told us the VC would be moving through. As usual, I was carrying as much ammunition as possible.

In 1964 I got my orders to report to Roosevelt Roads Naval Station in Puerto Rico and was assigned to UDT-21. As you can see by the photo UDT training was tough duty, every day was a real grind. Bud Thrift, kneeling in front of me, Bob Hrabak, squinting into the sun, and the rest of the platoon were heading out for a day of dive training in the sunshine and warm Caribbean waters.

After more specialized training, I finally arrived in Vietnam. Without further delay, I got right into the fight. Jim Finley (right) and I had just returned from a long, hot night op. We were filthy, tired, and chewed up by mosquitoes; furthermore, I'd burned through all of my ammo.

Here we are slogging silently through another canal on our way to position our-selves for a night ambush. Our corpsman, Doc Pecuric (left), Pierre Birtz (center), and I are avoiding crocs and attracting too many leeches. If you look closely you can see my LAAW rocket hanging across my back.

Big Al Ashton (left) with his M-60 and I with my Stoner get ready to head out for another night ambush operation.

Six members of our fourteen-man platoon based in Nha Be getting ready for an operation where our intel told us we would need a lot of firepower. Kneeling from left to right are Bob Calhoun, Mike McDonald, and Jack Squires. Standing on the left is Bob Moore, I'm in the center, and to the right is Jim Dilley.

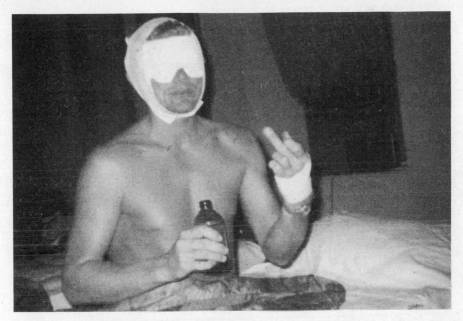

There is no such thing as a safe environment when you are a navy SEAL; even training can get you killed. Fortunately the docs in the hospital in Germany where I was treated thought that beer was almost as good as penicillin for flesh wounds. My face and hands were full of shrapnel caused by an accidental explosion while I was training a commando team in Iran in 1977.

This photo is of the commanding officer of SEAL Team 2, Commander Tom Williams (left), and me at the naming ceremony of the Jungle Warfare Camp on Isla Pineros.

Here is my platoon during training at Fort Pickett, Virginia. SEAL Team 2 never stopped training. I'm in the back row, second from the left.

The next couple of photos are of two of the jungle warfare classes I taught. Before I set up the course, I located an old set of blueprints for the island and was able to trace out all the old dirt roads, underground fuel tanks, bunkers, and gun emplacements. Though they had all been reclaimed by the jungle, I used these old relics (with what I had learned in Vietnam) as teaching aids for ten years to train some of the best warriors who ever came out of the jungle.

If they are lucky and tough, even the best warriors retire. I'm directly to the right of one of the finest warriors with whom I have ever had the honor of serving, Lt. Mike Thornton (in dress whites, standing, fifth from the right), on the day he retired. The ribbon around his neck is the Medal of Honor.

In Iraq, December 2004, this was another year that I didn't make it home for Christmas. I'm on the far right wearing a black watch cap. The team was recruited by and worked for Special Operations Consultants, Inc. You might notice that I'm the only man carrying what has become my favorite weapon: an AK-47.

Tomorrow night we would be taking on a tough, experienced enemy. This was real combat, and death could pop up from a spider hole in the flat earth, could be six feet away in the bush, or could come screaming out of nowhere. As the only veteran of a Vietnam tour, I was going to double-check everything I could to make sure that every man would be pulling his load and I would be pulling mine. When I was done and knew that everything was shipshape, I would double-check it.

Even though we would be operating with two separate platoons, covering an area about the size of the state of Delaware would keep us busy and might stretch our abilities a little thin. I was really glad to hear that we wouldn't have to depend on air cover from some other base. There was a Seawolf detachment based in Nha Be; if we called for air support they were right there. If we needed medevac pickup or if the shit was getting thick and we needed to extract under fire, the army helos wouldn't be far away or long in getting to us. There was also some other good news. Frank Thornton, a SEAL that we all knew and respected, was attached as an adviser to a sixty-five-man PRU team that was also operating out of Nha Be. The PRU teams always had the best intel network, and I was sure that we could depend on Frank to share the wealth with us or lend a hand to verify the intel that we dug up on our own. I was hoping that there would be more dependable intel and fewer long nights waiting to spring an ambush when the VC never showed up. I wanted to get back to operating, and to run more successful ops we always needed to get better intel. Unless there was something that we couldn't foresee, each platoon would be operating independently. If something really big was going to go down, we could all gear up and both platoons could work together. I couldn't imagine any enemy dumb enough to take on twenty-eight combat-loaded SEALs, but it would have been an awesome thing to see. With the briefing complete and the date and time for our first op as a platoon an established fact, all of us were ready to start running ops inside the Rung Sat Secret Zone. We had been thoroughly briefed about the area and wanted nothing more than to introduce the men with green faces to the local VC.

The Rung Sat was close to perfect for SEAL operations. Low-flying C-130 aircraft had sprayed millions of gallons of Agent Orange on every living thing in the entire area for over a year. The Rung Sat looked like a moonscape; nothing that had been covered with the chemical spray had survived. Dead vegetation, dying trees, bomb craters, and mile after mile of cracked, drying mud were all stitched together by large and small canals and the rivers. The lack of cover forced the VC to hide from aircraft in underground bunkers or under camouflage netting during daylight and to run all of their operations at night. From a helo during daylight, it didn't look like the VC would have even a blade of grass left to hide behind. They might be able to hide in tunnels, but when they came out on the ground they couldn't hide their trails and footprints. The SEALs owned the night; we would insert, find the trails, and track them down, or set up an ambush where the intel told us the VC would be moving men or supplies.

It was almost perfect, but there was a problem with running ops in riverine areas where Agent Orange had been heavily used. There were no longer any living roots of grasses, brush, or trees to hold the earth together. Sooner or later the dead root system would start rotting away, and over much of the area the dead earth could no longer support the weight of a man. There was nothing that would tell you that one chunk of dirt was any different than any other chunk of dirt. One minute you would be moving along silently, carefully putting your feet down where there were no sticks, branches, or leaves that might make a sound, and then the ground you were walking on would collapse under your feet in a heartbeat, dropping you a couple of feet, down into muck so thick that it would suck the boots right off of your feet.

Even with the earth disappearing under your feet, there was one thing that would make our ops a little easier. Most of the Rung Sat had been declared a free-fire zone. Anyone within our operational area was to be considered the enemy and was to be taken under fire; in the Rung Sat there were no civilians.

With our first op ready to go, and briefing the next day at 1800 hours, the first order of business was to get all of our gear sorted out and ready for the field. Having a full tour and over ninety operations under my belt, I didn't need to change the standard load out I would be using, but we all needed to get checked out on the brand-new LSSCs (Light SEAL Support

Craft) that had replaced the now obsolete STABs. LSSCs were the new boats in-country. The new boats and the converted Mike 8 boats were all run and maintained by COSRIVRON (Coastal River Squadron), a command out of our home base in Norfolk, Virginia. In addition to these new boats, we would also be able to request the PBRs for support anytime we needed them. With everyone checked out on the new boats and gear ready, Bubba and A-Y had decided that our first op would be with the full platoon. They wanted to get all of the new guys in the field as quickly as possible so that they would all have some combat experience behind them.

With nothing on the schedule until tomorrow morning at muster, it was time to check out the local nightlife. Bill Barth, a hard charger who was always the life of the party, Jack Squires, one of the guys you wanted at your back in a bar or the bush, and I headed out the gate and worked our way up one side of Main Street and down the other. Along the way we hooked up with Mike McDonald, a redheaded ladies' man, and Bob Christopher, a handsome blond "pussy magnet," at the place we decided would be the official home away from home for the 3rd Platoon, the Cho Duc Bar. Compared to My Lee's Tan Van Bar and Restaurant, it wasn't all that plush an establishment. It didn't have the most bar-girls on the strip, but it did have the best-looking, and it had a very nice touch from home— American beer! Budweiser and Miller could be had at a stiff price, and behind the bar were full bottles of real Jim Beam and Dewar's Scotch that weren't made in some backroom still. These would soon be close to empty. American beer and real American booze told us that the mama-san of the bar had some good contacts in Saigon.

Curfew was at 2200 hours, but when Frank Thornton, the SEAL PRU adviser, stopped by for a beer he told us that the SEALs were allowed to stay out past curfew as long as the doors to the bar were closed. Someone had convinced the navy that fraternizing after hours with the locals would get us better intel. It was clearly our duty to God and America to stay as long as we could with our piastres held out. So with the doors closed I concentrated on getting as much intel as I could from the lovely young hostess who just happened to be sitting on my lap at the bar. It was not that easy for the stalwart members of the 3rd Platoon to force ourselves to work on winning their hearts and minds and a key to one of the rooms upstairs, but we persevered. At first light, Squires, McDonald, Barth, and I collected what little was left of ourselves and, with not much spring left in our step, gathered downstairs in the bar for a toast to our new technique for gathering intel. It was my turn to lead PT back at the barracks, and I wasn't about to miss leading PT with a head the size of a half-grown watermelon. Warning order for the night's op, a canal ambush, was at 1300. I needed some rack time before we geared up.

15

First Contact—2nd Tour

No matter where in the world SEALs are based, we always try to have at least a few of the most basic comforts to remind us that there is someplace called home. Bob Moore and Jim Dilley took on the job of scrounging up a load of ammo crates and converting them into a functioning bar in our briefing room. With a couple of makeshift ammo-crate chairs and bar stools, it was almost as comfortable as half the joints that sold booze and warm beer in Nha Be. They had even stumbled across a freezer that wasn't nailed down, and somehow it ended up in our Quonset hut. With the freezer set to run at sub-Arctic cold level, our rum and Cokes tinkled with lots of ice. If we could have found a few good-looking hostesses it might have become one of the most popular nightspots that close to the Rung Sat. Even Mama-San and the girls at the Cho Duc Bar might have been envious.

Our first op had been a bust. Then, with a couple of cold glasses of rum and Coke in their hands, Lieutenant Brewton and Doc gave us the rundown on our next ops. Alpha squad would be going back out to the Cho Lan canal the next night to see if they could get lucky and ambush the VC who were moving supplies on sampans. Since we had had such lousy luck on the first op, we thought that a second insertion this soon might take

Charlie off guard. If Alpha got lucky, they might find that Charlie never expected that we would run two ops in the same place so close together. We were hoping that they would send in some heavy loads of weapons, ammunition, and supplies that Alpha could destroy while the VC thought we were looking somewhere else and before they were broken down into smaller loads and disbursed across the whole area. The night after Alpha hit the canal again, Bravo would be going out. We would be acting on some fresh intel that Brewton had gotten out of the Chieu Hoi center. We had learned the hard way that some of the Chieu Hoi who gave us intel were VC that had joined the Chieu Hoi program just to spread false intel, or worse. The VC were smart. They were ready to waste one of their men to feed us the kind of intel that they knew we couldn't ignore. The idea was for us to swallow the bait hook, line, and sinker and walk right into an ambush. Until the individual Chieu Hoi that had given us the intel proved to our satisfaction that he was not a VC plant, we took them with us on the op but kept them under tight control. If the op turned into an ambush, they didn't live long enough to regret the fact that they had made a very bad decision.

With a couple of days before our next op Alpha got busy building a weapons cleaning station, checking inventory, cleaning our cache of extra weapons, and getting our new base of operations shipshape. The briefing for Alpha squad was held at 1800 hours. All of us attended to make sure that nothing would be overlooked, and that if they needed our help we would know the op from one end to the other. If Alpha got in trouble they couldn't handle, we didn't have time to wait to be briefed before Bravo squad went out to lend a hand. Alpha headed out on the LSSCs that would insert and extract them from the Rung Sat, and a few of us decided that we would play a few hands of poker to pass the time. Around 0300 hours, the four of us still trying to win back what we had lost heard the engines of the Seawolves start turning on the helo pad on the far side of the base. Barth jogged over to the pad and came back with the news: It looked like Alpha had made first contact and had called in the helos to run a fire mission. At first light the LSSCs pulled slowly to the dock, and we got the good news; nobody had been hurt, and Alpha had mud-sucked a pair of big sampans, killing four VC and retrieving a couple of rifles and several bags of rice. Not much to show for a long, dangerous night's work, but there were now four less VC, a few less rifles, and some hungry bellies that wouldn't get that shipment of rice. On extraction they had started taking fire from behind them on the canal, so they called in the Seawolf helos to clear the back door and give the LSSCs open sailing down the Cho Lan canal. Alpha had their first contact, and it had gone well.

As soon as they had cleaned their weapons and gear, replaced grenades, flares, and anything that had been used up on the mission, reloaded magazines, showered, and changed clothes, we would start the debriefing. The longer it took, the better. The adrenaline that pulsed through your bloodstream when you were fighting to stay alive always took an hour or so to burn off.

The new guys couldn't help themselves; first contact with an enemy who is trying his or her best to make you dead only happens once in a lifetime. After surviving your first face-to-face combat, the adrenaline doesn't stop pumping until the rosy glow of being alive is finally overwhelmed by the realization that it could have been the other way around; it might have been you sucking mud. Both platoons claimed the glory of surviving the toughest part of the fight. I didn't care. The VC were all dead and both platoons had survived their first op with no casualties. Long run or short, that was the only thing that mattered. Every day is a good day when everybody comes home alive and in one piece. It wouldn't be long before the new platoon learned that all days are not good days.

For the next couple of weeks we ran low-probability canal ambush ops and waited for word to come in from the Tactical Operations Center (TOC) that there might be some new VC activity in the Rung Sat. When there was little or no intel we ran our nightly creep and kill ops that had no target but let us move silently through the Rung Sat until we knew just about every pile of buffalo shit, defoliated tree, and blown-to-kingdom-come hooch. We crossed trails that led from the bank of one canal to the bank of another, then disappeared. Obviously the VC were transshipping loads from one sampan to another overland, a smart move. Because the canals wandered around and turned and twisted back on themselves, moving material over short distances on dry land cut the total distance from point A to point B by many miles of pushing a pole into the toxic muck at the bottom of every canal. We found deep footprints in the goop that passed for earth in the Rung Sat that were made either by a giant with size eight feet or someone who was carrying a heavy load a long, long way, but contact was sporadic. The only thing we accomplished on most ops was one less sampan, a couple of dead low-level VC, and blowing up a load of food, weapons, and munitions when we got lucky.

After several weeks of hit-or-miss ops, we needed some good intel and a hot mission to run. Just as we were beginning to smell like the mud at the bottom of the canals in the Rung Sat, the TOC decided that it was time for us to take care of a little business that had been becoming a big problem. Somewhere in our part of the delta somebody was building water mines, and they were becoming a serious threat to the brown-water navy.

Water mines could be allowed to float free, barely breaking the surface, but the most dangerous mines were anchored to the bottom of a canal, just a foot or two underwater where they couldn't be seen until the bow of a boat struck one of the detonators and the boat and crew disappeared in a geyser of water, metal, blood, and body parts. Just a couple of weeks before my platoon had arrived in Vietnam, a mine had been found floating in one of the larger canals close to the base. Someone with too damn little understanding of explosives decided that instead of just blowing the mine in place, it would be a good idea to tow the mine back to the base. With the mine back at the base someone who had too little respect for what a couple hundred pounds of high explosives could do had, for a reason still unknown, decided to take a close look at how the mine was put together and how it would be detonated. It exploded, killing him and the base commander, who had been observing the operation. The flying shrapnel chewed up several other men, including a SEAL, who knew better but had been closer than he should have been to anyone screwing around with an unpredictable, homemade mine. Only this morning the crew of a PBR had gotten lucky and spotted a floating mine before they ran over it and got themselves blown to shreds. When they took it out with their .50 caliber machine gun, the two hundred pounds of high explosives packed into the makeshift mine blew a big enough hole in the canal that the shock wave of water had almost flipped the PBR over. It had been decided that, even though it was more than a little sketchy, there was enough intel for us to go out hunting for the mine makers. It was our job to go find these people, capture or kill them all, and shut down the factory for good.

There was not much good intel on the location of the mine factory. The best guesstimate was that the mines were being put together in an area just outside the Rung Sat. The entire area where the TOC thought the mines were being assembled covered six grid squares, far too much territory for one SEAL platoon to cover effectively. After talking to Tom Blais and Mike Naus from the other SEAL squad, the decision was made that both squads, a full platoon, would work the area until we had a better handle on the location of the mine factory; then we would put together an op to destroy it. There were two problems we needed to overcome. First was that somewhere in those six grid squares there were two villages. The second was that the entire area where we would be operating was outside the Rung Sat and could not be considered a free-fire zone. Lots of people might be wandering around; some of them would be VC, and some would be friendlies or, at worst, noncombatants. We wouldn't know who was friendly and who was VC until they tried to lure us into an ambush or started shooting at us. Always a good way to sort out the good guys from the bad guys, unless you were the one getting shot at.

To reduce the number of miles of bush and mud that we would need to hump, and to get a better handle on the entire area, Brewton and Bryson called up a Seawolf helo and did a flyover of the entire six-grid location with a Polaroid camera. They took photos as they flew, concentrating on the areas that looked like they would be a good spot for the VC to hide a mine factory. Bryson and Brewton thought that the only logical place for a mine factory was on a canal, where it would be easier and safer for the VC to move the final product without blowing their home base to smithereens. I guessed that they were right on the money; even the VC wouldn't like the idea of carrying a couple of hundred pounds of high explosives any farther than was necessary.

At daybreak the entire platoon would be inserting to search as much of the six-grid area as possible. The plan was to extract by Mike 8 boat no later than sunset. I met up with Squires, Barth, and McDonald at the Cho Duc

Bar, and over cold bottles of Ba Me Ba beer and bowls of rice and Chinese shrimp noodle soup we kicked around the potential for finally doing some serious damage to the VC. We were back in the barracks by 2200.

The briefing at 0500 was short and to the point, and we were saddled up and on the two army Slicks in just over a half hour. Using the Polaroid pictures, Barth and Brewton had picked an insertion point that would be about two klicks from the Tinh Long An River. After insertion we would work our way back toward the river to our extraction point, where the Mike 8 boat would be on station waiting for us. If we got lucky, we would find the mine makers hard at work on one of the canals somewhere close to the river.

The helos homed in on the LZ that Bryson had shown them on the Polaroid photos, and we were out and moving into the tree line before they were twenty-five feet up and pulling hard to gain altitude. When the helos are inserting or extracting troops, they are big, slow, easy targets, even for a man armed with nothing more than a bolt-action rifle. Helo pilots who like the idea of getting old enough to bounce their grandkids on their knees have as little appreciation for low airspeed as would a SEAL for a bright, tie-dyed shirt in the bush. The LZ was at the edge of a huge rice paddy, and there was now enough light to see people working the paddies and a couple of smaller sampans being used to load the crop of rice as it was pulled from the muck. With all those eyes and ears, we knew that we wouldn't have the element of surprise working for us. Word would get out and circulate quickly to the local VC that the men with green faces were in the neighborhood.

We moved out along the tree line with Alpha squad taking the lead. In only a couple hundred yards we picked up a trail that looked like it was well used. The footprints in the trail were fresh, and the impressions made by the rubber tire-tread sandals the VC favored were still sharp; they looked as if they had been made the night before. Even the ridges where the tire treads could be seen hadn't dried out or started to crumble. It was starting to look like we had gotten lucky; whoever it was that was using this trail was headed for the river. Maybe it would be the mine builders, and if we got lucky they would be within range of the 81 mm mortar on the Mike 8 boat.

We silently ghosted through the bush and trees that ran alongside the trail for only a couple of hundred yards, and suddenly hand signals called us to a halt. With the breeze coming directly into my face, I could smell the *nuoc mam*; I could also hear what sounded like people working and talking coming from the front of the platoon. We spread out in a line with all weapons pointed to the area where the voices were coming from. If the shit hit the fan fast, our firepower would be concentrated on the area to our front and none of us would be in the line of fire. As we moved closer and closer to the sound of the voices, we could see the outline of several hooches along the canal and people moving around the little village. It looked like the locals had just started getting ready for another long day of harvesting rice in the paddies, but we stayed hidden in the bush, hoping that any VC in the village might show themselves. After twenty minutes of observation we hadn't even seen a man, let alone a VC. As we evaluated the situation, a woman carrying a baby, with another child bringing up the rear, came walking down the trail right toward our position. She was only fifteen feet away when she finally spotted us. She stopped and stared as if we were ghosts or some kind of hallucination; her eyes were about the size of golf balls. Before she could move or make a sound, Bay An, our interpreter, walked up to her and pointed back at the village. They talked for a few minutes, both of them pointing fingers, and finally her baby started to cry. Bay An patted the kid on the head, and she turned and started back to the little village.

We circled up for security and listened in as Bay An briefed Brewton and Bryson. As it turned out, there were a lot more than two villages in this area. There were dozens of small hamlets with six or eight families doing their best to keep what little they had away from the VC. Now we were not only not in a free-fire zone, but we could expect to see lots of civilians, and the VC were masters at hiding among the civilian population. It always pissed us off when the magazines and newspapers or radio and television reports made it sound as if we enjoyed killing civilians. Innocent civilians did get killed, but it was the VC who used their own civilian population as shields because they knew that we didn't kill civilians when it was possible to avoid it. Bay An also found out that the reason we hadn't seen any men or even young boys was that they had left before daybreak to work out in the fields, on the river running fish traps or fish nets, or doing whatever they could to feed their families.

In a few minutes we were back on the trail that went right through the middle of the hamlet and continued toward the river. We had gone only three or four hundred yards from the edge of the hamlet when we came across another trail that crossed this one at a ninety-degree angle. It was a well-beaten path with fresh tire-tread sandal tracks. Bryson and Bay An slipped away to reconnoiter while we held our position to cover their back. It was only a few minutes before we got the signal to move out on the new path.

Now we were headed into very thick vegetation and slogging through mud and standing water where the mosquitoes built split-level mansions and the leeches grew to the size of toy poodles. The entire area was nothing more than a low-lying swamp. The vegetation quickly became so thick that it was almost like operating at the back end of twilight. Visibility was no better than twenty to twenty-five feet, so we looked hard for booby traps and moved slowly, silently, and cautiously. After half an hour and no more than six hundred yards, hand signals came back to halt, there were booby traps ahead. This was definitely bad news, but a good sign. In the deep bush, with visibility reduced to only yards, the primary uses of booby traps are to kill and maim, to warn the people who planted the booby traps that someone is coming in their back door, and, if they are experienced fighters, to push you into another booby trap while you are running away from the blast of the first. It was a good sign because nobody would waste a booby trap. Nobody puts out a bunch of booby traps unless there is something that is worth protecting.

At the first sign of booby traps, we would all start looking at every leaf, stick, tree, and lump of dirt. Barth grabbed me by the shoulder and pointed over our heads. Tied to a limb was a C-rat can with a grenade in it. From the can ran a long piece of almost invisible monofilament fishing line. At the end of the line was a small fishhook looped over a branch so that it dangled about shoulder high above the trail. The idea was for the point man to brush aside the monofilament line, just like the dozens of spiderwebs that we were constantly brushing out of our faces. If it worked as intended, the fishhook would get caught in his clothing and, as he moved ahead, the line would pull tight and tip the can over, and the grenade—with the pin pulled and the spoon only being held in place by the C-rat can—would fall free and explode. It was a simple, easy, and effective booby trap that would airburst right on top of whoever was passing underneath the tree limb. It was time to find another trail.

Experience had taught us that where there is one booby trap there are more, and it is close to suicidal to try to disarm booby traps. Half of the time one booby trap is set up so that it will be spotted and is booby-trapped itself so that anyone who tries to disarm it gets blown away by the second booby trap. We backtracked for about fifty yards and circled up in a security position with Bryson and Brewton in the center. This was getting interesting. Now we were almost certain that we were in the right place, or damn close to the right place. With all those sandal prints and the booby traps, there was something somebody was protecting, and whatever that something was, it wasn't very far away.

Even before Bryson could open his mouth, we heard something that you almost never hear in the bush, the sound of a hammer pounding metal. There is no sound in the bush that is more foreign than metal hitting metal. Even the sound made when the safety lever of an AK-47 slaps into the off position is so out of place in the bush that the sound alone has saved many men's lives, giving them a split-second warning before the VC could spring an ambush. When I heard someone swinging a hammer against metal, the first thing I thought was how glad I was that we had decided to take the whole platoon on this op. Anyone who wasn't afraid to be making all that noise must have the firepower to cover his ass and back it up in spades.

In almost less time than it takes to tell it, we automatically formed up in a T and were moving in total silence through the bush thirty or forty feet off of the trail. Alpha squad was the top of the T, and Bravo was in single file in the center. On first contact Bravo would split up; half would go left, half would go right to cover Alpha's flanks and to spread the field of fire. Nobody was expecting this to be anything other than the mine factory. Innocent fishermen or farmers don't hang booby traps in trees. We moved as slowly and silently as shadows through the mangroves. After ten or fifteen minutes we could hear another tinny transistor radio blaring out Vietnamese music, and we could smell smoke carried on the breeze right into our faces. There was only the sound of the radio, the hammer whanging away, and an occasional rustle of the trees as the breeze disturbed the leaves. Then, out of nowhere, a dog started barking, and Alpha opened up, shredding the jungle straight ahead of them. Bravo moved up, alternating right, left, right, left, and added our firepower to the fight.

From my position I could see the tops of two or more bunkers made out of mud and timber. We were all ankle- to knee-deep in the water, the muzzle flashes from the VC rifles were only thirty yards away, and bullets were skipping across the water and cutting the limbs off of the trees all around us. We all dropped to one knee in the water and got behind the biggest mangrove tree that we could find that didn't put us in our own line of fire. The impact of 7.62 bullets was kicking water in my face, and chunks of bark went flying from the mangrove tree as if a huge chain saw were chewing its way through the trunk. We were so close to the VC that we couldn't even use the LAAW rockets or 40 mm HE grenades because they wouldn't travel far enough to arm themselves before they hit the bunkers. With the rate of fire we were pouring into the bunkers and surrounding area, I couldn't believe that anyone could survive, but we were still taking fire from those bunkers. Even a few rounds were coming from VC who popped their heads out from behind the mangrove trees, yanked on the triggers of their AK-47s and SKS rifles, then ducked back behind cover. We were pouring fire into the bunkers and the swamp with two M-60s, two Stoners, two 12-gauge shotguns, and nine M-16s. The entire field of fire was being more or less systematically shredded, and somehow, at least a couple of the VC were still alive because we were taking return fire.

I let loose with another couple of short bursts into the bunkers and ran my drum magazine empty. I had just started loading a hundred-round belt of 5.56 mm linked ammunition into the rifle when I heard the call to cease fire. The silence was welcome—the VC were no longer firing at our positions—but it was a surreal scene. After we had all finished reloading our weapons, we formed up an assault line and started to move cautiously into the target area. As we walked into the area where there was better visibility we could see that we were right on a canal; there were three sampans tied up, two bunkers, a hooch, and some hammocks strung up in the mangrove trees. A dead VC, his rifle still slung over his back and most of his head gone, lay in one sampan. A second VC was splayed out, with blood seeping from what looked like a couple dozen bullet wounds, in the muddy dirt alongside an unexploded American 250-pound bomb with the snake-eye fins still attached. Lying at his feet was an innocent bystander, a mongrel dog that would never bark again.

We took up security positions around the camp, and the search team went to work. The hooch was cleared, and a tear gas grenade and a couple of smoke grenades were tossed into each bunker. Tossing a concussion or fragmentation grenade into a bunker that might contain more bombs or explosives would have been a really shitty way to end the day—forever. As the smoke and tear gas poured out of the entrances of the bunkers, we could hear coughing and choking coming from one of them. Bay An started yelling to them in Vietnamese to crawl out with their hands on the top of their heads, and it didn't take long before two men wearing the traditional VC uniform, black pajamas and tire-tread sandals, crawled out of the bunker. We blindfolded and gagged them, tied their arms together behind their backs at the elbows, and set them alongside the trail where Bay An could keep an eye on them while we completed the search. There was no way any of us was going to go into the bunkers to see what there might be inside. It would take at least an hour for the tear gas to dissipate, and we needed to haul our ass to our extraction point like immediately.

To simplify things, and to make sure that there wouldn't even be a bunker still there that could be reused by the VC, we carefully dragged the 250-pound bomb over to the entrance of one of the bunkers, which was still belching smoke and tear gas. I removed the back of one of our claymore mines and used my Ka-Bar knife to pry out the pound-and-a-half charge of C-4 it held. Then I wrapped it and taped it tightly around the nose of the unexploded bomb. We put all of the shot-up weapons and tools on top. I stood by while the platoon formed up with our new POWs in the rear. In only a couple of minutes we were squared away and ready to head back to the river. I inserted a chemical delay blasting cap into the C-4 and squeezed the copper capsule that broke the glass tube inside and released the acid that would eat through the copper wire. Then we headed out in the same direction we had come. We reached the main trail and headed for the river. I could hear Jim Folman on the radio calling the Mike 8 boat to stand by to extract the platoon. We were almost back to the river when we heard and felt the explosion of the 250-pound bomb. Two bunkers, whoever and whatever had been in them, sampans, trees, VC bodies, and everything else within five hundred feet of the mine factory had been converted to splinters and rubble.

At the riverbank, waiting for the Mike 8 boat, we realized that we hadn't warned them to expect the explosion of the 250-pound bomb. When the detonator blew, the crew on the Mike 8 boats figured that we were in deep trouble and were frantically trying to raise us on the radio, but our PRC-25 radio was as unreliable as ever. Ready for whatever might be coming their way, they had everything on board loaded and locked, ready for use. Everything that could shoot, from the .50 cal to the 105 recoilless and the 81 mm mortar, was manned and ready to save our ass. They didn't think it was as funny as we thought it was, but just knowing that we could depend on those guys being ready to cover our back always made us appreciate how important the boat drivers and their crews were to our operations. Fortunately, we didn't need bailing out that day.

With the Mike 8 boats even more crammed to the gunwales than they were on insertion, our extraction and the trip back to Nha Be with our prisoners was almost normal. We were wet, tired, sweaty, muddy, and getting rained on, but we weren't blue and shivering. That would have made it normal.

16

Dead Men Walking

After four months of humping the Rung Sat, sporadic contact with the VC along the canals, in their hidey-holes, and in the wonderland of jungle and swamp that hadn't been defoliated, the 3rd Platoon had become deadly guerrilla warriors. The local VC were getting their ass handed to them on a plate more and more often. As much as I was beginning to like smelling like mud, water buffalo dung, and rotting foliage, I couldn't stop myself from thinking about Australia, clean sheets, round-eyed women, and pools of clear water that were free of crocodiles, bugs, and leeches that latched on to you, chewed a hole in your skin, and sucked your blood. Halfway through my second tour I had become something of an expert on leech behavior and leech removal. Expert or not, no matter how well I secured my boots to the legs of my pants I always found a couple of hitchhikers somewhere when I showered off the mud and dirt. I hated the slimy little bloodsucking bastards.

SOP was for everyone with over six months in-country to take seven much too short days of R&R. We had our choice of where we wanted to spend that week: Hawaii, Bangkok, Thailand, the Philippines, and several other places where tourists were welcome and people didn't shoot at you. It hadn't been too hard for me to talk Jack Squires into coming along to sample the sights and sounds of Australia. To make sure that we wouldn't be screwing up any ops in the planning stages for the week we would be gone, we decided to clear our plans with Lieutenants Bryson and Brewton and put in our request for the next day. The next day was still one more op away, though; that night we would be going out with a PRU team led by Frank Thornton.

Frank never had to look too hard to find more than enough volunteers for his ops; his exploits and abilities in the bush had become almost legendary around SEAL Team 2. Frank briefed Lieutenant Bryson and let him know that there was room for another six or seven men on this op and he was looking for volunteers. The lucky guys drew the short straw, and Master Chief Tom Blais, Bill Barth, Jack Squires, Bob Moore, Mike McDonald, and I would be going along on what looked to be a high-probability operation. If Frank was going to be leading ten PRU and seven SEALs into the boonies, it was almost certain that his intel was rock solid. With seventeen men going on a single op, it also looked like Frank was expecting things could get very hot and very dangerous in a couple of heartbeats. One of the reasons that Frank had become almost a legend in the teams was that he never needed to preach to the choir. He understood the credo that kept us alive in the bush: There ain't ever no such thing as too much firepower!

That afternoon Frank came over to our digs to give the six guys that would be going out with his PRU team that night a personal briefing. It was an ambush operation that was intended to capture or kill a district-level VC and his five-man protection cadre. The intel was that they would be moving from Tieu Can village on the Tinh Long An River to Ke Sach, a village located on a canal about three miles from the river. The plan was for us to set up an ambush and nail them somewhere in those three miles. I always liked the idea of letting the enemy come to us. Fighting where we could stack the odds in our favor, on our chosen field of battle, not theirs, gave us an edge that was almost impossible to counter when the OIC hit the clackers and the claymores fired.

Even though most of the team had been in Vietnam for only four months, we had become very good at guerrilla warfare. Experience is the best teacher, and those four months had reduced most of the tactical advantages that the VC thought they had to no advantage at all. With months of operating in their backyard, we knew the turf as well as they did, most of the time better, and we had far superior training and weapons. We also had three other advantages: silence, stealth, and surprise. When we planned an op or an ambush, it was always assured that we would have total fire supremacy, and we almost always took Charlie by surprise. Damn near nothing could live for more than a few seconds when we opened up. The VC always ended up KIA unless we wanted to take them alive. Frank Thornton was a master at getting good intel, then figuring out how to put it to good use and the easiest way to get the job done. Frank told us that the shortest route between these villages was by cutting across the dikes between the rice paddies, not by running a sampan on the canals. The dike was where we would intercept the VC. We would use our two LSSCs to insert just after dark two klicks south of Tieu Can and sneak and peek through the bush to a trail that the usually reliable PRU intel sources said the VC would be using.

At 1800 we assembled at the pier and loaded up the boats. Smaller in stature, the PRU crammed ten of their men and two crew into one boat, and we loaded the second with seven SEALs and two crew. The PRU had learned a few lessons from the SEAL advisers. Like us, they all carried as much ammunition and other gear as they could hump and still move silently and fast. With all the men, ammunition, and weapons we carried, the boats were loaded to the gunwales. I didn't think that the LSSCs would be able to make much speed, but there was still plenty of daylight left to reach our insertion point on schedule. To my surprise the crew had figured out a way to get even a heavily loaded LSSC up on step. Being able to run on step, with most of the boat above the waterline, is a very nice thing, especially when you are hauling ass out of someplace that will soon be crawling with VC looking to take revenge for what you have just done to their command and control people. The boat crews could get those boats running at thirty knots, maybe a little faster with a light load, and at that speed the LSSCs are much harder to hit with an RPG, or even with small-arms fire.

These boat drivers knew what they were doing. The crew had figured out that if they stayed in the shallow water, close to the edge of the riverbank and out of the deeper main current, there would be less resistance against the hull. They hugged the bank until they were rocking and rolling and headed into the middle of the river and deeper water only after the boat was on step and running at full speed. Running flat out to avoid any unnecessary and unpleasant sniper fire from the bank of the river, we would be arriving while it was still daylight, too early for insertion. Frank gave the boat drivers map coordinates where they could slow down so that we could insert in darkness. Running slow and quiet, we approached our insertion point with no indication that the VC had figured out that they were soon going to have people hunting them in their own backyard. With daylight fading fast and the sun dropping like a rock over the horizon, the LSSC boats wallowed in the river until full dark.

As the bow of our LSSC touched the bank, we slipped into the shallow water and set up our security perimeter in the mangrove trees. After waiting fifteen minutes to make sure that the area was secure, Frank, using a red-lens flashlight, signaled for the second LSSC to move into position. With no indication of any VC activity in the area, the LSSC drivers decided that they would remain right at the edge of the mangroves in case we ran into serious trouble and needed them to relay radio messages for artillery or air support. Even though Frank had set up our extraction by helos at daybreak, the army pilots were always a little hinky about flying at night unless it was an emergency. If we started taking overwhelming enemy fire, the helos would come in to pick us up in a hot LZ, but even when they were covered by gunships they didn't like flying at night. So knowing that the LSSCs would be there to relay radio messages or to extract us as quickly as possible if we got into a real mess that we couldn't get ourselves out of was a comforting thought. Two escape routes are always four times better than one.

With nothing to disturb the sounds of the bush or the birds now roosting in the trees and no other indication of any VC activity, we moved out through another of the millions of rice paddies toward our objective. Frank was taking the point with Jack Squires and his M-60, the PRU were in the middle, and five SEALs were bringing up the rear. After a couple of hundred yards of swamp we struck dry ground and, with a half moon already in the sky, stuck to the shadows of the tree line. Frank moved two of his PRUs to the point because they had grown up there and knew every inch of this area as well as I knew Murphy Island back home in Florida. They would get us to exactly where Frank had planned to set up our ambush.

With the bright moonlight and the shadows of the tree line to hide our movement, we could really make some time. We could see for hundreds of yards, all the way across the rice paddy, but we remained invisible in the shadows, just the way I liked it. The intel was that the VC VIP and his cadre of bodyguards wouldn't be making his move to Ke Sach village until midnight or later. Moving as fast as we were, we would be there a couple of hours before the VC would show up; in plenty of time to set up our positions and get everything in place to welcome the VC with style. Then, just as I was thinking how nice it would be to arrive in plenty of time to get the ambush set up, the column came to a quick halt and we were all down on one knee covering our assigned field of fire from the deepest shadows we could find.

Before any word could be passed back, I could hear voices coming across the paddy. The voices were not loud, but over the hard surface of water even a little noise can carry for a long way, something I don't think the VC ever figured out. We could see several figures moving along the dike; they were coming from the direction of Ke Sach village. It was a long hundred yards from our position in the tree line to the VC, but in the bright moonlight they would make easy targets of opportunity. We were so well concealed and silent that the VC never knew that with every step they were centered in the front sights of seventeen rifles.

Even though this wasn't a free-fire zone, we knew that we were the only outfit cleared to operate in this sector. There wasn't any question in my mind; anyone else moving at night in this part of the Rung Sat was VC. We didn't need any more proof to know that these were bad guys on the move. As they got closer and closer to where we were hiding in the darkness, it was evident that they were all carrying weapons. Even after seeing it time after time, I couldn't figure out who the hell had trained these guys to carry their rifles resting on their shoulders while they held the front ends of the barrels with one hand. They were just tripping along like teenagers on a school outing, like they hadn't a worry in the world and the possibility of actually needing to use those rifles slung up over their shoulders was the furthest thing from their minds. These VC didn't know it yet, but we did: They were dead men walking.

There were nine of them spread out in single file with no more than forty yards between the point man and the last man in the ragged line. I knew that as soon as Frank opened up, all of the SEALs would drop the hammer and saturate their designated field of fire. Full-automatic fire from thirty-round magazines and hundred-round drums or belts would cut across the VC like a scythe through standing wheat. There would be enough flying metal in the air to ensure that they wouldn't get off even one round before they were all spouting blood from multiple wounds or KIA. While we were sweeping the dike with our machine guns and rifles, two of our guys would be firing 40 mm para-flares. The flares would turn the night into day, and anyone still standing or running away would be cut to pieces too small to be worth putting into a body bag.

I pushed off the safety of my Stoner and waited. Frank was OIC, and it was up to him to fire the first rounds that would get the proceedings under way. From the shadows, I watched as the VC just walked away into the gloom, still talking, and still carrying their rifles casually over their shoulders like golf clubs or umbrellas. It had been a perfect setup for an ambush, but Frank had bigger fish in mind. He didn't want to take out some local VC that had little or no strategic value and blow the chance to land one of the more important VC that was recruiting in the area. Capturing or killing a high-ranking VC was far more important than whacking the VC squad that we had allowed to disappear into the night and live another day. I put my Stoner back on safety.

Even with the long wait to allow the VC squad to pass into the distance, we were still running ahead of schedule. We arrived at the site our PRU guide had picked for us to set up our ambush at 2300, at least an hour before we were expecting the VC to show up. The ambush site was at the point where the trail that we had followed crossed a rutted dirt road that led to Ke Sach village, about four hundred yards away. We set up a security perimeter, and Tom Blais and I set out the claymore mine that would protect our left flank. The only tree that would allow us to hide the claymore was a little too close for our liking. We normally put the claymores out a hundred feet from our ambush position, but the only trees we could find were just barely fifty feet away. We would have to make do. While Tom and I were out on the left flank, two of the PRU team were setting out the claymore that would cover our right flank. When Tom finished attaching the claymore to a tree, about five or six feet above the ground, I fed the firing wire through the bush and back to Frank, now in the center of our position.

With the firing wires and clackers hooked up and Frank ready to fire the claymores to initiate the ambush, we all moved back into our positions. I laid out one of my OD green bandages on the ground and put a hundred-round belt for my Stoner on top, where it wouldn't get any crud on it that might jam the Stoner. In the bright moonlight, the linked belt would be easy to find and fast to load when I had emptied the drum magazine. Well concealed in the darkest shadows we could find, we waited in complete silence for the unsuspecting enemy to walk right into the middle of our killing zone.

It quickly became obvious that we had been lucky to get to the ambush site as early as we did. Hardly any time had passed when we heard voices coming from the trail that we had followed to reach the ambush site. It would be no more than a minute or two before the VC reached the dirt road where we were waiting. As the voices got louder and louder, I wondered what these guys had between their ears; it never failed to amaze me how the VC felt so safe moving around at night. It seemed as if they just couldn't stop talking, laughing, and, more often than not, playing one of their tinny transistor radios.

Even in the shade under his hat, I could see the face of the first VC coming toward me. He was no more than twenty feet away and was wearing black pajamas and one of the woven straw hats that looked like an upside-down funnel. I could hear the slap-slap of his rubber tire sandals as he walked into the center of our field of fire. Sure enough, he was carrying his AK-47 over his shoulder with one hand on the barrel, where it wouldn't do him any good at all when Frank touched off the claymores. Just as he was about to pass by my position he turned and gestured to someone behind him, then started laughing as he tripped and almost fell over a broken tree limb. Fifteen feet behind him I could see two glowing red dots that were bobbing up and down like crazed lightning bugs; two more VC smoking cigarettes passed by me at less than fifteen feet. A couple of yards behind the cigarette smokers there were three more VC who were obviously arguing over something. I don't know what they were thinking, or how these people planned to stay alive in the bush; they just couldn't seem to keep their mouths shut. To a man, all of their weapons were slung carelessly over their shoulders.

As the sixth VC passed my position, the claymores detonated. From only fifty feet away, the flash blinded me for a couple of seconds and the blast almost deafened me. Thousands of ball bearings went ripping through the VC at three times the speed of sound. Because sound travels only 1,100 feet per second, most of the VC were dead before they even heard the explosion.

My Stoner, almost as if it had a mind of its own, started sweeping the kill zone from right to left as Jack Squires swept his M-60 from left to right. A quick reload with a hundred-round linked belt and it was time for targets of opportunity. Tonight there wouldn't be any. The two white star para-flares floating overhead made it seem almost like daylight.

The ambush had taken all of twenty or thirty seconds, and in less than a minute all firing had ceased. With the enormous explosion of two claymores, the level of small-arms fire we were laying down, and the para-flares lighting up the night, it would appear to anyone within a mile or two as if an entire company had opened up. We all reloaded our weapons, and Frank and his three-man search team checked all of the bodies for anything that might be useful or provide us with more intel on other VC activities in the area. Meanwhile, Tom and one of the PRUs policed up the firing wires from the claymores. We always tried to make sure that there was nothing left behind that Charlie might be able to use against us. The only things we left behind were empty cartridge casings and bodies—and sometimes, as we would tonight, a surprise package for the VC who would almost always come looking for us.

I had gotten an "atta boy" from Frank to leave one of our little gifts, an instantaneous-firing fragmentation grenade taped to a tree about six feet from the ground. When we were ready to pull out, I would attach a length of almost invisible monofilament fishing line to the pin that held the spoon in place, then run it down the tree and along the ground and tie it to the arm or leg of one of the dead VC. I would carefully cover the line with whatever debris was handy that would camouflage it long enough for someone to turn the body over. If and when the body was turned or moved, the pin was pulled, the spoon flew, the grenade blew, and there were more dead VC to add to the pile.

We were all sure that the dead men walking that had passed us by only a couple of hours ago were still in the neighborhood and would probably be backtracking to find out who was making life a little shorter for their leaders. Estimating how far they would be from our location, based on how slowly they had been moving when they passed through our perimeter, they might not be more than a klick or two away. Frank gave the word to move out, and another white star para-flare was fired to give us a lot of light so that we could move fast and far. As I leaned over to tie off the line to the leg of one of the dead VC, I happened to see a pack of blood-spattered Camel cigarettes in the dirt. I guessed that the VC hadn't heard that smoking could be bad for your health.

To confuse the dead men walking and make it harder for them to catch up to us if they were humping in our direction, we moved out in a direction that was at a right angle to the trail we had followed into the ambush area. With Frank taking point, we kept moving fast to put as much real estate between us and any pursuers as possible. We humped away from the ambush site fast and silent for about an hour and a half and came to a road, a rice paddy, and another bombed-out pagoda. Frank decided that this would be a great place to hole up for the night. Just before daybreak, Frank would call up our flying chariots to come in and haul us back to base. With our perimeter secure around the broken-down walls of the pagoda, we had good cover and concealment; all we needed to do was watch and wait.

As the first blush of lighter blue started creeping along the horizon, there was an almost imperceptible sound, sort of a muffled pop, from the direction of last night's ambush. Somebody must have rolled over the dead VC and found the surprise package we had left behind. Within a few seconds of the grenade popping, we also heard the unmistakable sound of helo rotors in the distance. Frank got on the radio and gave them a compass bearing from their position to ours. With all eyes scanning the horizon, we spotted them coming in at three thousand feet, and Frank threw a colored smoke grenade that identified the area where they could come in, get us all aboard, and make their extraction. The pilots must have been guys with a lot of experience. They brought their helos in fast and touched down at the edge of the rice paddy, both teams loaded in under two minutes, and we were on the way back to Nha Be with another well-executed op under our belt. At our debriefing, Frank told us that we had captured and destroyed seven weapons and brought home a pouch filled with maps, documents, Vietnamese currency, and the positive ID of the now KIA district-level VC recruiter that we had targeted. We had accounted for six VC KIA, and not even one of us had gotten a scratch.

Now that the VC knew that we knew that they were operating out of Tieu Can, Frank figured they would never expect us to run another op in the same area so soon. They were wrong again. Frank was already putting together another op, and Tieu Can was the target. Missing that op was breaking my heart, but Australia was calling my name, and Doc Clark told Jack Squires and me to get packed. We were leaving for Australia on a big bird in the morning.

17

Australian Bliss

A t zero-dark-thirty hours, or half-past the middle of the night, Jack and I jumped onto a 4-by-4 truck commandeered by Doc, Bill Barth, and Mike McDonald, and the whole crew of misfits headed for Tan Son Nhut Air Base, arriving well ahead of our flight time. They dumped us out, told us to have a great time with the Australians, and headed back to Nha Be. Jack and I jogged into the military area of the airport to find that there was a throng of over two hundred soldiers decked out in civvies waiting in line to exchange their military scrip and piastres for real money. Even with a few disagreements over the exchange rate for piastres, the line moved along quickly, and in less than a half hour Jack and I had about two thousand American dollars stuffed into our pockets. With our R&R orders in hand, we wandered over to the departure gate for Sydney, checked our minimal baggage, and boarded the Pan American Boeing 707 that, five hours later, would be landing in Australia, a world away from canals, crocodiles, leeches, and the VC. The sight and smell of clean, beautiful, round-eyed women, the first we had seen in five months, was almost overwhelming, but those lovely stewardesses knew how to handle a plane load of rowdy men who were far from home. Those stews were real professionals. They managed to push a heavy cart up and down the aisle, serve drinks and food, and simultaneously evade the sometimes over-the-line attempts at fraternization by men who hadn't seen a woman dressed in a crisp white blouse and a tight, well-fitted skirt for months.

With the stewardesses wisecracking and entertaining all of us, the five-hour flight seemed much shorter than it could have. As soon as we landed and fought our way off the 707, Jack and I grabbed up our luggage, two small backpacks, and headed for the information booth. We needed to find a store where we could buy ourselves some real civilian clothes and get some leads on the hotels and motels. With our new civilian duds stuffed into our packs, we grabbed a cab, and the cabbie gave us the lowdown on the best bars (called pubs in Australia), beaches, and places to meet girls. As our cab bobbed and weaved through the traffic and wound easily along the sunny streets, Jack and I noticed something that really caught our attention. Somehow, while we were out in the bush getting shot at, someone had decided that the miniskirt was the required national dress of all of the attractive women that seemed to be scattered everywhere in Sydney. This, Jack and I quickly agreed, was one of the best ideas of this century, possibly of any century. Everywhere we looked there were long, tanned legs sticking out from under the shortest skirts we had ever seen in public. Beautiful women were strutting their stuff, shakin' and bakin' on every corner and in every park. Just about anywhere you looked there was another gorgeous Aussie lovely in a miniskirt. Watching all of those well-synchronized moving parts on all of those young ladies was enough to make a righteous young man like myself consider becoming a sinner of the first water—or opportunity. Jack was a different story. He might take a good long look now and again, but he was happily married to Barbara, a really beautiful woman back in Virginia Beach. Jack was smarter than I was; he knew a great thing when he saw it, and he was in love with his wife. He wasn't about to make any of the dumb mistakes that had destroyed my marriage.

Mel, who became our personal taxi driver for the next week, knew Sydney inside and out, and made sure that we would not waste our time looking for good food and entertainment. Mel suggested that we might like a motel that was owned by some friends of his. After a sightseeing ride around Sydney, and more gaggles of girls in miniskirts than I could manage to count, Mel took us to the Coogee Bay Hotel, just a short walk from the world-famous Bondi Beach and the rolling surf. After maybe too little negotiation over the cost, Jack and I each grabbed a room with an ocean view and sliding glass doors that opened onto a sandy path that led down to the beach—and to all of those lovely young women who spent all day on the beach in bikinis, baking themselves golden brown, and most of the night in the clubs or pubs. With the beach covered with gorgeous young ladies as far as the eye could see, I was almost feeling sorry for Jack, but I sure did respect his willpower. Whoever said that being shot at and missed was one of the most powerful aphrodisiacs must have been right. I had been shot at and missed a bunch in the last four months, and I was looking forward to spending as much quality time as possible with these beautiful women.

We unpacked, grabbed a shower, and headed out for some dinner. I was hoping that I could also manage a little one-on-one fraternization with the local beauties. Mel was waiting for us in the lobby and decided that Kings Cross was where we should start our evening. This area of Sydney was the epicenter of pubs and clubs and, most important to me, was populated by beautiful girls who were dressed to kill in every club where there was a dance floor and a bar. After an inexpensive dinner of fresh seafood and a few mugs of beer, we decided that it was time to do our recon on the local nightlife. Even at 2200 there were crowds of people moving from one dance club or pub to the next. Well scrubbed and dressed in our civvies, we blended right in. We looked long and hard at the California Bar but decided that the Texas Club, with two bars, a large dance floor, a live band playing the latest rock and roll, and wall-to-wall women, was a good place to start burning some of the money we had stashed in our pockets.

Somehow Jack and I got separated as we tried to bob and weave our way through the mass of happy, dancing, drinking Aussies without knocking anyone over or getting our feet trampled by the dancing couples. I quickly noticed that there were several pairs of women who were dancing together. There was actually a shortage of men in the club, and I figured that I could help change the ratio by at least one. I sidled over to the nearest empty spot at the bar and tried to get the attention of one of the bartenders who were slinging drinks as fast as they could. It looked like I was going to have to wait for half of the people in the room to be served before I could even get an order in. I was just about ready to move farther away from the dance floor, where the bar was a little less crowded, when I felt a hand on my shoulder. Figuring that it was another thirsty member of the crowd, I was about to turn around and tell him to wait his turn, but when I turned around I was staring directly into the eyes of a beautiful, tall, dark-haired girl whose smile and pearl white teeth struck me mute. That was a first, and before I could even pretend to be a smooth operator she got my heart beating with a simple question, "Where you from, Yank?" I'm sure that I was not the first American to fall under the spell of a beautiful woman with an Australian accent, and I sure wouldn't be the last, but no matter what anyone might say this wasn't just another quick fling with one of the local girls.

I introduced myself to Bonnie, and for the next couple of hours we danced, drank, and told one another about ourselves. Her name was Bonnie Ann Bliss, an Australian by way of Holland, and she was a sister, what we Americans call a nurse. She lived not too far from the hospital and worked three days on and two days off. She offered to show me all the sights and sounds of Sydney and its environs for the next two days. I remember looking at the clock over the bar just before two in the morning and ordering another round, but time didn't seem to be all that important just then.

I awoke the next morning to the sound of Jack banging on the door and a beautiful 5' 10" woman named Bonnie stretched out next to me on the bed. I considered yelling for Jack to go soak his head but thought that that would not be the way one SEAL should treat another, especially one who had spent the night alone, probably snoring loud enough to shake the shutters and beat the band! I jumped from the bed as quietly as I could, wrapped a towel around my waist, and opened the door to the room just enough to ask Jack to come back in half an hour. Like the gentleman that he was, Jack smiled and disappeared toward his room. Bonnie and I showered, then needed to shower again, and Jack, being smarter than your average SEAL on R&R, didn't return for almost an hour. When Jack finally stopped staring at Bonnie, now freshly showered for the second time that morning and dressed in her miniskirt and halter top, I introduced them, and Bonnie asked us if we were ready for breakfast. Bonnie, because she was always working different shifts, knew where to find a good breakfast anytime, day or night. She took us to a place that served breakfast around the clock. The food was good, the coffee was strong, and the sunshine coming through the windows reflected off of the mirror-polished trim just like it did in the diners back home.

We were discussing the local sights when Bonnie asked if we had ever heard about the Three Sisters in a place called Katoomba. We admitted that we hadn't even a clue, so Bonnie told us about the Aboriginal legend. It seems that long ago there were three sisters, Meehni, Wimlah, and Gunnedoo, who were members of the Katoomba tribe. Much to the dismay of their parents and tribe, the girls grew up as free spirits and fell in love with three men from the Nepean tribe, a definite no-no that led to a full-tilt tribal battle. To make sure that the girls wouldn't be carried off in the heat of battle—and knowing that the girls themselves might have become accomplices to their own kidnapping—the head witch doctor of the Katoomba tribe turned them into huge monoliths of stone. The witch doctor had planned to turn them back into human form after the battle, but battles don't always go as planned, and the witch doctor was killed. Today the Three Sisters still stand, each over three thousand feet tall, monuments to good intentions and the tide of battle. Bonnie assured us that it was well worth the two-hour train trip to see this natural wonder for ourselves. Jack and I agreed, so the three of us finished our breakfast and headed off to the outback for another adventure.

It seemed that no matter where you wanted to go in Australia there was a train that would, sometimes slowly, take you where you wanted to go. This train trip was accomplished by riding on the same train tracks that had been laid about a century before to haul coal out of the mountainous area. The tour guide told us that parts of the Scenic Railway are the steepest railway inclines in the world. After a couple of hours on the train, and looking down into what looked like the Grand Canyon, I wasn't going to argue the point.

It would have been hard to have a bad time with Bonnie as our personal tour guide, but the train trip across the wide open spaces was only the first act in a day that would give Jack and me the chance to see the wilderness that surrounded Sydney. It was going to be a wonderful day. The Three Sisters were enormous reddish rock spires, almost as impressive as anything you would find in Monument Valley or the Grand Canyon. One of the local tourist activities was to pay someone to take you out climbing up and down these ravines. The men who rappelled down them looked no bigger than ants against the immensity of the vista that we could see from the platform. I have no fear of heights, but those guys had to be pushing their luck to go up and down those spires day after day. Sitting outside on a platform while relaxing with a mug of beer at a local pub, we could see for miles and miles over sweeping mountains and valleys where the raw rock, the bones of the earth, stuck up as if they were the backs of prehistoric beasts. Bonnie was right when she told us that she couldn't describe it, we needed to see it for ourselves.

The return trip was, if anything, even more relaxing. As the train followed switchback after switchback, the ever changing panorama of wild Australia made me appreciate even more how astonishing it was that the Aborigines had scratched a living out of this wilderness and had created an oral history that went back thousands of years. Australia was a wild and beautiful place. I figured that at least we owed Bonnie a really great dinner for sharing it with us as our unofficial tour guide.

Mel, who obviously knew the train schedule and figured that we would be getting back well before dark, was waiting for us at the train station. We dropped Bonnie off at her apartment a couple of blocks from the hospital so that she could change into a fresh outfit and told her that we would be picking her up for dinner in about an hour. American women could learn a lesson from Bonnie. She was ready—and even more gorgeous than she was the night before—when Mel and I came to take her back to the beach for dinner. Jack joined us at the restaurant on the beach, and we spent a few hours listening to Bonnie tell us more about Australia as the surf broke less than a hundred feet away.

One of the things Bonnie said that surprised me was that Australian women generally preferred "Yanks," finding us, when compared to Australian men, to be well-mannered. Australian men don't open car doors, front doors, back doors, restaurant doors, bar doors, or any doors for a woman. They don't pull out a lady's chair or buy their girlfriends flowers, and it seemed that they expected a lot more than a good night kiss at the end of every date. I was very happy that my parents had taught me good manners. Had they not demanded that I learn how to treat a lady, I might have been eating dinner with nothing but Jack Squires to stare at all night.

The days when Bonnie was off duty we spent doing, going, seeing, eating, drinking, loving, and, much of that time, laughing out loud like kids having the time of their lives. When she worked her twelve-hour shifts I spent the day on the beach, wandering around and taking in all of the sights like a tourist, or just kicking back with Jack and Mel. Most nights I spent at her apartment. She didn't ask, but I promised her that I would come back to see her as soon as I could. I was pretty sure that I could wangle another trip not too far down the road. Time seemed to be moving faster than Einstein said it could. My last day in Australia, Bonnie was off duty, so we decided to stay at my place on Bondi Beach. Late that night, I took Bonnie Ann Bliss back to her apartment. She was working the early shift, and Jack and I were leaving early in the morning. It was a long good-bye.

For five hours I couldn't get Bonnie and Australia out of my mind, but there was something else that I couldn't shake: the feeling that the Australians knew more about the war we were fighting in Vietnam than most Americans. I had always made it a practice to read whatever American magazines I could get my hands on, and while I was waiting for Bonnie to get off duty at the hospital, I picked a few that were scattered across the waiting room. I couldn't believe that the news about the war published in *Time, Newsweek*, and all the others was about the same war that I was fighting. Reading the news in those magazines, it seemed that we were baby killers and wanton murderers and that the draft was nothing more than a curse on almost every young man in America. It was hard for me to believe that Americans were running to Canada to avoid serving their own country, but that was what all the magazines were reporting.

The air force was interdicting the VC supply lines, trying to stop the flow of weapons and munitions that were being used against the civilian population that wanted nothing more than to be left in peace to scratch a living out of the earth and feed their children. While the pilots and their crews flew high above the battlefield, the army, brown-water navy, marines, and SEAL Teams were slogging through the mud, running the rivers and canals under fire, and fighting an enemy who murdered their own people in cold blood because they wanted to be free. The peace movement, and the politicians they supported, took advantage of their right to speak their mind, a freedom that the men on the ground in Vietnam protected with their lives. Most of what I read was a load of lies, and I wondered if those reporters understood that if the American people lost the will to make sacrifices, like the sacrifices our parents and grandparents had made during two world wars, there was no way that we could continue to fight the aggression of the VC and Vietminh. I was almost back to Vietnam, and I wondered if the American people had lost the will to fight. Without the will to fight and win the war, I didn't think that anything we did would matter in the long run. I hoped that I was wrong. I hoped that the dead and wounded who had watered Vietnam with their blood wouldn't have sacrificed for nothing.

The thump of the wheels touching down and the screech of tires slowing the Boeing 707 told me all I needed to know. We were back at Tan Son Nhut, and the beautiful girl in the ruby slippers and miniskirt was far, far away. This was where the people who wanted to make me KIA were waiting, and all that had happened for the last week, and my doubts about what was happening at home, needed to be put away somewhere. Tomorrow I was going to be back at war. Jack and I turned in our cash and got back scrip and piastres, had our baggage searched, then found a convoy of trucks and hitched a ride into Saigon. We checked ourselves into the President Hotel, where Doc and a few of our gang of miscreants were meeting us to spend one last night of freedom. Tonight we would be bobbing and weaving through the hooker capital of Southeast Asia on the top floor while watching the war on the distant horizon.

My internal alarm clock went off at 0500. In the well-rumpled bed next to me was a cute naked woman with black hair and slanted eyes who couldn't have been more than 5'3'. I didn't remember her name, but it wasn't Bonnie. In Vietnam you never knew if you were going to be among the living from day to day, and that was, if I needed an excuse, enough of an excuse for me. After another hour or so of making sure that this last morning of R&R would be another morning to remember, taking a shower, and changing out of my civilian clothes, we mustered in the lobby at 0800 and loaded into a 4-by-4 that had been newly liberated from somewhere in Saigon. It hadn't even been painted navy haze gray. Jack and I got the lowdown on what had been going on since we left. Alpha was going out tonight, briefing at 1800. Welcome back.

18

Back to the Bush

It was too damn early to be bouncing along in a jeep headed back to Nha Be, but the trucks headed in our direction were all full, and these were the last two empty seats Jack and I could find. We tossed our backpacks into the jeep, climbed aboard, sat tight, and held on for dear life. As we bounced in and out of the ruts, passing the slow-moving buffalo carts and the people carrying piles of wood, bundles of straw, and sacks of rice on their backs, and wound our way through the little villages, I kept thinking about how much trouble General Curtis LeMay had made for himself. The general had suggested that if the Communists in Hanoi didn't pull in their horns and stop their aggression, we should bomb them into the Stone Age. If the general had been riding with us, he would have realized that the Stone Age wasn't much worse than what the VC, and most of the Vietnamese outside of the cities, lived through every day. The VC lived in bombed-out pagodas, dirt-floor hooches with leaking roofs, or caves and holes underground. They slept on beds made of branches only a few inches above the flooded mangrove swamps, dug tunnels and used them as hospitals and storage facilities for their food and supplies, and, as long as they had *nuoc mam* to pour on it, would eat just about anything that walked, crawled, slithered, grew, or flew. They were tough bastards, and, as much as most of us would have liked it, we could never defeat them by carpet bombing or fighting only from the air.

The draft had put tens of thousands of men into uniform, but they were draftees; they didn't have much interest in learning how to fight a guerrilla war. Some of the draftees were real fighters, ready and willing to take on the NVA and VC, but they were in the minority. Most of the draftees just wanted to stay alive. They went through basic training, served their tour, and headed for home, and another newbie took their place.

Somebody up the chain of command needed to understand that just putting huge numbers of armed men on the ground can't win a guerrilla war, and the VC had been fighting a guerrilla war for decades. They knew that we would always have air superiority and could keep dropping bombs until the cows came home. Like all guerrilla fighters, they adapted and found a way to survive even the most devastating bombing runs. It didn't take the VC long to figure out that the only way to survive the rain of bombs falling day and night was to go underground. They dug out tunnels and bunkers and lived right under our feet.

To defeat the NVA and VC, we didn't need more draftees. We needed warriors who were well trained, dedicated, and tough as nails. Men who would dig the VC out of their bunkers and kick their ass no matter where they thought they could hide. It seemed that somebody was trying to make it look like there was an easy way to win this war, but we knew better. Every man who survived Hell Week and became a SEAL knew that the only easy day was yesterday.

Even before we passed through the main gate of Nha Be, we could see that there was something going on that probably wasn't going to be good. Both SEAL platoons and Frank Thornton, with a couple of members of his PRU team, had gathered in a group between the chow hall and sick bay, and nobody was laughing or smiling. They all looked to be in a somber mood. The jeep hadn't even stopped rolling when Master Chief Tom Blais waved at us and came over to let us know what had happened. Frank's replacement as adviser to the PRU team, Aviation Electrician's Mate First Class Curtis Ashton, had taken out a PRU team on a canal ambush last night. Although Curtis had been back in-country for only a couple of days, he had already served one tour, and he was anxious to get the team out into the bush so that he could get to know the men and how each of them operated. Their first op was a standard canal ambush op; there was nothing unusual about it. They had inserted, set up an ambush, and placed their claymores in the trees that would protect their flanks and the back door. The VC had walked right through the front door. When the PRUs opened up, Curtis pulled the pin on a concussion grenade, and either it was knocked out of his hand or he dropped it. Before he could find it and throw it into the canal, where it would have detonated harmlessly, the grenade, equal to a half pound of TNT, went off, killing Curtis and wounding two of the PRU team. Curtis was on his second tour of duty and had over a hundred ops under his belt, but it didn't matter how good you were or how many ops you had survived—sometimes it all came down to the luck of the draw. Vietnam had more ways to kill you than anyone has ever cataloged, and last night Curtis had drawn the short straw. I didn't know Curtis very well; we hadn't worked together, and now we never would.

While Jack and I were hiding our civilian clothes from the platoon and getting the rest of our normal gear and weapons out of our lockers, Doc Clark came in and told us that there would be a briefing after chow at 1800; we were headed out on a full platoon ambush operation. Chow time was usually when we would have expected to be grilled about the wine, women, and song found in Australia. Tonight there wasn't much chatter to keep us in the mess hall, so I went back to the weapons locker, stripped and oiled my Stoner, checked my normal load out for an ambush, and finished just in time to get to the lounge for the briefing.

In the past couple of months, the VC had started to harass two small towns, Ben Luc and Tan An, that were about ten miles apart. They had started using the same tactics that they had used in My Tho: set up as close as they could get to the village, drop a couple or three rounds down the mortar tube, and hustle their ass out of the area while the rounds were still in the air. The civilian population was taking a beating, and when they were scared shitless we could never get any intel out of them. If we wanted more good intel, we were going to have to see to it that the mortar crews were captured or became KIA.

We were going to insert by helo at last light, hump a couple of klicks, and set up our ambush on a dirt road that connected the villages. If the VC showed up, we would kick ass and take names; if not, we would spend another long night with the bugs, leeches, and snakes and extract at first light on Mike 8 boats. When two squads went out together, it was SOP for us to take turns in the lead. Tonight it was Alpha's turn, and that meant that Lieutenant Bryson would take the point or would be right behind the point man with an M-60 or Stoner operator right behind him. SEAL officers were always on point or as close to the point man as they could get without tripping over his heels in the dark. No officer can lead from the rear, and SEAL officers were almost all natural-born leaders who never expected their men to do anything that they hadn't, couldn't, or wouldn't do themselves. Warriors can smell a fake from a mile away downwind, but we would always fight alongside a man who was willing to put his own life on the line on every op.

Tonight I would be sticking to Brewton in the middle of the patrol, and our M-60 gunner, Bob Christopher, would be covering our backside in the rear. "Chris," as he had been nicknamed, always wanted to get as close to the point man as he could. He was constantly pestering me to let him take my spot behind the point man while I hung out at the back of the patrol. I wouldn't have minded that too much, but the fact was that Chris was too big a target. He looked like a damn Viking warrior that had come back to life to fight in another time and place. At six feet plus, with curly blond hair, blue eyes, and an open, mischievous grin that was always quick to come and slow to go, he had the women falling over themselves to get next to him when we were on leave. Chris was from California, and he could have been the perfect Hollywood movie model for a surfer, but he had none of the California attitude that was becoming so popular back in the world. He was as solid as a rock and as deadly as they come in combat.

The op would start with a half-hour trip and insertion by helo, and we would extract just after first light. The Mike 8 boats headed out at 1500 to make sure that they would be on station in the Tinh Long An River in case they needed to cover our ass or extract the platoon in an emergency. The Mike 8 boats were originally converted LCM Mk-6 amphibious landing craft (similiar to the LCM Mk-3 used in Normandy and the South Pacific landings). They were big, heavy, and slow, but they had been adapted for use by the SEAL Teams. They could only make about nine knots with both of the Detroit Diesel engines running flat out, but they were more like floating gun platforms than landing craft. After being converted to SEAL specs, they were renamed HSSCs—heavy SEAL support craft—but we called them Mike 8 boats, from their LCM Mk-8 designation. The Mike 8 boats were heavily armored and carried twin .50 caliber Browning machine guns mounted on either side of the bow, a 7.62 minigun in the back of the boat, and an 81 mm mortar and 106 mm recoilless rifle on the top deck. This was more than enough firepower to really light up the night and cover our extraction.

Like all of the navy boats that were attached to the SEAL teams, they were crewed by the Boat Support Units (BSUs), the guys that called themselves "the Brown-Water Navy." The blue-water navy may have looked down their noses at these crews and called them "river rats," but they were real operators in their own right. Having these guys on station, locked and loaded with enough firepower to turn the bush and anyone foolish enough to be chasing us into nothing but shattered tree stumps, smoking grass, and dead bodies gave us another back door where we could extract when the helos couldn't get us out. Knowing that the heavily armed Mike-8 boats were ready and able to cover our ass and haul us out of harm's way made a lot of long, wet, cold nights in the boonies seem a little shorter.

The army helos touched down about two klicks from the dirt road where we would set up our ambush at last light. We faded into the trees like green-faced ghosts, set up our security perimeter, and let the bush settle back down. After half an hour of listening for any noise that didn't belong in the bush and sniffing the breeze for the faint smell of *nuoc mam*, we moved out in the light of a quarter moon toward the village of Ben Luc. Looking for trip wires and booby traps, slipping through the low-growth bush as silently as possible, and remaining in the shadows of the trees, we were making good time when we heard voices, then could see the flickering glow of lanterns coming our way along a paddy dike that paralleled the trail that we were skirting. We all disappeared into the deepest shadows we could find, went down on one knee, and swung our muzzles to cover our assigned field of fire. Without a word being spoken, we were ready to handle whoever was wandering around in the dark. Not even thinking about it, I had taken off the safety on my Stoner, and my muzzle was following the sound and bobbing lights as they approached our position. The light from the quarter moon was strong enough that it became apparent that these were just some local villagers who were heading to one of the small hamlets and were going to be getting home a little late. Several of the men were pushing ancient bicycles with bags of what looked like rice slung under the handlebars and tied to the frames; none of them carried any weapons. There was a gaggle of kids and a group of women, several of whom were carrying what looked like heavy bundles on their heads, bringing up the rear. Like mothers anywhere on earth, they were encouraging the kids to keep up and shooing them along. Even if this had been a free-fire zone, we would have just let them walk on past our position and disappear into the night. After all, it was their country, and a big part of why we were here was to help them get it back from the Communists and the VC. We waited until they had disappeared into the distance and the signal came to move out.

As we closed the distance to the road, our progress was slowed because we needed to be constantly checking for trip wires and booby traps. The VC didn't usually waste explosives and booby traps out in the bush. Like us, they usually would deploy these devices in areas or along trails or roads to cover their back door, or where their intel told them we might be patrolling. The locals knew where they could move freely and where the VC had stuck their nasty surprises, but we had to move slowly enough to have eyes always looking for a VC trip wire, a pit with punji stakes at the bottom, or any other VC trap. It took us another hour to navigate our way to the road and to choose a good place to set up our ambush.

There were five things that we always wanted to be able to do when we set up an ambush: have concealment so good that we would have the element of surprise on our side, set up in positions that gave us a dominant field of fire, be able to see at least thirty to forty yards in all directions when possible, cover our flanks and back door with claymores, and have an escape path toward the evac point that we had already scouted to make sure that there were no trip wires or booby traps. There was never a guarantee that we would be able to do more than one or two of these at any ambush site, but that was why we were paid the big bucks; we got to pick the best of a few lousy choices and hope that our superior firepower would make up for any lack of cover, concealment, or advantage in the terrain. Somebody said that it was a Hobson's choice: We could ride the horse that was right in front of us, no matter how old or swaybacked it was, or not ride at all. I'm not sure who Hobson was, but he sure did have that one right.

With our three claymores placed, wire strung, and clackers handed over to Lieutenant Brewton, we picked the best spots for individual concealment and got ready for the VC mortar team that we hoped would be coming our way. Everything we might need in a hurry was laid out where we could grab it up instantly without having to take our eyes off of the killing field. When the claymores were tripped to initiate the ambush, there wouldn't be any time to be looking for flares, grenades, ammo, or anything else. With nothing moving as far as we could see, Jim Folman got on the radio and checked in with our Mike 8. It was 2300 hours, and we were all set up and ready for what was, most often, a long wait.

Where we were sitting in the first plateau of mud, just above the water of the canal, the mosquitoes and leeches were doing their own recon in force. Ignoring the squadrons of hungry, bloodsucking damn mosquitoes wasn't easy, but we couldn't make any movement. Slapping a mosquito that was trying its best to suck our last drop of blood could easily give away our position and compromise the op. We had gallons of insect repellent available, but we didn't like to use any in the field because if we could smell it, so could the VC. We didn't want the VC to be able to smell us like we could them when they had been eating *nuoc mam*. Leeches were not as much of a problem while we were out in the bush, but when we crossed canals or had to spend the night in the water we usually found them on our legs, chests, and backs when we were cleaning ourselves up after the op. We discovered that the easiest way to get rid of leeches was to spray them with mosquito repellent—the damn stuff worked like magic. When they got hit with it they squirmed, dropped off, regurgitated our blood, withered up into a slimy little black sack, and died.

As the mosquitoes tried to suck us dry and the hours dragged on, the moon set, and starlight was all the light we had to illuminate the roadway. It always surprised me how well we could see by starlight. Even thirty yards away, I could make out the undulating movement of a snake as it crossed the road and slithered into the grass that bordered the rice paddy. At 0500, after six hours of donating blood to the bugs, I figured that this was going to be just another of the hundreds of no-contact ops. Pretty soon we would be stashing our gear, gathering up the claymores and wires, forming up, and heading for extraction on the Mike 8 boat waiting for us on the river. At 0530 the eastern horizon was starting to turn the peach-orange that only lasted for a couple of minutes before the sunrise. In a few minutes it would be time to break our cover and move out. I was almost relaxing my attention when I heard a sound, a clink of something metal coming from the road on our left flank. I was sure that the rest of the platoon could hear it because I could see heads slowly swiveling toward it. In less than a minute I could hear voices coming from the same direction. The muzzle of my Stoner tracked them as they walked right in front of my position. Their rifles, AK-47s, were slung over their shoulders on slings, and they were talking as if they were on their way to the local fairgrounds for a weenie roast on a Saturday afternoon. They didn't even look where they were walking; they just kept trucking along and jabbering as they wandered down the middle of the road. Two more VC were lagging behind the main group, trying their best to keep up. One carried a wooden box that looked like it could be a case of mortar rounds; the second man was humping what looked like a mortar tube with a big baseplate on it. I was surprised at first that the VC were moving around in daylight, but it made sense. Ben Luc and Tan An, like My Tho, were getting hit with mortar rounds when the VC could do the most damage, in daylight, when the streets were full of people. The two VC carrying the tube and ammunition were now past me and moving to my right; there was nobody following behind them to protect their rear. Lieutenant Bryson hit the clackers, and the right and left claymores blew. Even with no VC centered in my field of fire, I laid down a hundred rounds of ammunition into the kill zone to be sure that anybody hiding in the grass or tree line on the other side of the road was not going to live long enough to pop up and start shooting back. Following the flying steel buckshot from the claymores, hundreds of tracers streaked through the air and ripped through the bodies of the VC. In thirty seconds the ambush was over.

The sun was now rising above the horizon, so there was no need for firing para-flares. Our search team did a quick recon of the dead VC, searched them for documents, and grabbed the mortar tube and ammunition, then we formed up. It was time to head back to the river for extraction. Bryson hollered a warning and blew the claymore that had protected our back door, and we headed for the river three klicks away. As we humped back to the boat, Brewton called in to the Mike 8 boat and asked the crew to fire a WP (white phosphorous) round on the ambush position, now several hundred yards behind us. We weren't taking any fire yet, but Brewton was a firm believer in closing the back door well before any fire could come our way. The WP round sailed overhead, impacted exactly where we had been only a few minutes ago, and threw up a huge cloud of white smoke. Knowing that the WP round had landed exactly where he wanted it, safely behind us, Brewton immediately called in for another round. The second round would be an HE (high explosive) that would terminally discourage anybody that might even be thinking about trying to catch up to us.

Every minute or two he called in for another HE round to be fired a couple of hundred yards behind our current position. With full daylight we could really hump, and soon we could see the river in the distance and hear the boom of the 81 mm mortar on the Mike 8 boat every time it fired another HE round behind us. We stopped at the last canal we had to cross just long enough to throw the ChiCom mortar rounds and two of the weapons that had been so badly shot up that they were useless into the water. They would sink deep into the soft mud at the bottom of the canal; even if the VC tracked us back to the canal, they would never find them. We held on to the bag of documents and the mortar tube and baseplate. We crossed the canal, set up a perimeter, and called in the Mike 8 boat to pick us up. It had turned out to be a good op: six VC dead, one mortar tube permanently out of action, and a bunch of documents that would go over to the TOC and might provide some good intel for another good op real soon. I just hoped that we would get lucky and find ourselves a larger target, more VC, and more strategic material that we could destroy. I would soon find out that it was wiser to be a little more careful about what I wished for.

19

A Little Walk
in the Bush

It turned out that the documents we had brought back were paying off in some fresh intel that looked solid. A-Y and Bubba would get the first shot at using it to plan and run a hot op as soon as the intel boys at TOC had completed their evaluation and we had confirmed their findings. That would take the bureaucrats at least a day or two, so it was time for most of the guys to hit the Cho Duc Bar for some serious R&R. I was sitting at the bar with Squires and Barth, who were arguing about how many VC they had whacked and how they could have won the fight single-handed if only everybody else had stayed out of their way.

Sitting on the bar stool next to me, Bubba Brewton was doing his level best to deplete the local supply of cold beer before he headed to Tan Son Nhut to spend the night with his girlfriend, Cheryl, an airline stewardess. Some of the SEALs could tell a good story, but Bubba was the best, a real first-class raconteur.

I enjoyed shooting the shit as much as anybody, but I couldn't listen to Squires and Barth trying to top one another anymore. The facts were too simple to argue, and the facts are this. In the middle of a firefight, your training and experience take over. There is no time for fear or for planning what you are going to do next. Nobody is counting, and nobody knows who shot who or who shot how many. When the first round is fired or the claymores are triggered, the shit hits the fan. Even when we initiate the ambush and dominate the killing field, there is so much shooting going on, so many grenades going off, flares lighting up the black night, magazines and belts being stuffed into weapons, and red and green tracers in the air, that nobody knows what happened until it is all over and, when the op goes the way we planned for it to go, we are searching the dead for intel. Even then, claiming a personal body count is only a SWAG—a systematic wild-ass guess. Hell's bells, most of the time, if we have a choice, we work at night, and even in daylight it's damn near impossible to know with any certainty who killed how many of what or who.

Taking enough cold beer with him to hold him over on the trip, Brewton headed for his night with Cheryl. We had nicknamed her "Wonder Woman" behind Brewton's back. I was about ready to tell Squires and Barth to shut up or move to another bar stool where I didn't have to listen to them bullshitting one another when Little Suzie, a nickname I had given one of the lovely young ladies that worked the Cho Duc, came over and sat down next to me. Little Suzie was almost as small as a child, only a couple of inches over five feet tall, but she was perfectly proportioned, curvy where women should be curvy, and had the face of an exotic angel. I held up a finger to order her a drink and noticed that she looked perplexed, as if she was trying to figure something out that was completely alien to her. She smiled at me and waved to a group of river rats who had bought her a few drinks before I showed up. Suzie told me that they had told her that I was a SEAL, and that to become a SEAL we had to be experienced divers. Further more, that the real SEALs, the SEALs fighting in Vietnam, were even more experienced—we were all highly experienced muff divers. Seems that Suzie didn't have a remote idea what that meant—and she wanted me to explain it to her. The river rats were watching me squirm a little and laughing their asses off. Suzie, with the innocent look of a schoolgirl, was staring up at me waiting for me to explain what made SEALs such good muff divers. I wasn't about to give those brown-water boat drivers the pleasure of watching me try to explain this to Suzie, but when I left her room the following morning I think she understood.

At 0800 Brewton, looking like he had been run hard and put away wet, was leading PT in front of the barracks. I can't swear that this is true, but I think the sweat running down his face and soaking through his T-shirt had about the same alcohol content as 3.2 beer. As I waited for Bubba to finish our daily workout I noticed a SEAL leaning against a truck, relaxing and watching us go through our paces. He was older than most of us and was built like a fire hydrant, short and heavily muscled. It looked like it would be tough duty to move him even a foot if he didn't want to move that foot. I had never met him, but I was just about dead certain that this was Erasmo Riojas, called Doc Rio by anyone who had ever met him. Doc had spent over a year as a corpsman in combat with the marines in Korea and had spent six months in Vietnam with the 7th SEAL Platoon. He was almost twice my age and was still a warrior in every way. Doc Rio had proven himself and survived on the field of battle almost as long as I had been alive. There was no question about it; Doc Rio was respected by everyone that knew him and was as close to being a legend as you can get in the teams.

With PT painfully concluded and a new op being run tonight, Brewton started chewing the fat with Doc. Since I wanted to meet him, I walked over. As I approached, I heard Brewton tell Doc that the intel was pretty good and that if he wanted to go for a nice little walk in the bush he could grab up anything he needed from our platoon storage locker. In the SEAL Teams, our corpsmen were unique. While all enlisted men in the teams were expected to advance in their specialties, the corpsmen were the only SEALs who actually worked in their specialties and were qualified SEALs to boot. Briefing would be at 1800 hours, and we would be inserting by LSSCs at 0200 and extracting by helo at daybreak. It was always good to have another doc along, and having a legend like Doc Rio along was a rare experience for me. Before the op was over, I would see for myself why Doc Rio had become a legendary combat medic.

At 1830 we were aboard the LSSCs and headed down the Tinh Long An River. At 0200 the first LSSC headed in to the riverbank and Bravo, my squad, taking our turn in the lead tonight, set up security and signaled Alpha squad to come on ahead. Doc Rio was with my squad, and Doc Clark was in the rear with Alpha squad, that was running security on our back door. The intel we had captured and brought back said that the VC were using one specific canal that was about a klick and a half away to transport sampans full of supplies and munitions. If this intel wasn't better than most of the intel we captured, it would probably be another walk in the bush with no contact, but good, bad, or indifferent, we were always looking for contact with the enemy.

With only a klick and a half to hump, Brewton decided to take the point. I was right behind him with my Stoner, and Barth, Squires, Doc Rio, and the rest of the squad walked in our boot prints through the thick bush. The quarter moon was high in the sky, and we could move fast and make good time because there was more than enough light to see trip wires or booby traps. The plan was to be set up and ready to ambush anything that moved by 0300. On the way to the target canal, we had to cross two canals that were almost up to my neck. Now I knew that I was really at home—I was wet and cold again. Brewton led us to the place where we hoped the VC would show up ahead of schedule. Barth and I set out the claymores on the right flank and brought the wires and clackers back to Bryson and Brewton just as Jim Dilley was bringing his in from our left flank. From my hidey-hole in the dense cover I had good visibility for at least twenty yards up the canal, so I would probably be the first person to see the VC coming. With all of my ammo and grenades spread out on an OD green triangle bandage just in front of my crossed legs, everything was SOP. I was wet, cold, and feeding every mosquito and creeping crawling thing within half a klick that was hungry for human blood.

At 0400 nothing had moved except the moon as the earth spun around on its axis and flew through space. My eyes were almost crossed from watching for any minute movement, because I was sure that that night we were finally going to get to pull off a solid ambush of more than one or two sampans. I was looking for sampans so hard that I almost missed what looked like a twelve-foot-long log moving up the canal. It was a good night to be sitting on the bank of the canal, because a twelve-foot crocodile could really ruin the crease in my Levi's. Where there was one croc there might be more, so I passed word up the line to hold fire. Opening up on a croc would ruin the ambush and waste the whole night of waiting for the VC.

After six hours of nothing more than a croc moving up the canal, dawn was breaking on the horizon, and word came from Brewton to bring in the claymores. We were breaking our busted ambush and heading for our extraction point. With all my ammo and grenades stashed and the claymores back in their bags, I signaled that I was ready to pull out. Brewton took point, and as Chris passed me he told me that Brewton wanted him up front with the M-60 and then me right behind him. It was almost like Brewton was expecting that the shit was going to get deep and wanted the heavier M-60 close to home if it did.

Barth, Doc Rio, and Squires were right behind me, and the rest of the squad followed our lead. We were patrolling through knee-deep water in the mangrove swamps looking for a rice paddy where we could call in the helos for our extraction. With fifteen men patrolling along the edge of the canal and swamp, it wasn't just difficult to move silently; it was impossible. The constant sound of our legs swishing through the water was not loud, but any constant sound that isn't caused by wind, rain, birds, or animals can alert your enemies that something isn't right. Brewton spotted something out in front of him that I couldn't see and halted the patrol. As we crept ahead a few more yards, we could then see three sampans that had been pulled up on the bank of the canal and several boheos, platforms made of branches and vines that let the VC sleep a foot or two above the waterline.

Chris was about five yards in front of me, and Brewton was about fifteen yards in front of Chris and off to our right when Brewton opened up on full auto. Instantaneously Chris opened up, and in a heartbeat there were green tracers coming at us from every direction. I was painting the bush and the trees with rounds from my Stoner, putting out as much controlled fire as I could, when I saw Chris go down hard. The water around him was being hit by so many rounds of full-auto fire that it looked like it was full of piranha in a feeding frenzy. I didn't know if anyone else saw Chris get hit, but he was less than ten feet ahead of me, so I could get to him fast. I started to run through the muddy water to pull him to safety, but I got only two or three steps before I was hit so hard that I spun around in almost a full circle and dropped to my knees in the canal like a puppet with its strings cut.

My left hip was screaming with pain, but I managed to grab a mangrove root and drag myself to my feet. I was drenched with something that was running down my face and dripping from my fingertips. I figured that I had been hit and was covered with my own blood and that scared the hell out of me. I was the only one who could get to Chris, and I didn't know how much blood I could lose before I blacked out. Looking down at my hip to see how badly I was bleeding, I was amazed that I couldn't see any blood. Then I realized that it was water running down my body. My metal canteen had been shredded, and only the jagged remains of aluminum were hanging from my web belt. The round that had knocked me off my feet had struck the canteen hard enough to make it explode.

Without realizing it, I had started firing over Chris's prostrate body in the water as I moved as fast as I could to get to him. When I reached him I was running short on my second belt of ammunition. He was lying facedown in the mud, blood, and filthy water, and I could see a gaping hole in the side of his head.

The whole platoon was now firing to our front, but so many green tracers were coming out of the tree line that it had to be several RPK machine guns; even twenty-plus AK-47s couldn't put out that much fire. There were so many tracers flying past that I was amazed I had not been hit again. With a hole the size of a baseball in his head I figured that Chris was dead, so I grabbed his M-60 to fire into a bunker complex that I now could see only a couple of yards in front of me, but the gun had taken three rounds through the receiver and was totally useless. As I loaded another belt into my Stoner, I could see two bodies on top of one of the bunkers from which we were taking fire.

I knew that my LAAW rocket wouldn't arm on a target that close, so I opened up on them with the Stoner. Barth and Squires were now at my side, and I could hear Brewton calling, screaming above the sound of gunfire, for help. "Rio, I'm hit. Come get me." Bubba had been hit in the first seconds of the firefight. As I found out when we debriefed, Doc Rio heard Brewton call, threw his M-16 to the man behind him, and, without a weapon, instantly started running through the knee-deep water toward the incoming fire and his wounded friend. Tracers were streaming past him like deadly green fireflies; the water boiled at his feet from the impact of hundreds of rounds of enemy fire, and he never broke stride. Legs churning through the water, he ran on. Doc Rio reached Brewton and grabbed him by his collar and web belt as if he'd been made of papier-mâché.

Like a madman, Doc Rio ran back through the raging storm of VC bullets, dragging Brewton through the water to the safety of the rear of our line while tracers were chewing everything to pieces and the battle raged around him. Barth had run his Stoner dry and was out of ammunition, so I passed him one of my belts and started throwing every grenade that was passed up the line into the bunkers. How I saw him move in the insanity of that firefight I don't know, but Chris, lying in a pool of his own blood that was spreading across the water, raised his hand, and I could see that there were two fingers hanging loose. The only things keeping them attached were ligaments and skin. I had to suppress the VC fire, so I screamed for the doc to get up to my position and get Chris. With Brewton in very bad shape, Doc Rio told Doc Clark to stay where he was and take care of Bubba. Doc Rio, still unarmed, headed back through the firestorm he had just escaped. I almost didn't believe my eyes when I saw Doc Rio flying toward me through the water and tracers a second time. It looked like a tracer went right through him, the impact spinning him around and dropping him in the water. In a split second Doc was on his feet and still coming, hard charging all the way to get to Chris. Rio rolled Chris over and handed me a grenade that Chris had held in his right hand. I could see the blood spurting out of his neck as Doc Rio started to clamp it off. With a bandage held in place and the bleeding from his neck wound stanched, we grabbed Chris and dragged him back to the rear with Brewton. We now had two docs working on our wounded.

Lieutenant Bryson had called in Seawolf gunships as soon as the shooting had started, and they were finally overhead. Now we had their overwhelming fire plastering the bunkers and the tree line with 2.75-inch rockets. The staccato M-60 fire from their door gunners was added to the fire that we were still pouring into the bunkers and tree line. The medevac helos were on the way, and the fire from the bunkers and tree line slowed, then stopped completely. The medevac helos tried to set down in a clearing, but it wasn't big enough for their rotors. The only place they could get close to the ground was in the middle of the mangrove swamp, where a bomb had landed and blown away most of the big trees. The major problem was that the only open area was right in the middle of the bomb crater that was now filled with reeking, stagnant water. The helo hovered overhead with its skids almost touching the water. Doc Rio and Doc Clark, with as much help as we could give them, dragged Brewton and Chris to the edge of the crater, inflated their UDT life jackets, and swam out to the middle of the flooded bomb crater, dragging Brewton and Chris behind them. The door gunner pulled Doc Rio into the Seawolf and together, with Doc Clark pushing from below and them pulling from the hovering helo, they managed to get both men aboard. Doc Clark was then pulled aboard. As the helo gained altitude, they both worked to keep Chris and Brewton alive until they could get them to a MASH unit or hospital.

Lieutenant Bryson called in another airstrike on the bunker complex, and we headed out for the LZ, where we would extract as fast as we could. We had two men down, and it was a silent march back to the rice paddy and our evac point. With gunships covering our extraction, we loaded on the helos and headed back to Nha Be.

Bubba Brewton was too damn tough and stubborn to throw in the towel. Bubba had been shot seven times with an AK-47 at point-blank range, and he survived. Doc Rio managed to visit Bubba almost every day at the hospital in Saigon. In the end it would be the infections caused by all of the water and filth that had saturated his wounds that wore Bubba down and finally took Bubba away.

The day Bubba died, Doc Rio got himself stinking ugly drunk at the Special Warfare Group Club in Saigon, and, after tearing the place apart, he was taken to the same hospital where Bubba died. They injected Doc with a sedative, paraldehyde, and knocked him out. There wasn't any other way that he could be handled without several members of the shore police ending up in the trauma ward. Two days later Doc escaped from the hospital. He was seen sitting by himself in the courtyard of the hospital. It was reported that one of the toughest men I have ever seen, in combat or out, was crying. No disciplinary action was ever attempted.

Ten years later, Bob Christopher visited with Doc Rio at Doc's home in Texas. Chris had been awarded the Silver Star and Purple Heart and, aside from being a little forgetful, was doing well. Doc Rio was awarded a Bronze Star and a Purple Heart. Doc Clark was also awarded a Bronze Star. I always wondered why Doc Rio was awarded a Purple Heart and Doc Clark wasn't. Years later I found out.

After he got Bubba to the hospital, Doc Rio went back to base and decided that he needed to shower off the mud and blood. While he was showering, someone told him that he had a leech on his leg. When he tried to scrub the bloodsucker off with a brush, it hurt like hell. Then Doc looked closely and realized that it wasn't a leech at all. It was the bullet hole from an AK-47 round that I had seen hit him in the leg and spin him around as he ran toward Bubba. He had just forgotten about it.

20

First Command

Debriefing was short and right to the point. We had walked into a hell of a mess, had won the fight, but had two men seriously wounded and out of the fight for a long time, maybe forever. In a squad of only seven men, we couldn't afford to lose anyone. Lieutenant Bryson decided that we were going to stand down for a week so that we could set up a schedule to visit Chris and Bubba in the Saigon hospital. All Lieutenant Bryson could tell us was that Chris had been hit in the hand and the neck. The hand wound was bad—Chris lost a couple of fingers—but the neck wound was much worse; the docs didn't know if he was going to make it. The bullet had entered his neck and exited through the side of his head, blowing away a piece of his skull. Chris was drifting in and out of consciousness, and it would be several days before they knew how bad the trauma to his brain was. Bubba had been hit seven times at point-blank range. He was still alive, and that was just about all we knew, or his doctors could tell us.

Some of our guys were religious—not Bible-thumping, go-to-church-every-Sunday religious, but they believed in God, and I think that some of them prayed whenever they remembered or got the chance. In most wars there seems to be a lot of praying in battle. When the shit gets deep, some men will try to make a deal; they pray to God to just let them live and they will never go whoring or drinking again, or they will start going to church every Sunday. I had done what SEALs do in battle; I had killed everyone who was trying to kill me and my teammates. I had done everything in my power that would help Bubba and Chris stay alive long enough to get to the docs in Saigon who might be able to bring them through it all alive and able to lead a good, long life. Nobody has ever called me a religious man. I don't pray and I don't try to make deals with God, but with Bubba and Chris both shot up and fighting for their lives, I came close to saying a prayer that day. The way I look at it is this. If there is a God he isn't a SEAL, and if he isn't a SEAL he wouldn't know what the hell I was talking about.

As soon as the debriefing was over, I cleaned my weapons, reloaded my magazine, grabbed another couple of belts of linked 5.56mm ammunition for the Stoner, four grenades, and a couple of para-flares, and stashed everything in the team locker so that I would be good to go if anything came up in a hurry. I wanted nothing more than to get the crap and crud off of my clothing, then scrub myself down and check for leeches in the shower. Still fully dressed in my combat gear, I washed off all of the dirt, burned powder, blood, and pieces of debris and vegetation buried in my gear that had been thrown up by the impact of the VC rifle fire all around me. With my clean gear piled in a heap on the floor of the shower, I started soaping up and removing the bloodsuckers. As I scrubbed my left hip, it hurt like hell. I looked down—there was a black and purple bruise the size of a softball. Only then did I remember that my canteen had been KIA. Looking at that bruise, I realized that it was just the luck of the draw that the bullets had hit the canteen and missed the three grenades hanging next to it on my web belt. It also reminded me that human bodies are not much more than big, soft sacks, canteens made of skin and full of blood instead of water. The physics are easy to understand. When your body gets hit by a bullet, the blood, bone, and tissue almost explode trying to get away from the pressure of the bullet as it rips through your body. Your own bone, blood, and tissue become projectiles that tear you apart. Had the VC aimed better and the bullets landed a couple of inches to the right, I might have been on that medevac helo with Chris and Bubba. My hip hurt and looked ugly, and I needed a new canteen, but I still had a left leg. I could still fight.

With only two months left on this tour, Lieutenant Bryson didn't think that there would be the time or the need to replace Bubba and Chris before we headed back home for our required stateside rotation. Doc Clark was now the senior man in Bravo squad, and there was no question that he was more than capable of leading us into combat, but he was also our corpsman, and I believe that he always saw this as his primary duty. He had no objection to me taking over command of Bravo squad for the next couple of months. It was time for me to apply some of the lessons that I had learned in my first tour and that had become even clearer in the last couple of months. First: Always be ready and able to handle the unexpected. Make doubly sure that you have artillery or air cover dialed in, on notice that you may need it right now, and waiting for your call, because the force with the most firepower almost always wins. Second: Never bet your life, or the lives of men under your command, on anything you did to make sure that Rule 1 was covered—always have a backup plan. Overconfidence will get you killed. Telling yourself that you've got it all covered and under control is like sending an engraved invitation to Mr. Murphy to drop a big rock on your head—right now.

Lieutenant Bryson decided that a week was as long as we could be out of the bush and running back and forth to Saigon to try to visit Bubba and Chris. Bubba was always disoriented and at best semiconscious, and Chris had stabilized with no apparent brain damage and would be getting shipped off to a stateside hospital on a medevac flight as soon as one was available. It was time to get back into the bush, and Bryson told me that he had picked a simple canal ambush for our first op under my command. When he said that this would be a simple canal ambush, I started to worry. I couldn't keep myself from thinking that there wasn't ever a simple operation. Remembering our last simple canal ambush operation, I hoped that Mr. Murphy wasn't at home when the invitation landed in his mailbox.

TOC told me that there was a patchwork of canals that ran through an area covered with dense mangroves. I wasn't surprised to find out that this was where we would be operating; rumors of VC activity in those Rung Sat swamps had been coming in for weeks. My first op in command would be to find and stop the VC from using small sampans to run supplies and munitions all across the Rung Sat. Hell, the TOC was really being useful; they even had maps and aerial photos of the entire area. The maps that overlaid the canals looked like somebody had dumped a couple of pounds of skinny black spaghetti on top of the topographic map of the Rung Sat. Everywhere I looked there were little lines that represented another canal. The lines on the map were so close together that it looked as if there were more little canals than there was dry land. The photos were even worse. I couldn't find anything that resembled more than a few square meters of dry ground anywhere in the area of operations where our five-man squad could hide out and be able to dominate even a half-decent field of fire. As we were finishing the briefing and I was folding the maps, I thought that I could hear someone with an Irish accent chuckling to himself just outside the briefing room.

With our squad now down to five men, we didn't really need a lot of room or a big boat for our insertion. We could insert and extract with only a small LSSC (Light SEAL Support Craft) and the crew of two boat drivers. The lightweight aluminum-hulled LSSC boats were relatively new, and they were almost perfect for squad-sized ops. At only twenty-four feet long with a nine-foot beam, they were powered by a pair of diesel engines that drove jet pumps. Even in very shallow water they could almost fly. The cockpit and crew compartments were protected with ceramic armor plating, and there was plenty of space for mounting guns, including a .50 caliber machine gun on the stern. After looking at the maps again and again, I didn't see any good alternatives, so I gave the boat crew and the squad our ops plan. We would leave at last light and cruise for about a mile down the Tinh Long An River until we hit a canal that, at least on the map and in the aerial photos, looked like it should lead to about the center of the suspected VC activity. We would go as far into the mess of dinky waterways as we could, hide the LSSC in the mangroves where we had a decent field of fire, and watch for the sampans with starlight scopes.

There was no moon, and even starlight was in short supply due to cloud cover, but, using the starlight scopes that turned night into green daylight, we slipped up the main canal and found a smaller canal that gave us a wide-open field of fire up and down about a hundred yards of the main canal. We backed the LSSC into the mangroves against the fast-flowing current and tied her up. For three hours the only sound we heard was the mosquitoes buzzing around our ears; the canal was empty, and it was looking like another no-contact op was well under way. I had just turned over my starlight scope to Barth or Squires when I heard the familiar sound of a push-pole smacking on the side of a sampan, maybe more than one. I was sure that everyone else heard the sound because the boat crew, Squires, Barth, McDonald, and Folman, were all now positioning themselves to make sure that they had a good field of fire and that nobody would block another's. We listened and waited motionless in the darkness as the sound faded into the distance. It was that sampan driver's lucky night; he chose to turn off of the main canal before we had him in our sights. As far as I could tell, the ambush hadn't been busted, so we untied the LSSC and let her drift in the fast-running current. Hoping that we could drift faster than mosquitoes could swarm after us, we found another little canal where we could slip in and hide the boat. It didn't have as good a field of fire, and the mosquitoes never stopped sucking our blood, but we would have to make do with what we could find because even before we had tied the LSSC up we heard that same *thunk-thunk-thunk* sound again. More sampans were coming down the main canal, and the current would be helping them move along with good speed. In a couple of minutes we could see the outline of one sampan coming our way; behind it, and a little farther out into the middle of the main canal, was a second sampan that was picking up speed. With the first blush of dawn starting to climb over the horizon, we didn't even need our starlight scopes. As the sampans reached the middle of our fire zone, I touched off my Stoner, and everyone instantaneously cut loose. With a Stoner, two M-60s, and two M-16s running, I didn't think that anyone would be alive, but to be on the safe side and make sure that we had neutralized everyone on the sampans, I fired two white star para-flares that lit up the mangroves and canal like stark daylight. I couldn't believe what I was seeing. A single VC in black pajamas and rubber tire-tread sandals had somehow survived and was trying to get away from the canal. I almost admired him; he was running as fast as he could, bobbing and weaving through the dense mangroves. Barth took him apart in midstride with a long burst from his Stoner.

With the para-flares lighting up even the shadows, we untied the LSSC and headed out into the main canal. The sampans were now floating upside down, and there was no longer any cargo visible. Whatever they had been carrying had sunk to the bottom of the canal, where it wouldn't be doing the VC any good. We had seen four men, two on each of the sampans, and we were sure that they were all KIA, but there were no bodies floating anywhere. They had probably sunk in the fast current and would soon become croc snacks or fish food as they rolled along the bottom of the canal and drifted downstream. Even though we would have liked to search the dead for documents or other intel, we decided against going into the canal or the mangroves to look for the bodies. Based on our personal observation and experience in the canals, we knew for a fact that crocs would eat anything they could grab with their incurving teeth that pull everything down their throats. It had been a good ambush, and nobody had even gotten wet or had a single leech anywhere on his body. I figured that it didn't make much sense to push our luck any harder on my first command.

Knowing that our para-flares had been spotted by every VC within five or so miles, we decided that it would be a good idea to haul ass out of that particular piece of Rung Sat real estate before the local welcoming committee had the time to set up a little surprise party for us on our way out. With enough light to steer the boat, and five SEALs and two boat drivers the only cargo in the LSSC, we almost flew down the canal to the Tinh Long An River. At only a little after 0300 we were safely back in Nha Be. I debated interrupting Lieutenant Bryson's sleep but figured that he would want to know how we did on the first op under my command, so I woke him up and did a quick debrief.

By SEAL standards it was way too early to hit our racks, so we decided that a couple or three serious nightcaps were the order of the day and headed to one of our favorite watering holes to decompress. It hadn't been a big ambush, and we hadn't captured any VC or documents, but we all came back in one piece without even letting the VC get off one round, and I considered that a good omen on my first command. I hadn't made any big mistakes, and I thought that my decision to get out of Dodge fast was the reason that we had not drawn even one round of VC fire as we extracted. I would keep that in mind for the future. Hit and run, hit and run. Overwhelming firepower and hit and run; I hoped that this tactic would keep working as well for us in the future as it had this morning. After half a dozen nightcaps I sacked out until almost noon and was heading for the chow hall for lunch when I ran into Doc Clark. Doc let me know that my squad should be geared up, reloaded, and ready for briefing at 1800 hours. We would be going back out on a full platoon patrol and ambush op that night.

The op was planned to take out a VC mortar team that had been dropping rounds on the small villages that hadn't paid their taxes to the local VC tax collectors. We would run down the Tinh Long An River on a pair of LSSCs, slip up a canal that led toward An San village, insert the platoon, then patrol to a dirt road that led from the canal to the village. The intel was as sketchy as most was, but we hoped that tonight would be the night when the mortar team decided that the defenseless taxpayers needed a little reminder that they were late on paying Uncle Ho. The VC mortar teams were effective at terrorizing the villagers; there was no way they could defend themselves against the rounds that came falling out of the sky. The ChiCom mortars were simple, cheap, and powerful weapons that carried a pound and a half of TNT inside a finned steel tube that turned into shrapnel when the TNT exploded on contact. They blasted a hole a foot and a half deep in the ground, and anyone within fifteen or twenty yards of the impact was either killed or wounded. Used as a weapon of terror, the mortar let a couple of VC sneak through the darkness, drop a couple of rounds down the tube, then disappear before the rounds had even hit the little villages. The mortar was a coward's weapon, and we didn't like cowards.

Tonight A-Y would be taking the point, and Doc Clark would be right behind him as we humped through the free-fire zone to our ambush site. The LSSCs inserted Alpha, and we followed them as soon as they had established a security perimeter with A-Y and Doc Clark in the middle. There was now a sliver of moon throwing just enough light for us to see the entire platoon in the shadow of the palm trees at the edge of the canal. The LSSCs had been gone for only about ten minutes and we were still in our security perimeter, letting our eyes adjust to the moonlight, looking and listening for anything that might reveal the presence of the VC, when word was passed back that there was a "duffel bag" listening device hanging twenty feet high in a tree about fifty yards in front of us. It was right over the path that we had planned to follow to get to the area where we would set up our ambush site. The "duffel bag" was a nickname given to a listening device that was used by the army. It looked like an old army duffel bag, but it contained some sophisticated electronics that could detect movement and sound and would radio back anything detected to the TOC. The army would leave these listening devices in trees or along paths, or drop them in by parachute in areas where there was suspected VC movement. Seeing the duffel bag hanging in our path wasn't a cause for alarm. We knew that they had been deployed all over the Rung Sat, and SOP was for us to clear our area of operations with TOC. We knew that we didn't have a problem because we had cleared six grid squares and everyone knew that there were friendlies operating in the area.

The platoon was just about ready to move out when Mr. Murphy opened his mailbox and got his invitation. We heard one of the sounds that could chill blood. There was incoming artillery headed our way, right now.

The Rung Sat Secret Zone was one of the most desolate places on earth, but it had become almost the heart of VC activity in South Vietnam. To interdict and kill the VC where they lived, the Rung Sat had been ringed with both American and Vietnamese 155 mm artillery emplacements— and listening devices. Someone hadn't gotten our op clearance and was firing 155 mm artillery on the grid square where they thought there was VC activity. The first round hit about fifty yards to our front. The duffel bag had probably picked up the sound of the LSSCs when we inserted and radioed back our position to the closest TOC. The second round landed closer, and the platoon scrambled into what looked to be a water-filled crater dug out of the earth by a bomb dropped by a B-52. A-Y was holding on to the rim of the crater with one hand and calling the LSSCs on the radio to tell them to relay a message to the TOC to immediately cease fire, they were firing on a friendly position. Two more rounds landed, throwing shrapnel in every direction and blowing up debris, mud, and water that covered us from head to foot. After another three or four rounds, the artillery fire stopped. Poor fire discipline and communications had screwed this op over in fine style; no VC would be anywhere near here tonight.

We called in the LSSCs, loaded aboard, and headed back to Nha Be. A-Y was up in the bow of the lead LSSC and looked as cool as a cucumber. I had never seen him lose his cool, and even in the worst situations he was as solid and unflappable as any SEAL could be. I don't think that he had a temper. On the other hand, Doc Clark and I were ready to chew a second asshole right through the middle of somebody's forehead. Whoever had called in artillery fire on our position was lucky that A-Y was OIC, because he wouldn't do what Doc Clark or I would have done to whoever had been playing with his dick when he should have been covering our ass.

We were back at the base in an hour, and some of the steam coming off Doc Clark and me had been drowned in cold beer. A-Y was over at TOC requiring a detailed explanation of who had tried to kill our entire platoon and why. Any of the 155 mm rounds that fell near our position could have killed us all if it had fallen ten yards closer. Had one of those rounds landed in the bomb crater, there wouldn't have even been parts of us left to scrape up with a shovel and bury.

Some TV media asshole who had never been within fifty miles of combat had decided that he would come up with a new phrase, "friendly fire," that would make it easier for the brain-dead public who let the media think for them to understand what had happened when Americans were killed by what were supposed to be the good guys. There isn't, and never will be, any such thing. Dead is dead, and there's nothing friendly about dead.

21

Last Dance—Second Tour, 1969

For the next couple of weeks we ran canal ambush after canal ambush, with no contact and nothing to show for our long nights spent in the mud and bush with the crocs, bugs, and snakes. Doc Rio let us know that Chris was on his way home, but the bad news was that Bubba's right leg had to be amputated and his kidneys were failing. The bad news didn't do much for our morale. The only thing that kept us going was the desire to kill some of the people who had shot us up so badly.

With no hot intel, A-Y decided that we would take matters into our own hands and set up our own op. A couple of weeks ago we had patrolled through an area where we came across a well-worn trail that led from a village all the way into a dense mangrove swamp. There was no reason for the local villagers to be going back and forth to the swamp, so we figured that there was a high probability that it was VC who were making use of that trail. With the wind in our faces as we patrolled, we thought that we could smell the distinctive odor of *nuoc mam* coming from the mangrove swamp. As much as we would have liked to go hunting whoever was stinking up a perfectly good swamp with the *nuoc mam*, we were on our way to extract from an all-nighter, another canal ambush that had been a dead end, so we didn't have time to investigate any further. It would soon be daylight, and it is almost impossible to move silently through a mangrove swamp; the VC would almost certainly hear us coming and disappear into the mangroves long before we could dig them out. Added to the difficulties of moving silently in broad daylight was the probability of finding booby traps that would slow our progress to a crawl almost everywhere. There was no question that if there were VC using the swamp as a hidey-hole, they would have booby traps set up all the way along the trail. This area would have to wait for another op at some later time.

A-Y decided that tonight would be the night to go run a sneak and peak op and maybe catch Charlie off guard. It had been decided that trying to find a VC hideout at night in a mangrove swamp full of booby traps wasn't going to happen. The way we figured it was that the VC would follow the trail to the village at night and return to the swamp on the same trail right after sunup. The idea was to insert on one of the new MSSCs (Medium SEAL Support Craft) that could carry a whole platoon, patrol to a small path that ran alongside a rice paddy that was just across from the village, and set up our position so that we could catch the VC heading out of the mangrove swamp just after sunset.

After an hour on the river, the MSSC pulled up to the bank and lowered the boarding ramp right onto dry land. This hydraulically operated ramp may have been a little bit noisy, but it was a real improvement in the way we could at least start an op. Not even one member of the platoon was starting this op wet or muddy; all of us were dry and ready to hunt. With a cloudless sky and a bright quarter moon, we had plenty of light to navigate silently through the mangroves to the tree line where we had decided we would set up what we hoped was going to be a hot, high-body-count operation. After our SOP twenty-minute wait to make sure that we had inserted without attracting any attention from the VC, it was time to hump. A-Y took the point with Alpha squad and moved out toward the target village. Bravo covered the back door. This was one of a very few ops in which we moved out on the high ground. Not having to worry about the sound of our legs and feet swishing through the water made moving silently through the bush a lot easier.

With no idea of when the VC might decide to head for the swamp, we wanted to reach the village and get our ambush set up as quickly as possible. The plan was to catch the VC in the open and take our revenge; we didn't want to meet the VC in the swamp where they could hide and scatter before we could kill them all. Hugging the tree line, it took us about a half hour to reach the edge of the paddy. A-Y halted the platoon and went to check out a bunker that we had passed several times before on other ops. It had been deserted and half fallen in, and still was. From where we were, we could see that there was almost enough cover to hide behind if we had been mice or snakes, but there was not a damn thing that could offer us even a little concealment. We decided to set up right out in the open, facing the direction of the swamp the VC would be leaving just before or right after sunset. We would be depending on our silence, stillness, green-painted faces, and camouflage clothing to let us keep the element of surprise on our side. We also were betting that until we opened fire the VC would be as relaxed, undisciplined, and unaware of their surroundings as most of the VC we had run into had been. They wouldn't know that we were anywhere within a mile of where they were going to die.

To give us the biggest possible field of fire, we set up our ambush positions in a straight line with both platoons facing the mangrove swamp. Barth and I set up our claymores on the left flank, and Bob Moore and Phil Perzanowski, a second class quartermaster, nicknamed Ski, set theirs out on the right flank. With open field to our rear there was no place to put a claymore, and we figured that there was really no need to cover the back door. Hell's bells, the way we had set up the ambush we had an open, almost unlimited field of fire behind us. To get behind us, the VC coming from the swamp would need to overrun our position. We were sitting on fresh mud and muck; it smelled like everything under my soggy ass was rotting as I sat there. The mosquitoes were the biggest and hungriest I could remember. They could have snatched babies out of their cradles and carried them away. They were so thick that they flew up our noses and into our mouths and ears. It got harder and harder to stop myself from swatting them; seven in one blow would have been easy. I could have killed at least twenty in a single swat. No matter how slowly you moved to shake the flying bloodsuckers off of your head so that you could hear and see, it was close to impossible to keep yourself from swatting at them when they started swarming every inch of exposed skin. There were so many on my ears that I couldn't hear anything but their constant buzzing and droning. After almost an hour of being dive-bombed by the bugs, I was sure that A-Y was suffering as much as I was and thinking to himself that it might be time to move to another position before the VC showed up. That would have been a good idea, but before he could give the order I saw Jim Folman, our radio man, grab hold of his arm and squeeze hard. Jim was sitting right next to A-Y, but he was covering our back door, facing to our rear. He either saw or heard something that none of us had picked up on yet. In a couple of seconds we all started hearing voices, and the voices were coming from the wrong direction. We were in very deep shit. The VC were behind us.

Figuring that the VC would be coming from the swamp and heading for the village, we had laid all of our gear out in front of us. We didn't have a claymore at our back. We were like sitting ducks out in the open. Everyone but Jim was sitting cross-legged in the dirt, facing the wrong direction. Somehow we all would have to turn ourselves around without the VC spotting us. As silently and slowly as I could, I placed my Stoner in my lap and gathered up my ammunition, para-flares, and grenades. Moving in slow motion, I lay down on my back, took all of my gear from my lap, reached out as far as I could, and placed it all behind me. If the VC didn't spot our movement and open up while our backs were still turned, it would be where I could grab it up when I turned myself around. With everything now where I could get to it, all I needed to do was to get myself turned to face the VC without being heard or seen. Very slowly I flattened my hands against the ground, dislodging a cloud of mosquitoes, pushed hard, and raised my body straight up while using my crossed legs to keep my Stoner out of the dirt. I pushed myself up and very slowly turned myself around to my left. I moved counterclockwise so that if the VC saw or heard anything, the muzzle of my Stoner would be pointed right at them and I could start laying down fire. I could clearly hear voices and even their feet slapping on the mud. They were too close, but even if they saw us move I would be able to get a hundred rounds downrange before I needed to worry about my grenades or how fast I could get to my linked belts to reload.

In two painfully slow movements, I turned myself to face the village and the VC. The VC were even closer than I had thought; I could see their point man coming right at me. I couldn't believe that he hadn't seen me. I was out in the open, only twenty yards away, and he was closing fast. He stopped at thirty feet and was looking hard in our general direction when A-Y dropped the hammer and turned him into a noncombatant. In half a heartbeat the whole platoon started covering their assigned fields of fire, para-flares were fired, and VC were dropping like mowed wheat. Even though we had been facing the wrong way, we had taken them by surprise. For the first thirty seconds of the firefight it looked like this op was going to work out the way we had planned; then we started taking fire from our right flank. I didn't know if the fire was coming from a different VC cadre or another part of the patrol that we had engaged, and it didn't really matter. Bullets were flying everywhere. There was a shitload of green tracers coming our way from two directions, and we had no place to hide. Bill Barth and I got up onto one knee so that we could move to counter the incoming fire more effectively. Bill went down hard, and his weapon went flying away. In midburst my Stoner was hit in the receiver, and I could feel searing pain in the left side of my face as I fell into the muck. The Stoner had saved my life by taking a couple of rounds through the receiver, but now I was almost defenseless. Bill had been hit bad, and I had shrapnel buried in my face, ear, and left hand. I pushed myself out of the mud and got back up to my knees. Green tracers were thick, slamming into the ground, skipping along, and plowing up the dirt all around us.

Jack Squires, from his position on our right flank, opened up on the muzzle flashes to our right and laid down a nonstop shitstorm of red tracers from his M-60. In a few seconds the firing from our right flank stopped, but now we were taking fire from the left flank. I didn't have time to think about how many VC were shooting at us, or where they had all come from; all I could do was get myself back into the fight.

With the para-flares lighting up the entire area, we couldn't see any VC still standing in our field of fire, but we were still under heavy fire from the tree line and left flank. It was either me or Squires who had yelled for Doc Clark, but he appeared out of nowhere and started working on Barth as best he could under heavy incoming fire. We were still taking heavy fire from our left flank, and the platoon was trying to suppress the incoming fire by covering their fields of fire with belt after belt of 7.62 ammunition from the M-60s and magazine after magazine of 5.56 ammunition from the M-16s. I took my only weapon, my LAAW rocket, from its sling on my back and, using my improvised sighting system, let it fly toward the muzzle flashes I could see coming from the tree line seven or eight hundred yards across the field. I watched it impact and airburst on the trees just above the position where the green tracers were coming from. The incoming rounds from the tree line stopped, but we were still taking fire from the low bush.

Kneeling next to Doc Clark as he worked on Bill, I yelled as loud as I could so that the platoon could hear me over the firefight to toss me all the grenades they could spare. I threw my three frag grenades into the bush where the VC fire was the strongest, then three more that someone passed to my position. I started to grab the frags off of Bill's web belt while Doc was working on his face. Bill grabbed my hand with a grip of iron and wouldn't let go. Even though he had been hit in the face and was bleeding like a stuck pig, he was trying to talk and wouldn't let go of the hand that was holding one of his grenades. I couldn't understand what he was saying, and it took me a couple of seconds to figure it out, but suddenly I knew what he was trying to tell me. I had grabbed up one of the instantaneously exploding grenades that we frequently left behind as booby traps for the VC. He was trying to tell me that we would all disappear in a cloud of red mist if I pulled the pin and let it rip. As shot up as he was, Bill was still covering my ass and wouldn't let me have the grenade until I understood. I yelled that I wouldn't pull the pin, and his grip relaxed. I threw the grenade as far as I could, a little gift from Bill for any VC that might come along and find it in the muck or bush.

When the shit had hit the fan, A-Y had called the MSSC and told them to scramble some navy Seawolf gunships for a fire mission and to send along a medevac helo to evac our wounded. The helos flew dark at night so that the VC couldn't see them coming or have a defined target for small-arms fire, but I could hear that wonderful sound of high-speed rotors coming from a good way off. Doc handed me his M-16 with an M-203 40 mm grenade launcher slung under the barrel, half a dozen loaded magazines for the rifle, and two bandoliers of six rounds each of HE rounds for the 40 mm. After what seemed to me a long, long time, I was no longer defenseless. Thanks to Doc, I was well armed and back in the fight.

A-Y told the helo drivers where he wanted them to place their munitions, and they didn't try to save any taxpayer money. They burned up 2.75-inch HE rockets as fast as they could, and the door gunners showered the mud hole, bush, and tree line with thousands of empty 7.62 cases from their door-mounted M-60s.

With the Seawolf helos chopping the VC to pieces, and no fire coming our way, the medevac helo landed, loaded Doc and Bill, and, with the Seawolf helos flying cover, headed for the hospital in Long Bien or Saigon. Now that every VC for a long way knew that there were bad guys in their backyard, it was time to form up, take a head count, and hump the shortest route we could to our extraction point. Forget the booby traps; the shortest route to the extraction point would be right though the mangrove swamp. A-Y called the MSSC and told them to keep firing white star paraflares over our heads so that we could see where we were going in the darkness of the swamp and could find any booby traps on our way out. It didn't matter if we gave away our position; we would be moving fast, and half of the NVA and VC knew where we were anyhow. I was bringing up the rear and thanking Doc every couple of hundred yards by lobbing a 40 mm HE round behind us. I didn't give a rat's ass whether I took out any VC or just blew up some snakes or crocs. I just figured that high explosives tearing the shit out of everything behind us would kind of discourage anybody that might be thinking about following us through the swamp.

We fought our way through the vines and knee knockers and got back to the river in record time with no more VC contact. We reached our base at Nha Be just as the sun was painting the sky the red-orange that would have been beautiful if I hadn't had pieces of my Stoner and AK-47 rounds buried in my face and hand. After our debriefing we showered off the mud and blood, replaced the gear that had been lost in the firefight, cleaned ourselves up, and, with most of the platoon rearmed, headed for the chow hall, hoping that we would hear some good news about Bill's wound. We knew that Doc would let us know as fast as he could, but his first responsibility was to make sure that Bill was getting the best treatment available or possible, not babysitting us. I was pretty sure that Doc had found only one wound when he checked Bill over in the middle of the firefight. It had been a head wound, but Bill had remained conscious or semiconscious and seemed pretty damn coherent when he grabbed my hand to warn me about the instantaneously fused grenade. My wounds didn't hurt too much, but I figured that since my face wasn't all that good to look at in the first place I had better have somebody take a look at the damage and do whatever he could to make sure that it didn't get any worse. I reported to sick bay after breakfast, and the corpsman patched me up with butterfly bandages, gauze, and Band-Aids.

When I got back to the armory where we stashed our weapons, it was apparent that my Stoner was in worse shape than I was. The receiver, where it had been hit by a couple of AK-47 rounds, was shot to hell, and the barrel had been completely blown free of the receiver. It couldn't be put back together, but it wasn't a total loss. I always kept a couple of complete sets of parts in the armory, just in case something broke or what happened last night happened. I disassembled what was left of the Stoner and assembled all of the parts I needed to put it all back together and get it up and running. In a couple of hours it was as good as new. I went to our improvised firing range and emptied two drum magazines without even a hiccup. After I cleaned and oiled the Stoner, we were both ready to go back out.

Doc jumped onto a helo headed to Nha Be and got back to base in the afternoon. Bill was in stable condition with a single wound to his mouth; the surgeons had removed a .45 caliber slug from the back of his head. The bullet had smashed all of his teeth on the right side of his mouth, and that was what had probably saved his life. The bullet fired from a .45 ACP cartridge is big and heavy, but it is a low-velocity round that doesn't reach even nine hundred feet per second in velocity at the muzzle. At close range it will smash flesh and bone and drive a man to the ground, but the big, heavy, round-nosed bullet sheds velocity quickly as it flies through the air. Fired from a submachine gun a couple of hundred yards away, the bullet might have been going less than five hundred feet per second when it hit Bill in the face. He was alive because his teeth had slowed the bullet down before it could go all the way out the back of his head and kill him. It didn't come as much of a surprise to any of us that Bill had been hit with a .45 caliber bullet that had probably been fired from an American-made Thompson submachine gun. There were more U.S. weapons left over from World War II floating around Vietnam than you could shake a stick at. Bill had been hit in the face, but, everything considered, he had been lucky. If he had been hit with a 7.62 bullet from an AK-47 in the same place, he would be in the morgue, not recovering in a hospital full of good-looking nurses.

Our platoon had now lost three of our finest warriors. With only weeks left on this tour, there wouldn't be any replacements, but we would soldier on. With the other SEAL platoon, our eleven-man platoon, and a full PRU team stationed in Nha Be, we could handle anything that needed handling. Frank Thornton was still waiting for his replacement and running ops with his PRUs, so we decided that we would tag along whenever we could until it was time to rotate home. Between ops we managed to visit Barth a couple of times before he was loaded onto a medevac flight to the States. He was expected to make a full recovery. With only a couple of dry ops, and without any more VC contact, our date to rotate home loomed. We said our good-byes around the base, spent a long fare-thee-well night with all of the girls at the Cho Duc Bar, and loaded up our gear to convoy to Tan Son Nhut for the long ride home.

22

Grapes of Wrath

Even round-eyed, curvaceous stewardesses wearing miniskirts bringing us drinks to help level out the excesses of the previous night would not have relieved the long, boring flight. After four round-trips that covered close to a hundred thousand miles, the trip had become almost routine. With a couple of mandatory overnight stops for the air crew to get a good night's rest, we had ample opportunity to get an early start on our R&R. Most of us never missed an opportunity to spend some quality time revisiting the local bars and restaurants we had come to know so well. We might have been a little the worse for wear when we dragged our ass back to the air base, but with a fresh aircrew ready to lift wheels, we got aboard and settled in. This, the final leg of the long flight, would end up at Coronado Naval Air Station in sunny California, only one long flight from home. With nothing else to keep us busy while we were in the air, we got the sack time we needed to recuperate from our overindulgence the previous night.

Some of the men from SEAL Team 1 met us as we landed at Coronado and transported us to the naval amphibious base where we were supposed to lay over for the night before heading to Norfolk Naval Air Station the following morning. From what I could see even before we left the air base, the miniskirt had become as popular in Coronado as it had been in

Australia. Hot damn; there was nothing better to raise our spirits than round-eyed women wearing teeny, tiny miniskirts. Someone suggested that we might like to spend the evening in a joint called the Mexican Village right down the road. They served delicious Mexican food and had several different brands of tequila, and women wearing miniskirts had been known to stop there for dinner or a drink. An added bonus to us was that there was a motel right next door that rented rooms on short notice. The next morning several of us had proven the hard way that we could not drink more tequila than the bar had stashed in the basement. SEALs hate to fail, but there were at least a couple of bottles of tequila still behind the bar when our SEAL Team 1 escorts dumped us off at the naval air station. I think I kissed someone wearing a miniskirt and too much lipstick good-bye, because I had the remnants of hot pink Revlon lipstick from one end of my body to the other. I hoped that whoever she was, she had as much fun that short night as I did.

Our welcome home party at Norfolk, always attended by fifty or more friends, girlfriends, kids, family members, and wives, was close to the top of the list of homecoming events to which even the confirmed bachelors and battle-hardened SEALs looked forward. After hugging our wives, kids, mothers, fathers, and girlfriends, we unloaded all of our gear onto the waiting trucks and headed to our amphibious base at Little Creek. With the trucks and gear secure on base, I had planned to spend the night in the barracks. We had been given the whole night off; we had until 0800 to kick back and relax. Tonight nobody would be shooting at us, no mortar rounds would come falling out of the sky, no leeches would be sucking us dry, and no mosquitoes would be swarming our exposed flesh. Even the prospect of bars full of round-eyed, curvaceous women wearing miniskirts wasn't going to lure me away from a long, quiet, uninterrupted night's rest. After a couple of days of listening to the constant drone of aircraft engines whining like a thrumming insect, even the worst snoring of a barracks full of SEALS is like a lullaby.

Bright and early the next morning we would unload our equipment, check it back into inventory with each department, and store our personal gear, and then everyone would be heading out on leave. Mike McDonald and I had decided that for the two weeks of leave we had requested we would share a bachelor's paradise as close to our favorite SEAL bar, the Casino, as we could get. Mike had already gotten a lead on a place right on the beach and only two blocks from the Casino. With a long-term rental struck with a landlord that gave us a great deal, Mike was ready, willing, and able—to spend a couple of weeks with Diane, his girlfriend. I was planning to spend my time consorting with as many of those American beauties with miniskirts and lovely long legs as I could find. Sometimes, though, life throws you a curveball instead of a slider. It didn't work out quite the way I had planned it.

It was just about dark when we finally touched down, and, as usual, there was a crowd in the hangar waiting to greet us. As I walked across the tarmac, I saw a face that I hadn't expected to see this far from her home. Donna Sexton was a schoolteacher from Blackstone, North Carolina. We met while I was going through some training in her hometown just before I left for my second tour. Donna was a tall, black-haired beauty with an hourglass figure who had run track and field in college. She kept herself in top shape by running just about every day and could keep up with me on any long run. While I was in training in North Carolina, we had struck up both a romance and a friendship. We had written to one another several times while I was in Vietnam, and I had always looked forward to getting her letters, but I never thought that she would be waiting for me in Norfolk. I don't think that I have been luckier than most SEALs, but when I do get lucky I get very lucky. Donna was taking a course at the local community college and would be in Norfolk for the next couple of weeks. My plans changed faster than Superman could snap his fingers; as sure as the sun rises in the east, I wasn't going to be sleeping in the team bunkroom tonight! Donna told me that she had already booked a room at the Oak Leaf Motel, and we figured that we could let Mike and Diane have a whole week to themselves before we showed up at the beach house. While Mike and Diane were getting to know one another again, Donna and I would hang our hats at the motel. I grabbed my overnight bag, forgot all other plans, and told Mike not to expect me for a week or so, and we jumped into Donna's VW Bug and headed for the Oak Leaf Motel as fast as that little four-cylinder engine could get us there.

While Donna was busy with her classes, I decided that I should keep in close contact with the SEAL Team so that I could find another platoon that would be heading back to Vietnam in the near future. While I was scouting for another platoon I heard about a three-week-long training course for PRU advisers that was going to be run by the Naval Special Warfare Group in Coronado. By then Donna would be on her way back home, so, along with another SEAL, Clay Grady, I signed up.

Maybe it was Donna that started my streak of good luck, maybe not, but since seeing her on the tarmac I had been on a hot streak. Clay and I completed the PRU training course and were put on the waiting list for an opening. Then I found out that I had been accepted into the 9th Platoon along with Mike McDonald, Jack Squires, and Boomer, who had been with me in the 10th Platoon on my first tour. Everything was shaping up well for my third tour. When we mustered the platoon, I saw that my good luck was getting out of control; every member of the platoon had at least one tour under his belt, and most had two or more. Lieutenant Dick Moran and Master Chief Bob "Eagle" Gallagher, one of the SEAL Team legends, would be leading us into combat. During the Tet offensive Eagle had won the Navy Cross, the second-highest award given for valor. More than a few of the men who had been there, and had seen with their own eyes what Eagle had done to lead them out of that firefight alive, thought that he should have received the Medal of Honor.

With more than a little experience in the bush, Eagle had been picked to be assistant patrol leader of SEAL Team detachment Alpha that was going to run a night combat operation against a VC base camp located somewhere deep inside a battalion base area. After insertion the patrol had to hump about five klicks through the bush where they knew there was a battalion of VC hiding out for the night. The squad was looking for the command and control center, but they ran into a big barracks building. Somebody decided that Eagle should take three men and do a quick sneak and peek to see who or what was inside the silent building. There were about thirty VC in the building, and somehow a VC sentry heard or saw some movement and the shit hit the fan. In the first couple of seconds of the firefight Eagle got hit in the legs, but he never fell. He kept his head and took out at least five VC before he and his guys could haul ass out of the barracks. All of the sleeping VC were now wide-awake and grabbing their weapons, and it didn't take them long to start throwing a shitload of small-arms fire in the general direction of the SEAL squad. With an overwhelming VC force all emptying their AK-47s, there were so many tracers in the air that sooner or later somebody was going to catch a round. Before the squad could even get out of the direct fire from the VC and into the bush, the squad patrol leader was hit. In a heartbeat Eagle, wounded and bleeding, had to take command, step up to bat, start swinging, and lead the squad as they fought their way out of Dodge. As the squad fought their way back a thousand yards, Eagle got hit again, but that didn't stop him from calling in fire support and evac helos and directing the fire of the gunships until the squad could load aboard the helos and get airborne. Even in the SEAL Teams, men like Eagle Gallagher are few and far between. Eagle was a fearless, skilled warrior and natural leader who was always where the fight was raging and who brought his men home, alive or dead.

With guys like Lieutenant Moran and Master Chief Gallagher leading the platoon, it was easy to see why some of the best operators in SEAL Team 2 had signed on. Chief Frank Moncrief, an E-7, was platoon chief, backed up by three E-6s, six E-5s, and a pair of E-4s. With all this talent and experience in the 9th Platoon, our predeployment training would be more or less a walk in the park. Every man in the platoon had already been through the Army Jungle Warfare School in the Panama Canal Zone, and we had all been cross-trained on every weapon from slingshots and crossbows to the AK-47. All we needed to do was to work out our SOPs until they were instinctive and running as smooth as a fine-tuned race car. During the four weeks we would spend at Camp Pickett, we would work out and eliminate any bugs that came up in our patrol and ambush tactics. At the end of a month, we would know how far any of us could chuck a grenade, who was the most accurate with a LAAW rocket, and even which hand a teammate used to wipe his ass. When we were done training, each man would be an expert with every weapon carried by the platoon. We would burn up thousands and thousands of rounds of ammunition; every weapon would be tested as hard as we could test it, sometimes to failure. If a weapon was going to fail, it was better that it failed where we could rebuild it or replace it and test it again. Failure of any weapon in a firefight could get all of us DOTS—dead on the spot. We didn't ignore the ordnance that we would be using, including some ChiCom grenades that had been captured and sent back for evaluation and study. Everything new or old that we might use was put under the microscope of hard use in the intense, monthlong refresher course.

Putting together a platoon, or a squad, that works like a single complex machine is almost like building a high-performance engine for a race car. When you finish building an engine, you start it up and run it slow. As the new parts begin to wear against each other, they fit better and better and the horsepower increases until all of the parts are running so smooth and tight that the maximum output is greater than it was when every part was bright, shiny, and new. When we were done with those four weeks, the 9th Platoon would be one powerful, scary, deadly engine capable of running wide open on all cylinders.

With a month of living out of each other's pockets complete, we were ready for deployment. Our platoon would be relieving a West Coast SEAL Team 1 platoon in someplace that I had never even heard of—Ca Mau. Before we loaded up for the trip back to Vietnam, though, there were a few loose ends to tie up. One of those loose ends was a formal awards ceremony that was scheduled for the day after we got back to our base at Little Creek. SEAL Teams 1 and 2 were becoming two of the most decorated outfits in Vietnam, and awards ceremonies were held on the parade ground with all of the pomp and circumstance that the navy could muster. With the band playing, the flags flying, and a couple of hundred friends and family members gathered to honor their husbands, sons, and buddies, these awards ceremonies were impressive events. Looking like officers and gentlemen in our dress whites, half of the platoon lined up to receive awards that the navy had decided we had earned. I was almost embarrassed to be standing there as I was awarded my second Bronze Star with the Combat *V* for Valor, a second Navy Commendation Medal with the Combat *V* for Valor, a Navy Achievement Medal with the Combat *V* for Valor, our second Presidential Unit Citation, and the Purple Heart. I was honored to be receiving these awards, but, like most of the SEALs that were standing there that day, I was only doing my job, what I had been trained to do. As far as I was concerned it was men like Bubba and

Chris who should have been standing there beside us to be honored and awarded.

Even though people outside of the teams thought that what we did was dangerous, I couldn't agree. To my way of thinking, there were only two things that made combat in Vietnam dangerous. The first was to be doing something that you hadn't been trained to do. The second was to be fighting like II Corps or I Corps was in the north. The army and marines were taking hilltops, fighting the VC head-on, then trying and dying to hold the ground they had won. In that kind of fight indiscriminate death was the rule, not the exception. No matter how well you were trained, an artillery or mortar round could turn you into a red spot on the jungle floor, or some teenager or a sixty-year-old rice farmer with an SKS could pop up out of a spider hole or from behind a tree and whack you before you even knew he or she was there. SEALs didn't charge into enemy fire to take and hold ground; we were guerrilla fighters. When we fought it was in the enemy's own backyard; they didn't know that we were there, how many of us there were, how we got there, or how we would extract. We were masters of surprising the VC before they even had a clue that we were within miles of the ambush site. If the op was compromised, we hit the VC before they could hit us, then faded into the bush or the swamps and disappeared into the darkness like nightmares—nightmares that would come back again and again. We fought fast and hard with overwhelming firepower on ground of our own choosing, and always remembered the rule that a young SEAL with a kind of wild gleam in his eyes, Dick Marcinko, had added to the SEAL rules of engagement before my first tour in My Tho: "The *only* rule of unconventional warfare is that there are *no* rules."

With the medal ceremony concluded and our dress whites hung in a closet where we wouldn't get them covered with crud, we reconvened at the Casino Bar for our own ceremonial toasts to our fallen and those who had been wounded and survived. With only a few days of R&R remaining, we made the best of the time available. We would soon be back across the Pacific Ocean to Saigon and Tan Son Nhut airport, where we would have to scrounge up transport to our new digs in Ca Mau.

As we made our approach to Tan Son Nhut, nothing much had changed. The vegetation was still brown, killed by Agent Orange, and the bomb craters were starting to become a too familiar pattern. While the platoon was unloading our gear, Eagle and Lt. Moran were checking out available transportation to Ca Mau. They had bad news and good news. The bad news was that there wasn't any transport available until tomorrow and the good news was that we would be spending the night in Saigon. Tomorrow morning the platoon would be hitching a ride on an army Caribou transport plane headed to the army base at Quan Long City, Ca Mau province, Republic of Vietnam. Until 0800 we were on our own. Even though it was only late afternoon, it didn't take long to find a couple of married guys who, more or less, volunteered to stand guard duty over all of our gear, and the rest of the platoon was off to our favorite watering hole in Saigon, the President Hotel! The rest of the platoon decided that they would get settled in their rooms, but I headed up to the top floor to see if anyone I knew was hanging out and to see if there had been any additions to the crop of beautiful ladies of the evening since I had last awakened with "Suzie." This early in the evening there were not many GIs, but there were enough lovely ladies to empty the pockets of my entire SEAL platoon. It seemed that day or night, there was never a shortage of extraordinarily good-looking, willing women. As it was a little early for bringing the night to an end, I looked around and saw a guy wearing a flight suit sitting all by himself at a table on the balcony. Thinking that he might have been a member of our aircrew, I went over, pulled out a chair, and introduced myself. As it turned out, he wasn't one of our flyboys but was an air force pilot named Gabriel "Gabe" Penagaricano. I ordered both of us a drink, and we talked about our experiences in Vietnam. I told Gabe that in the morning I was heading down to Ca Mau to relieve a SEAL platoon that had just about finished their tour of duty. That piece of information seemed to light up his face.

Gabe was an F-100 pilot with the Air National Guard out of Puerto Rico, and he had a little experience with the SEAL platoon in Ca Mau. On the way back from a recent mission in the U Minh forest, with a full load of bombs still aboard, he heard a SEAL platoon calling for fire support and the TOC telling them that there wasn't anyone available. He cut in on the conversation and volunteered his immediate services. With the SEALs giving him directions to their position on the river over the radio, and then marking the area they wanted to turn into flying debris and dead VC with flares and red tracers, he rolled in and dropped everything he had. His F-100 empty, he did a flyover above the platoon's position and headed back for Tan Son Nhut. He figured, and I agreed, that it must have been the SEAL Team 1 platoon and the boat detachment out of Quan Long City that he had helped out. I couldn't let a pilot who had helped out a SEAL platoon in trouble buy his own drinks, and our glasses were almost dry. While we waited for another round, I asked Gabe if he had any other stories as good as the last one. He looked at me kinda like I wasn't going to believe him; then he started to talk.

Yesterday afternoon Gabe had stopped at the President for a couple before-dinner drinks and to watch the war out on the horizon, almost like I had done. Like I did, he looked around the room and spotted one older-looking guy wearing green fatigues who was sitting by himself out on the balcony. Gabe didn't want to drink alone, so he walked over and asked the guy if he could join him. Gabe ordered a round of drinks and noticed that the stranger wasn't wearing any insignia on his fatigues at all. Gabe introduced himself, then asked the stranger why he was in Vietnam. The stranger told Gabe that he was just about to leave for home but that his two sons were serving in Vietnam and he was a journalist for *Newsday*. He had come to see his sons and to see for himself what we were doing to help the Vietnamese keep the Communists from overrunning their country. He had been able to track down his sons and had even been allowed to spend the night in a machine-gun bunker at a firebase where one of his sons had been deployed. Gabe listened, fascinated, as this unknown journalist asked Gabe's opinion about the stories he was planning to write when he got back to the States.

After a couple more drinks, an hour had disappeared and Gabe had to get back to the air base. He stuck out his hand and said, "It's been great to meet you, and to hear about what you're going to write. Maybe someday I'll read one of those stories. Don't forget, my name is Gabe—Gabriel Penagaricano." The journalist shook his hand and said, "Thank you, Gabe. It was a pleasure to meet you. My name is John—John Steinbeck."

The rest of the platoon showed up a few minutes later, and I waved them over and introduced our new friend. After a last night in Saigon for what would probably be at least a few months, we headed for our rooms and mustered in the lobby at 0600. The weapons carrier that we had commandeered the day before was right where we left it, so we loaded aboard and headed back to Tan Son Nhut. Boomer and Squires had already loaded our gear on the Caribou, a smaller, twin-engine version of the C-130, so we were ready to head for Ca Mau.

This would be the first time that one of our platoons would be split up and would work from two different bases. Six other guys and I would be part of Alpha squad, which would be led by Lieutenant Moran and Chief Moncrief. Alpha would be based at the army garrison in Quan Long City. Bravo, led by Master Chief Gallagher, would be living and operating out of a small outpost in Ha Tien village. Ha Tien was still in Ca Mau province, but it was located on the banks of a canal way the hell and gone out into the Mekong Delta. Ha Tien was an easy thirty miles away, and the only way to get there was by boat or helo. Looking out the window as we landed on the steel mats that made up the runway, I could see two helo pads with navy Seawolf gunships. I hadn't known that we would have two gunships from a detachment in Can Tho covering our ass here in Ca Mau, but it was a very nice surprise, and I looked forward to meeting the pilots as soon as I could arrange it. At the end of the runway our boat support team, MST-2 (Mobile Support Team 2) Det Foxtrot, led by Lieutenant JG Roger Berg, was waiting to greet us, give us the skinny on the local area, and take us to the army garrison less than a mile away. Checking into the base was quick, and we found ourselves all living in one of the single-level barracks. The Seawolf pilots were at one end, the boat crew was in the middle, and we were up front. It wasn't as nice as the other places where I had been stationed, but I didn't expect too much; after all, it was an army compound. Our area was one large room with double bunks, lockers, a small room for our lieutenant, and an oversized map of our area of operations on the wall behind the well-constructed bar. SEAL Team 1 had its priorities well squared away.

The garrison itself covered about seven square acres and was surrounded by what could have been called a moat, a ten-foot-wide hole filled with water. It was better known as, and was always called, "the shit ditch." Inside the protective shit ditch were four sets of barracks like ours, a mess hall, several small general purpose buildings, a magazine for ammunition and munitions storage, and a TOC. Outside each of the barracks, there was a pair of level sandbag bunkers for use in case of mortar attack or an attack on the base. Talking to the boat crew and looking around at the surroundings, it was as clear as Bombay gin that this was not going to be anything like My Tho or Nha Be. There were no local bars with beautiful, available women. Even in town, where we were told there were several good restaurants, there just weren't enough military people to keep a strip club profitable. Now I knew why SEAL Team 1 had bailed out of Ca Mau as fast as they could.

Lieutenant Moran and Master Chief Gallagher checked in with the TOC, gave us a rundown on the do's and don'ts, and told us that we would be the base QRT (quick reaction team). In the morning, Master Chief Gallagher and his gang would be taking a helo ride to their base at Ha Tien, and Chief Moncrief and Lieutenant Moran would be looking hard for something nasty that we could do to let the local VC know that there was a new squad of SEALs in town. We were going out hunting.

23

Welcome to
the Neighborhood

The West Coast SEAL platoon was on their way home to the land of miniskirts, well tanned long legs, and sunny California beaches. Master Chief Gallagher and his squad had headed for Ha Tien on helos to set up their base of operations. It was time for our squad to get settled in and then get out into the bush. The order of the day was to start lining up some solid sources of intelligence for our first op in Ca Mau. John Fallon, an E-6 now on his third tour, had developed almost a sixth sense for digging out the real intel and separating it from the bullshit that led to too many long nights with nothing to show for them other than leech and mosquito bites. With no CIA interrogation team available here, as there had been in My Tho and Nha Be, finding good, actionable intel wasn't going to be easy. Fallon found out that there was a PRU team operating from the other side of the city and that their acting adviser was a CIA field agent he had known during his second tour. We got lucky; the CIA agent remembered Fallon and was willing to help us out whenever we needed intel or verification of intel that we had dug up ourselves.

Most of what we got from the Chieu Hoi program on my first two tours had been pretty spotty intel at best. Based on our own experience, it was difficult for us to have much trust in most of the Chieu Hoi who claimed to be able to lead us to good targets. Recently, though, more and better intel had been coming from the Chieu Hoi program, and we didn't have much choice—we had to start getting intel from somewhere.

A recent Chieu Hoi recruit named Wang So told Fallon that he knew there was a weapons cache in a bunker in an old French cemetery very close to the village of Muc Wa. Wang So not only knew about the weapons cache and exactly where it was located, he was from the village of Muc Wa. If he wasn't bullshitting us, he could lead us right to the spot where the VC had dug the underground bunker in one corner of the graveyard. Wang So also told Fallon there was a local VC cadre of about twelve men who used the cache to hide weapons, grenades, and ammunition that they used for resupply whenever they needed to top off their combat load out. The downside of this intel was that he didn't know when they would be using the bunker to resupply. The op would have to wait for a couple of days to allow Lieutenant Moran to get back from Ha Tien, where he was checking on how Master Chief Gallagher was getting along, and for us to get settled in our new digs.

While we were making sure that our new quarters were well supplied with the liquid refreshments that would help make our after-action relaxation more enjoyable, Chief Moncrief and Fallon asked the Seawolfs to do a flyover of the Muc Wa area with a Polaroid camera to snap some photos that would give us a good lay of the land. Even from three thousand feet, the standard altitude for helos that were not running a fire mission or evacuating troops, the photos gave us a crystal-clear looky-see at the entire area. By tacking up the photos on the wall in a grid, we had a panoramic picture of the canal where we would insert and extract from the MSSC boats, the rice paddies, the village, the tree lines, and the French cemetery where the bunker was supposed to be located.

Lieutenant Moran got back to base earlier than expected, and the planning with Moncrief and Fallon got under way as soon as the skids of the helo touched down on the pad. We would be inserting around 1900 tonight from the MSSCs, right at last light. With Wang So as our guide, we would patrol through the bush and along the tree line to the area of the cemetery and set up a security perimeter so that we could keep the cemetery and bunker under observation until daylight. We were hoping that the local VC might decide to resupply while our new welcome wagon was ready to throw them their last party. If nobody showed up before daybreak, we would set up a security perimeter around the bunker itself, and the search team, Moran, Moncrief, Fallon, and Wang So, would proceed to the bunker to check it out.

In addition to my normal load out I would be carrying three two-pound blocks of C-4, twenty-five feet of det cord, and my chemical time-delay blasting cap kit. Even when we hadn't planned on blowing anything up I always made it a practice to carry my blasting cap kit. It came in handy for use with claymore mines and grenades whenever we wanted to leave behind a time-delayed surprise for anyone trying to track us to our extraction point. The C-4 and det cord would be used to blow anything found in the bunker that we couldn't take with us. It didn't matter what was stashed in the bunker, when the six pounds of C-4 exploded, there wouldn't be much left but a smoldering hole and pieces of whatever we found in the bunker would become useless scrap falling from the sky. Lieutenant Roger Berg briefed his boat crew, and we all headed for the dock.

The MSSC that Roger's detachment was running was one of the newest models in-country. It was a powerful river rocket and a beautiful thing to behold: twenty-eight feet long, ceramic armor on the sides, twin 428-cubic-inch Chevrolet engines, Mercruiser outdrive, underwater silenced exhaust system, and a concave dished bow for easy loading and unloading. It also carried the kind of firepower that could get our ass out of just about any jam we got ourselves into. Even with two .50 caliber machine guns, two M-60 machine guns, a 7.62 mm aircraft Gatling gun on the stern, plenty of ammunition, and thirteen men aboard, Roger could get the MSSC from dead in the water to thirty-five knots in thirty seconds. The MSSC was one hell of a boat. With the sun setting and seven SEALs and six members of the boat crew on board, we were rocketing up the Song Ong Doc River like a well armed, aquatic bat out of hell. We wanted to get to the Long Tay canal with enough daylight left to find where it branches off of the river before we went flying past it and needed to double back.

The plan was to follow the Long Tay canal to a bend where we could insert about a half mile from Muc Wa. From that point on the canal, the cemetery was only a mile past the village, an easy hump that would get us there with more than enough time to set up what we hoped would be an ambush for a dozen or so VC. Lieutenant Berg had put in a lot of hours on the river and was a skilled boat driver. He knew the river and canals as well as he knew his boat and crew. Swinging in close to just skirt the mangrove roots and brush that lined the sweeping curve of the riverbank, he started to slow the MSSC as we approached a bend in the river. Even in the fading daylight we could see the entrance to the Long Tay canal just beyond the bend. It wasn't exactly what we had expected from looking at the maps and Polaroid photos. It looked like Roger would need a shoehorn and maybe some Vaseline to get the MSSC into the tiny canal; at best it was going to be a very tight fit. If the shit hit the fan on the way up the canal, there was no place for the MSSC to turn and run and gun our way to the river. Roger and Moran talked it over and decided that the only thing that made sense was for Roger to tie up where he could hide the boat in the bush at the entrance to the canal and we would patrol the extra five hundred yards. A small bonus was that there was a well-used path along the canal that probably hadn't been booby-trapped. We could make good time on the path, but the point man would have to really focus on any surprises the VC might have left.

Roger pulled the MSSC tight to the left bank of the canal, and we filed ashore to provide cover for the crew as they tied up the boat and concealed it in the bush. With a quarter moon rising and a clear sky covered with stars, we moved out with Fallon and Wang So on point. Following them was Lieutenant Moran, Ron Rogers with his M-60, and the rest of the patrol separated by ten or fifteen yards between men. I was covering our back door with my Stoner. It took us an hour of silent, careful humping to reach the bend in the canal where we had planned to insert. From our position we could see lights in the village in the distance; someone was still awake and might be watching for anything that moved in the night. The canal ran right through the middle of the village, and the village was dead center between us and the cemetery. To reach the cemetery on the other side of the village, we would have to skirt around it as best we could, using the tree line along the edge of the rice paddies for concealment and cover. With more than enough moonlight to see the village, we figured that there was enough light for anyone on watch to see us.

We decided that we would get as close to the paddies as we could and then, to reduce movement to a minimum, cross them one man at a time and slip into the tree line. Fallon and Wang So reached the tree line and signaled back with a red-lens flashlight that it was all clear and they were ready for us to follow. One man at a time, crawling through the rice paddy, the patrol snuck into the tree line and headed toward the cemetery. We moved as silently as possible and stayed in the shadows because our line of march would take us within seventy-five yards of the nearest hooch. We were forced to halt as we got closer to the village. We could see a couple of flashlights coming our way along the paddy dike that ran parallel to the tree line where we were hiding. We all slipped off into the bush as far as we could get, slowly moved down onto one knee to be ready to cover our field of fire, and waited to see if Lieutenant Moran opened up or we were fired on. In the moonlight we could see that the flashlights were carried by a couple of villagers returning home to Muc Wa after a day of hard work in the fields. They were carrying no weapons, but they did have one of the ubiquitous radios that was playing tinny Vietnamese music. They were talking a mile a minute, laughing, and the slapping of their sandals made enough noise to wake the dead. They strolled right on past us and out of sight without ever knowing that instant death and destruction was only a couple of feet away.

With no more lights bobbing through the night, Wang So told us that we were within a mile of our target. Hugging the tree line, we could see a dirt road that we had noticed in the aerial photographs. It would lead us right to the front gate of the old French cemetery. With the moon now lighting up the landscape, we approached the area and from over a hundred yards away could see the wrought-iron gate with a large sign over the entrance to the graveyard where the bunker was supposed to be located. Moving as close as we could while remaining in the cover of the deepest shadows we could find, we set up an ambush position facing the cemetery. From only twenty or thirty yards, we could almost read the names that had been inscribed on the tombstones by some now long dead and forgotten stone mason. Tim Baron and I set up a claymore on our right flank, and Fallon set up the claymore that covered our left flank; the clackers were handed over to Dick Moran in the middle of the ambush position.

With a couple of hours of relative darkness before we had planned to hit the bunker, we hoped that the local VC using the bunker might give us a chance to capture or take them all out. Wang So had told us that there was no schedule that the VC followed, so we weren't expecting much action, but we never fully trusted the Chieu Hoi, and Wang So was no exception. There was nothing to lose but a couple of pints of blood to the mosquitoes. We would stay as dry as we could on the high ground and hope that we got lucky and the VC showed up. If not, we would break the ambush at dawn, when we could see the entire area and be sure that the VC hadn't set up an ambush of their own, and check out the bunker.

Just as the first blush of sunlight lit up the horizon and we were about to break the ambush, we heard voices coming from the road that went past the cemetery. Hoping that it was the VC, we were disappointed when four rice farmers went walking right through the middle of our ambush. Two of them carried large bundles of rice, and the other two had a long bamboo pole; nobody had any weapons. Hanging from the pole by their tails were half a dozen of the biggest rats I have ever seen. I had heard that the farmers trapped rats for food, but I had never seen a rat as big as these. I didn't have any doubt that a man who had been crippled by a severe wound and left behind could become prey to the rats as soon as he couldn't defend himself.

As soon as the farmers disappeared in the distance, Lieutenant Moran signaled for the claymores to be brought in; we were going to break the ambush and head out to set up security around the cemetery. Then with all of our gear packed up and ready to move out, he signaled us back into cover. Someone was heading our way from the village. Melted as far as we could into the bush and the rapidly disappearing shadows, we watched as this guy walked right into the cemetery and headed for the bunker. The bunker wasn't hard to see because it was only half underground, and there was no question that this guy knew exactly where he was going. When the suspected VC got to about ten feet from the bunker, Fallon stepped out of the bush with the sights of his M-16 centering on the VC's back and told him, in Vietnamese, to halt and put his hands on the top of his head. Surprised and probably scared half silly, the VC turned around to see who the hell was talking to him. All that poor bastard could see was seven green-faced devils and seven muzzles, all pointed at him. He became very cooperative. Lieutenant Moran and Fallon walked up to him, tied his elbows together behind his back, walked him over to the bunker, blindfolded him, and sat him down where he would be out of the way. Fallon spoke a little Vietnamese, but not enough to do a field interrogation, so Charlie would be joining us on a boat ride when we had completed our mission.

With security set up on the four corners of the cemetery, Moncrief and Fallon checked the entrance of the bunker to make sure that there were no booby traps before going in to see what the VC had stashed. Meanwhile, Fallon and Wang So were keeping an eye on the VC prisoner. In a couple of minutes, Moran and Moncrief exited the bunker with four rifles and a backpack full of documents. Lieutenant Moran motioned me over and told me that there were several more weapons inside, but they were old, rusty junk not worth taking along when we extracted. There were also a couple of cases of ChiCom mortar rounds and AK-47 ammunition that we didn't want to hump back to the MSSC. With Tom Burton holding a flashlight so that I could see what I was doing inside the bunker, I piled up everything that Lieutenant Moran left in place, topped off the pile with six pounds of C-4, and tied it all in with det cord. Pulling ten feet of det cord out of the bunker, I capped it off with two fifteen-minute chemical-delay blasting caps. Moncrief told me to booby-trap the bunker so I used an instantaneous frag grenade and monofilament fishing line to leave behind a terminal surprise for anyone foolish or careless enough to try to get the munitions out of the bunker before the C-4 blew. With the squad formed up under the cemetery sign, Lieutenant Moran signaled me to start the chemical clock. When I crushed the two glass-lined copper tubes, the acid would start eating the thin wires inside the chemical delay caps. In fifteen minutes, the wire would let go and detonate the det cord, firing the C-4, obliterating everything in the bunker. With the C-4, the mortar rounds, and a couple of cases of ammunition, the blast would turn the bunker into a bigger muddy hole in the ground.

Fallon and Wang So took the point and headed right down the middle of the road toward Muc Wa village. Right behind them was our prisoner with two SKS and two AK-47 rifles strapped to his back. Tim Baron had tied a five-foot-long piece of parachute cord to his elbows, so he wasn't going to go anywhere. We had removed his blindfold so that he could keep up with us and nobody had to guide him. There was no reason to reduce our firepower by detailing one of the squad to babysit a prisoner. If we ran into the VC on our way to the extraction point, he would be the first casualty of the firefight. As we entered the village, we could see women, kids, pigs, and ducks everywhere; the men were already out working the fields and rice paddies. As we passed through the village, Lieutenant Moran got on the radio and let Roger know that we had placed a time-delay fuse on a bunker full of VC munitions. There was going to be a big explosion in a couple of minutes, and we didn't want Roger and his boat crew to think that we were in deep shit.

As we hastily left the village behind us, the bunker blew sky high. Now that everybody for miles around knew that we were in the area, we moved off of the road and back into the tree line. Even though it was now broad daylight, there was no reason to take any unnecessary risk on our way back to the extraction point. Wang So was still out on point, and it looked like he might be one of the Chieu Hoi that could turn out to be a real asset. Fallon, by making sure that Wang So and our prisoner were seen by everyone in the village, had assured that the local VC would know that we had good local intel and were going to use it to find them no matter where they were hiding.

Roger and his crew were where we had left them last night. They were ready to get away from the mosquitoes, so we secured our prisoner in the boat and manned the guns for the trip back to base on the Song Ong Doc River. Fallon had a short talk with Wang So while we prepared for the ride home and found out that our prisoner was a member of the VC company that was working in the district. Wang So also told him that the backpack that Lieutenant Moran had grabbed up from the bunker was full of identification packets and other documentation. With one VC prisoner for further interrogation, a pile of documents and four rifles captured, the destruction of a munitions cache bunker, and nobody injured, this first op had been a success. Roger got the MSSC out into the river and humming along at full speed. I hoped that all of our missions would be as well planned and as productive, but we never forgot that Mr. Murphy is always waiting somewhere out in the bush.

24

Looking for Trouble

Before we cleaned ourselves up and headed for breakfast, we stashed our still tied, gagged, and blindfolded prisoner in the calaboose, the lockup on the second floor of the TOC. Fallon asked Wang So to hang around to act as our unofficial backup interpreter. Fallon was one of the best interrogators in the SEAL Team, and he never waited long to start interrogating our prisoners. To get some solid intel that would let us hit the VC before they realized that they had been compromised, we needed to squeeze the captured VC dry as fast as possible. As soon as the VC realized that one of their guys might have been grabbed, they wouldn't wait around for us to show up; they would move their operations to a new location. The VC had figured out that the SEAL chain of command was only about two men deep. We didn't wait for some numb-nuts in Saigon to make up his mind to approve an op, we just got the job done.

If Fallon got anything out of a prisoner that made putting together an op look worthwhile, we would almost always try to get some confirmation from a Chieu Hoi or the CIA before we headed into the bush. Getting fresh, reliable intel was always the most difficult and important part of any successful op. On the really shaky ops, it was almost SOP to insert into the general area, grab one of the local rice farmers to see if he had any information that could corroborate the intel from a prisoner, then figure out how to get in, kick ass, take names, and get out fast. Sometimes we got information on VC movement or weapons caches that was only hours old, but damn seldom. The local farmers always knew what was going on in their area, but they were so afraid of VC retaliation against their village or families that most of the time they wouldn't even tell us what day of the week it was.

The prisoner didn't tell Fallon anything but his name and the name of the village where he lived. His story was that he was just an innocent farmer visiting some of his relatives in the village. The problem for him was that he couldn't give us the name of the people he was supposed to be visiting. The poor bastard was a lousy liar; he couldn't even come up with a good reason for being in the cemetery and headed for the bunker. Wang So, who had grown up in Muc Wa, told us that he had never seen the guy before but that he was sure that he was part of the VC contingent in the Muc Wa area. If that VC prisoner had had any brains at all, he would have told us everything that he knew. With no information after a couple of hours, we didn't have much choice; we had to turn him over to the Vietnamese police force for detention and further interrogation, and they really didn't like the VC. That poor asshole was in for an interrogation that would make his little chat with Fallon and Wang So look like a Sunday afternoon tea party.

With no good intel to run an op right away, we were hoping that the documents we had found in the bunker might have something we could use to target a valuable VC asset. That wasn't going to happen. The documents were so old that they could have been in that bunker when the French were still fighting the Vietminh. It was looking like all that we had to show for our bunker op was one lousy prisoner captured and the destruction of some munitions and rifles that wouldn't be used against us. Hoping that the local VC hadn't headed out of town, we spent a week looking for more intel, but there wasn't even a whisper of VC movement. More out of frustration than anything else, and to try to take advantage of what the VC might be thinking now that they knew we had one of their guys in interrogation, we ran two canal ambush ops with Wang So guiding us in. Our hope was that we would be able to hit the VC that were working in the Muc Wa area while they were trying to find someplace to hide from us by moving men and material around in sampans. We didn't get lucky. The VC had either hauled ass out of the area fast or had dug in so deep that nothing and nobody was moving. We fed the bugs and got some exercise while Lieutenant Moran was digging for intel everywhere that might let us catch the VC off guard.

Moran got lucky. Through the CIA PRU adviser he got a lead on a VC POW camp that was located down in Nam Can, a long way down the coast of the Gulf of Thailand in the U Minh forest. The intel about the POW camp came directly from an escaped prisoner and was just about as good as it could get. The downside was that it had taken him almost two weeks to find his way out of the U Minh. Two-week-old intel is usually not worth much, but with the possibility of freeing POWs we had to make sure that our intel was as solid as possible. If we screwed up the intel, we might actually endanger the people we wanted to set free and get some of us KIA in the bargain. Although the SOP of the VC was to move anything and everything if a prisoner escaped, we figured that even if the op was a long shot it might be the only shot for us to free the men being held prisoner.

The U Minh forest is a big piece of real estate, mile after mile of waist-deep, swampy marshland that is crisscrossed by canals and covered by dense triple-canopy trees that grow to over a hundred feet tall. The treetops were so dense that nothing could be seen from the air, so flying an aerial recon mission wasn't worth much. It sure wasn't worth the delay in getting the op set up. We had been in some remote, nasty places, but the U Minh forest was as desolate a wilderness as you could find just about anywhere on earth. In 1953 an entire company of the French Foreign Legion, a group of experienced, resourceful, very tough fighters, had been ordered to go into the U Minh forest and find the Vietminh who were using the wilderness as a base of operations. The whole company of well-armed, experienced men simply disappeared and was never seen again.

After the disaster of the Tet offensive, when American forces had thrown back every VC assault, killed more VC than survived, and destroyed a large part of the VC arsenal of heavy weapons, the VC had almost disappeared from the Mekong Delta. General Giap realized that if his troops stayed in the delta we would dig them out and destroy them. The VC needed a place to nurse their wounds and rebuild their strength, so Giap ordered an enormous pullback and moved thousands and thousands of VC into the U Minh forest, where we hadn't yet begun to concentrate our military force. The VC, their ass kicked decisively and thrown back on every front in the Tet offensive, had no place else to go; they soon became the overwhelmingly dominant population in the U Minh forest. We were going to go pull the tail of the tiger in its lair and let them know that, even in that wild morass of VC-controlled territory, there was no place for them to hide. The search for more recent intel was going to take more time than any of us liked, but there was nothing else that we could do. Pulling the tiger's tail would have to wait.

It looked like it was going to take at least a week before we had any new intel that we could use to put together a solid op, so Tim Baron and I asked Chief Moncrief if we could fly over to Ha Tien for a few days and go out with Master Chief Gallagher and his squad. The navy Seawolf helo pilots were easygoing guys, and it wasn't too difficult to talk them into giving a couple of SEALs a ride that afternoon. Since we were going in the right direction, we hauled a couple of cases of ammunition and grenades that my pal Dickey Cyrus had requisitioned over to the helo pad and loaded them aboard for the trip. Eagle was happy to see us, ammo and grenades are always a bonus, and there were a couple of ops in the pipeline that looked promising. Eagle was never opposed to adding more firepower when he was out hunting the VC, so we were welcome to go out when the op intel all came together. Until then we could relax and enjoy all of the sights, smells, and nightlife we could stand.

Calling Ha Tien a village was almost like calling Gauley Bridge, West Virginia, a major metropolis. Two canals snaked past a couple dozen or so hooches where thirty or forty local fisherman and their families tried to eke out a living. In the center of the village was a Vietnamese Army outpost, a single helo pad, and one big hooch where Bravo lived. It was all self-contained and reminded me of some of the Special Forces camps we had visited out in the boonies. With no mess hall or local bistro, Bravo did all of their own cooking, housekeeping, cleaning, laundry, and anything else that needed to be done.

The poor bastards didn't have even a single MSSC or LSSC; there wasn't a boat detachment at all. The entire transport capability of the base was a nineteen-foot Boston Whaler with an outboard motor, three sampans, and a thirty-two-foot Chinese junk with an ancient diesel engine that they rented from a local fisherman. Earning a living was so difficult that the fisherman who owned the junk would hire on as boat driver any time that Eagle needed to use it. We guessed that he went along to make sure that his only source of income came back in one piece, but he knew every little canal and backwater in the area and could repair the banging, smoke-belching engine when it decided that it was time to break down. It was a good deal all around and let Eagle get everyone to the same place at the same time. I'm sure that Eagle would have rather inserted by helo, but with a single helo pad they couldn't get everyone out into the field in one trip. About the only bright spot was that Eagle could call up virtually unlimited navy and army gunship support from Can Tho whenever Bravo needed to make sure that the deck was stacked in their favor.

Two of my good friends, Dickey Cyrus and Bob "Oz" Osborne, met us at the helo pad, and Dickey took the ammunition and grenades over to the hooch to check them into inventory. While Dickey was busy, Oz gave us the royal tour of the village. As we were walking along the top of the dike that kept the canals from reclaiming the village, the sound of a pair of rounds came from the tree line a hundred yards away. Mud flew as the rounds smacked harmlessly into the dirt berm behind us, and Tim and I hit the deck. Oz looked down at us in the mud, kinda chuckled, waved at the tree line, and told us that it was safe to get out of the dirt. One of the more entertaining events that everyone looked forward to here in Ha Tien was the daily sniper attack by "Sure Shot Charlie." It seemed that about this time, every day, this "sniper" took a couple of shots from across the canal. When he got lucky he hit the dike. So far, punching holes in the earthen dike had been the most damage he had been able to do. Out of curiosity, Oz had dug a couple of the bullets out of the dirt, and they turned out to be 9 mm. Oz figured that old "Sure Shot" was shooting at us with either an old British Sten or a Swedish K, submachine guns that had been plentiful and easy to find in the early days of the war. Both of these weapons were designed for the close-range "spray and pray" school of fighting in dense jungle. The manual of arms went something like this:

1. Point the muzzle in the direction of the bad guys.
2. Mash down on the trigger.
3. Hang on to the weapon until the magazine is empty.
4. Replace empty magazine with full magazine.
5. Recock weapon.
6. Repeat steps as needed until the enemy is dead, you are dead, or you run out of ammunition.

Good Luck.

While this style of "spray and pray" wasn't ineffective in the heavy bush when applied with a powerful cartridge like the 7.62 mm, the 5.56 mm, or the 7.62×39 mm round, the Sten and Swedish K were designed around the underpowered 9 mm pistol bullet. By the time this little bullet had smashed its way through the leaves, branches, vines, and other crap, it was just about out of gas. There were a few instances of men being hit with 9 mm bullets that didn't even break the skin. Sometimes they didn't even know that they had been hit because the bullet was moving so slowly that it hit their web belt or some other gear, bounced off, and landed at their feet, leaving only a small bruise. To make them even less effective at ranges past a couple of dozen yards, the Sten and Swedish K had almost worthless sights, fired when the bolt slammed into battery, and had universally lousy triggers that made accurate, aimed fire virtually impossible. If someone was shooting at you from a long way off using the Sten or Swedish K, the chances of getting killed were about the same as winning the Irish Sweepstakes.

Oz let us know that we had just experienced one-half of what could be called entertainment available in Ha Tien. The real fun started when Dickey Cyrus got a couple of drinks in him and started taking bets on what had become his almost legendary ability to eat and drink things that would make a vulture or hyena gag. Nobody even tried to equal Dickey's exploits, but we never stopped betting and he never stopped winning. The old trick of snorting a strand of spaghetti up his nose and letting it dangle out of his mouth was just the opening act. Dickey had won a bundle by drinking half a glass of still hot urine, swallowing gobs of fish entrails that had been lying in the sun all day, and biting the heads off lizards and eating them. When he was drunk, Dickey had the strongest cast-iron stomach in the teams, but the next day the real entertainment started.

When Dickey sobered up and we told him what he had done the night before, he showed off his other, and even more entertaining, talent. In only a few seconds Dickey would start getting a little green around the gills; then he'd start to sorta gurgle. It didn't take more than ten seconds for him, like Clark Kent turning into Superman, to become the Vomit Volcano! Everything that he had downed the night before would come back out in a stream that would reach, in some extraordinary displays of projectile vomiting, ten or twelve feet. Even the Vietnamese kids would gather around to watch. Dickey was a great operator, fearless and deadly in combat, always throwing out one-liners that broke everybody up, but it was his gastronomic deeds that kept us all laughing.

With the daily sniper attack over and nothing more to look forward to until tomorrow, Oz, Dickey, Tim, and I caught up with Boomer and Mike McDonald, and they escorted us to the guest quarters where we would be hanging our hats for the next few days. In the back end of the SEAL hooch were a couple of cots draped with mosquito netting where we would stash our gear and get some rack time. In Ha Tien this was what passed for living the high life, but there are a few conveniences that are appreciated by all concerned.

The bar was nothing more than a jury-rigged setup of ammo cans and some scrap wood that served as a top, but there was no shortage of Ba Me Ba beer, booze, and mixers. A SEAL hooch, even a second-rate hooch, just couldn't be called home without a good supply of rum and Coke. Before we could start trying to get Dickey drunk enough to eat lizards, though, we heard Eagle whanging away on the official dinner bell, banging a pot to let everyone know it was time for chow.

Judging from the village and the SEAL hooch, we didn't have high hopes for the local cuisine. We were about to be surprised with fresh salads and all the T-bone steaks and lobster we could eat. Being accomplished doggie-robbers, Osborne and Jack Squires had figured out how to make sure that Bravo ate like this every day. A couple of times a week, they took their beat-up Boston Whaler out for a run to the navy supply ships that were anchored at the mouth of Song Ong Doc River in the Gulf of Thailand. The navy guys, far away from the ground war, were almost desperate to get their hands on anything that they could take home as war trophies. Captured ChiCom SKS and CKC rifles, U.S. World War II .30 caliber carbines, and, best of all, bullet-riddled VC battle flags that one of the mama-sans in the village made for the SEALs were in high demand. Take a nice new fake VC battle flag, drag it around in the dirt, sprinkle it liberally with chicken blood, and it was worth cases of steaks and boxes of lobster and responsible for all of the fresh fruit that Bravo sent over to us on the Seawolf helo every week. Ha Tien may have been lacking in some of the more enjoyable aspects of SEAL life, but when Eagle banged the dinner gong, everybody ate till they were ready to burst.

One of the other advantages of having the navy supply ships so close at hand was that they got daily radio contact from the fleet and could get Armed Forces Radio and even the BBC. It was from these guys that we could get some of the news that took weeks or sometimes months to reach us in the bush. It was from the supply guys that we heard that President Richard Nixon was bombing Cambodia. It was supposed to be a secret, but the word had spread like wildfire. We might have been the last to know, and it didn't make our ops any easier or more effective. We just hoped that the bombing might cut down on the flow of weapons and munitions into South Vietnam. One piece of good news that we celebrated long and hard was that Ho Chi Minh had cashed in his chips, but that good news was followed by some bad news, news that we had a tough time believing. It was reported that massive antiwar demonstrations in Washington, D.C., had attracted over a million protesters. Even worse news was that there had been a massacre of women and children by American troops. It was hard to believe, and even more difficult to understand. We had always done everything that we could, many times risking our own lives, to make sure that noncombatants didn't get caught in the middle of a firefight. But when you cut right down to the bone and ignore all of the pronouncements by people like Carl von Clausewitz about war being politics by other means, the purpose of war is to make the enemy dead, and innocent people die in every war.

The poor peasants all over Vietnam had been killed left and right by the VC and NVA. It took four weeks of house-to-house fighting before the U.S. troops fought them to a standstill and forced them to retreat from the city of Hue. In the rubble of what once had been a beautiful, peaceful city of 120,000 people, the VC left over 2,800 civilian dead behind them when they finally broke and ran. Those innocent people were not caught in a crossfire or killed by random fighting; they were murdered to send a message to every man, women, and parent in Vietnam: Oppose us and we will slaughter you, your children, and your grandchildren. The civilians who died in Hue were victims of premeditated, well-planned summary executions and mass murder, but the newspapers and TV reporters never reported those facts. Nobody liked the idea of innocent people getting killed, but I decided that when it came time for me to mourn the dead, I was going to mourn the men who fought and died for freedom.

After dinner, Eagle Gallagher and Harry Constance, another old friend, let us know that Bravo would be running a GTG, good-to-go, op the next morning, and we were welcome to go along. Briefing would be at 0600, and, as with most of the ops we ran, we had no intel. We were going out looking for trouble.

With only a single helo pad, the platoon would be inserted round robin; Gallagher, Boomer, Harry, and Doc John Myers inserted first and set up a secure perimeter in an area where there had been some rumors of enemy movement. The rest of the platoon, with me and Burton sitting in the doors riding shotgun, inserted as soon as the helo could get us there. The twenty-minute flight was uneventful. We didn't draw even the usual small-arms fire as we sailed along toward the insertion point. With all of us on the ground, close to a small hamlet on a canal, the helo disappeared into the distance. We formed up and patrolled down the trail that ran along virtually every canal in Vietnam. Operating in daylight, moving in plain sight of one hamlet and humping toward a second, was almost like sending an invitation out to the local VC. Every farmer on the rice paddies and fisherman poling a sampan down the canals would send out word that the men with green faces were out hunting. With no intel, that was what we were hoping would happen. We wanted the VC to come looking for us. On this op we got our wish faster than we thought we would.

We hadn't gone more than a few hundred yards when all hell broke loose up at the front of the platoon. Tim and I instinctively dropped to one knee. We could hear rounds ripping through the trees and foliage just above our heads. Even before we could locate any muzzle flash or open fire, Squires gave us the hand signal to move forward and get online so that we could lay down effective fire to the front, the origin of the incoming rounds. As we moved up toward the front of the platoon, I could see Constance with his Stoner and Osborne with his M-60; they were both laying down a withering stream of fire across an open field and into the hamlet we had passed after we inserted. Tim got his M-60 up and running, and I added to the incredible volume of fire being laid down on the hooches and bunkers. Doc Myers and Dickey Cyrus were on either side of me firing 40 mm grenades from the XM-148 launchers slung under their M-16s.

Even with all of us online, firing controlled, effective fire into the hooches and bunkers, we were still taking heavy automatic weapons fire from the tree line—and these VC weren't wasting any ammo. It was close to suicide to stick your head above the dike to return fire for more than a few seconds. Bullets were whanging off the hard ground and turning the dirt into dust. The embankment was high enough to give us some good cover, but we didn't have enough ammunition to maintain the high level of fire forever. Eagle grabbed the handset from the radio Boomer had strapped to his back and started calling for some help. Our first fusillade had reduced our ammunition supply by about half, so we slowed down our rate of fire and returned fire only when we could see a muzzle flash from the tree line that gave us a good target.

Eagle had told us that we were going out looking for trouble, and we sure as shit had found some. Whatever or whoever we had run into had us seriously outnumbered and outgunned. The VC had at least two RPK belt-fed machine guns in the tree line, and it didn't seem as if they were worried about running low on ammo. In the middle of the fight Boomer, paying no attention to the incoming rounds, started crawling around in the dirt on his hands and knees. I couldn't figure out what the hell he was doing, but in a couple of minutes he had laid out the big orange *T* that we normally used to signify an LZ where we wanted a helo to set down. I didn't figure that any helo pilot in or out of his right mind was going to drop onto that LZ, so I grabbed a quick look behind our position to see if there were any gunships headed our way. No helos, but I could see that the VC were in for what would be a terminal surprise for most of them. At about two hundred feet off the deck there were two Black Ponies coming right at us. Boomer had laid out the *T* to show them where our lines were and the location where we would like them to put down as much fire as they could muster. With the marker showing our position and the Eagle giving them distances and directions over the radio, it would be only a few seconds before the Black Ponies started doing their thing.

All of a sudden I heard the familiar, wonderful sound of the wing-mounted M-60s opening up, and it started raining hot 7.62 brass down on our position like a heavy hailstorm. I stuck my head up to get a good look, and the tree line started to turn into boonie salad; pieces of trees, dirt, leaves, and shredded VC were flying all over the place. It's amazing how many rounds those wing-mounted M-60s could light up in a few seconds. At that, the M-60s were only a small part of the weapons that the OV-10A Broncos carried. The Black Ponies were small single-engine, fixed-wing aircraft with dual tails that gave them a predatory, sharklike look. Flown by both navy and marine pilots, they were flying gun and rocket platforms, armed to the teeth. Each Pony carried two M-60 machine guns, a pod of twelve 2.75-inch rockets, and another pod of five 5-inch Zuni rockets under each wing. If the VC had any idea of the kind of hell that the Black Ponies could lay down, they would have pulled up stakes and headed for anywhere not where they were. The VC made a very bad decision; they stood their ground and started trying to shoot down the Black Ponies with small-arms fire as the pilots swung around for a second run. With the VC tracer fire giving them good targets, the Black Ponies made a second pass. For what seemed a long time there was nothing but the howling, growling sound made by the endless stream of M-60 fire. From under their wings an arc of red tracers slammed into the tree line. Then, as they screamed over our heads, they fired their rockets. The sound of rolling thunder as rockets exploded on the VC position almost drowned out the sound of the machine guns. In little more than a minute the Black Ponies had hammered the VC hard, and they were now turning for another run. With only sporadic fire coming from the tree line, Eagle decided that after their next run there wouldn't be anyone left alive to capture and interrogate, or enough left to waste our time trying to find some documents that might be useful. It was time to make a hasty retreat to the rear while the larger VC force was being sliced, diced, and turned into fresh fertilizer by the Black Ponies.

We extracted in a pair of army Slicks, and in twenty minutes we were cleaning our weapons and gear. Over dinner of steak and the biggest shrimp I have ever seen, we got the lowdown on what had happened. It turned out that Eagle was walking point with Constance right behind him with his Stoner, and they had walked right up on two VC sentries that were obviously really lousy at their job. With no time to count VC heads before they decided to engage, they took out the sentries, and the whole company of VC opened up on us. We were outnumbered by about three to one, but like the old saying goes, "Sometimes you get the bear, and sometimes the bear gets you." Thanks to the pilots of those Black Ponies, it was our turn to get the bear.

25

Down Under Op

When we arrived back at our hooch, there was a surprise waiting for us. Two Australian SAS commandos had been attached to our squad. More firepower is always better than less, so Tim and I shook hands with Otis Warren and his chum Victor Kemp. We bought them a couple of cold Ba Me Ba beers and pointed out a pair of cots with mostly intact mosquito netting where they could sack out and stash their gear and "rucks," as they called their backpacks. The unit designation SAS, Special Air Services, might sound like they were some type of paratroopers, but they were really Australia's version of SEALs.

There were a lot of Australians fighting in I Corps and II Corps up north, but I hadn't met any SAS guys until Otis and Victor showed up in our hooch. Someone way above our pay grade had decided that a few SEALs should work with SAS units and a few of them should come spend some time with us. The idea was that maybe we could learn something from one another that would help both of us add to the VC body count. Seemed like a good idea to us, so we dragged out more Ba Me Ba beer and got down to the very serious business of defending the honor of our respective countries. After about an hour, I decided I would never again bet against an Aussie in a beer drinking contest.

As the beer disappeared, they told us that their SOP was usually long-range reconnaissance. They would helo-insert a squad or platoon into some godforsaken shit hole in the middle of East Bumfuck, then spend a week to ten days looking under rocks and into tunnels, caves, bunkers, and any building they came across until somebody shot at them or they found something or somebody that wasn't supposed to be where they were. It seemed like these guys really got their rocks off by planting big charges of C-4 and blowing up tunnels and bunkers full of VC or munitions and supplies. It didn't seem to matter to them which it was as long as the explosion could be heard back home in Australia. On most of their ops they covered a couple of klicks and then called in the extraction helo.

When it was our turn to tell them what they could expect on our ops, they were a little surprised at how different it would be working with a SEAL squad. We almost never did anything but direct action ops based on the best intel we could get from the Chieu Hoi, PRU, or TOC, dig up in the field, or drag out of a prisoner. What really opened up their eyes was that it was common for us to cover two klicks on a single op that only lasted overnight. I told them that they would be getting an advanced degree in balls to the wall, overwhelming firepower, and ambush tactics as soon as we got more good intel worth turning into an operation.

Setting another empty bottle next to the dead soldiers at my feet, I started counting and realized that I had done all I could to uphold the honor of my country, at least until I made some more room in my bladder. It was getting almost dark, so I figured that I could kill two birds with one trip. I hit the head and then went to find Chief Moncrief to see if he had any new intel and find out when we might be able to take Otis and Victor out into the bush. Someone told me that the chief hadn't gotten any new intel, so he was running a one-man, private ambush out in one of the bunkers. I found the chief sitting in a bunker that offered an excellent view overlooking the shit ditch, there was a floodlight up on a pole that gave him a good look at about thirty or forty feet of the ditch and the dirt piled up on both sides. I was a little worried that the chief had gone over the edge, so I ducked in quietly and asked what he was up to. With a smile and a wicked gleam in his beady eyes he said, "Rat ambush. Got three so far, and I'm waiting for the king rat to show up. He's the size of a small dog, and I'm going to skin him and make us a rug for the hooch."

I thought about it. I had been sitting less than twenty yards away from the bunker for the past hour or two. I hadn't heard any shots fired, and I was sure that, even if I had missed hearing it, the chief wouldn't have been so dumb as to fire a rifle that would give the VC a target for a mortar round. I had to ask. "How are you killing them, Chief?" Frank didn't answer; he just held up a silenced .45 caliber grease gun. Well, there is never too much firepower, and the fully automatic, .45 caliber grease gun would certainly repel any rat boarders that tried to rush the bunker. I decided to hang with Frank and watch the festivities in rat land while Tim upheld the honor of our squad and country by drinking as much beer as he could hold.

Before long, a rat the size of a small cat started slinking along the edge of the shit ditch. It was like watching our squad on patrol. Emulating our sneak and peek tactics, he or she stayed just inside the shadows. If that rat had never moved, we would never have known it was there. I guess the odor of fresh C-rats wafting from the open can that Frank was using for bait got the best of the furry piece of vermin, because it kept on skittering along the shit ditch. Then I heard the sound of the bolt of the grease gun smacking the chamber. By just gently tickling the trigger until a single round went off, Frank was able to put a big .45 caliber bullet amidships. The big bullet smacking the rat and dirt sounded like a baseball bat hitting a sack full of sand, drowning out the sound of the grease gun firing. In Vietnam, nothing, not even a dead rat shot through the guts, went to waste. Sooner or later the dead rat would get chomped down by even bigger rats.

Without saying a word, Frank handed me the grease gun and pointed at the shit ditch. Now it was my turn. Taking turns, we depleted the rat population for an hour or so, but the king rat that Frank was hoping would show up must have been too smart. He was probably back in the deep shadows waiting for us to leave so that he could get to all that freshly dead rat meat. If I had been the king rat, that's where I would have been.

Starting to get a little thirsty, we decided to call it a night and head back to the bar in our hooch. Before we could get the welcome-to-the-squad party really rolling, Fallon rang the last call bell and told us we would be briefing at 0700 with liftoff from the helo pad around 0800. Tomorrow morning we were going back into the U Minh forest looking for another POW camp.

Otis and Victor looked sort of sheepish when they stopped me at the bar. It seems that they both had fifteen magazines, but they were short on ammo. Each of them had only enough to fill three magazines with 7.62 mm ammunition for their standard-issue FAL rifles. If we ran into the VC tomorrow, sixty rounds of ammunition per man wasn't going to be anywhere near enough. The problem was that the only 7.62 ammunition we had in the armory was linked into the belted ammo we used to feed our M-60s.

Our SOP for all of our belts and magazines was to load one red tracer, then three standard ball rounds, then another tracer and three more ball rounds until the magazine or belt was full. Even in the dark, when it was impossible to see our sights, the tracers made an almost continuous stream of glowing red bullets that let us adjust our fire into the enemy positions. More than half of the time we didn't need to use our sights at all because we had set up our ambush at close range. On most of our ambush ops, enemy contact was measured in feet or yards; the fight was over before the VC could react or return fire. When the ambush didn't go as planned and we engaged the VC at longer range—across a rice paddy, firing from the protection of a dike, or holed up in a tree line or bunker—the stream of tracers let us adjust our fire in a couple of heartbeats.

I left them alone to delink the M-60 ammunition and load up their magazines. I don't know how long it took them, but they delinked two cases of M-60 ammunition and filled up all of their twenty-round magazines while I was getting some rack time. Even with raw, blistered fingertips from stripping all of those links, they were smiling, civil, ready to go, and even cracking jokes about the Yanks at 0600 the next morning. Having fifteen full magazines, plenty of extra loose ammunition, and a couple of grenades in your ruck has that effect on most people who are heading into VC controlled territory.

The briefing was short. We would be inserting on two helos at Nam Can in the U Minh forest. This was as close to the location where the latest intel said the POW camp was located as we could get without letting them know that we were headed in their direction. From our insertion point, we would patrol a little over a mile past a couple of small hamlets, where we would do our best to get more hot intel from the locals. Fallon had arranged for a combat interpreter named Fong, an experienced member of the PRU team, to come along to interrogate the local farmers. Fong would also come in handy in case we found the POW camp and needed to extract prisoners who only spoke Vietnamese. Not many of us spoke Vietnamese, but we had figured out that no matter how loud you yelled at people who don't speak English, the added volume never seemed to help. With Fong, Otis, and Victor going along on the op, we now had ten combat-tested-and-proven ass-kickers who would be hunting for the POW camp. Otis and Victor didn't know what to expect, but I was sure that if we found the POW camp or made contact with the VC, the way that SEALs fought would be a new experience for the guys from "down under."

The squad, all carrying as much ammunition as we could hump and still move fast and quiet, loaded onto two army helos and headed south. As we approached our insertion point, the pilots dropped down to treetop level, and Fong and Lieutenant Moran pointed out a field near a six-hooch hamlet right alongside another canal. Almost before the skids of the helos were off the ground, we were formed up and headed for the hamlet and the welcoming party that had stopped what they were doing to eyeball our approach. While we waited in our security perimeter, Fallon and Fong had a chat with what appeared to be the headman of the hamlet. After fifteen or twenty minutes of palavering with the headman and just about everyone else in the hamlet, they headed back to where we had set up our perimeter with one of the farmers in tow. With Fong and the farmer out front on point, we headed out across the field in the direction of the tree line. The shortest route across the field would take us past half a dozen water buffalo that looked like they could get nasty and a herd of ducks that squawked, flapped their wings, and shit just about everywhere as they dusted off for the edges of the field. Even out here in VC territory I kept an eye on the buffalo. The last thing I wanted was to be the only SEAL KIA by a glorified cow.

At the tree line, the farmer pointed out a two-foot-wide trail and told Fong that it would take us into the area where the intel said the POW camp was located. Of course, he had never heard of a POW camp, so we should let him get back to his chores. Not today, pal. I would bet that the poor bastard was so scared of retaliation that he probably wouldn't admit that he had ever heard of the VC, either. With the farmer and Fong still out front, we headed down the trail along the canal and ran into some of the thickest bush I have ever seen. Even the dense jungle of the Panama Canal Zone wasn't any worse than this three-tiered morass that turned daylight into twilight in only a couple of yards. As we patrolled through the dank, gloomy bush, I started thinking to myself that this must get to be a really interesting place after the sun goes down. Even the brightest light from a full moon wouldn't have a chance of reaching the ground; it would be like patrolling blindfolded in the bottom of a coal mine. Even the idea of close air support in this crap was out of the question. Artillery or naval gunfire support might penetrate the trees, but there were no ships or artillery bases anywhere close to being in range. If the shit hit the fan in here, we were all alone, and help wasn't likely going to be on the way anytime soon.

In the gloom we humped silently along, closely watching every step for booby traps and snakes. The farther we got from the hamlet, the smaller the trail became and the wider the canal grew. About a mile into the jungle, the canal was now about twenty feet across, and I was hoping that we didn't have to get to the other side. The dark water didn't look inviting, and the local leeches probably hadn't had a good meal for a long time. I was thinking that being a POW in this dark, depressing, seemingly endless gloom would be enough to make most men lose their will to fight, and maybe their mind, when the signal came back that a booby trap had been discovered. Booby traps are only used by people who have something to protect and who don't want anybody sneaking up on them, or who want to get an ambush off to a good start. It made sense that a POW camp would be located near a canal. It would provide easy access by sampan for resupply and a source of drinking water for the VC and the prisoners. It was only a minute or two before word was passed back that the booby trap was old and probably nonfunctional, but there was no reason to take any unnecessary risks; we were going to move off of the trail.

We formed up into an assault line and moved slowly through the trees and bush. We hadn't gone much more than fifty yards when we found ourselves almost standing on the perimeter of what once must have been the POW camp. Although POW ops were at the top of our list and we would always go after them no matter the cost, none of us had ever seen a POW camp before. It looked as if the whole camp had been built on the spot with material that could be gathered up by the prisoners right there in the jungle. We went down onto one knee at the edge of a well-constructed double fence made of lashed-together bamboo poles that encircled the whole perimeter. We listened and waited for a couple of minutes to see if there would be any movement or sound. From my vantage point I could see two hooches, a bunker, and several sleeping platforms made out of bamboo that were three or four feet above the ground. It looked like another dead-end op; there was nobody home and no sound.

When the farmer and Fong started walking toward the camp, I was sure that it was long deserted. The farmer wouldn't have gone anywhere near the camp if it was dangerous or he might get his ass shot full of holes. The farmer took the lead with Fong right behind him as we walked along the fence. We came to what had once been a gate, also made of bamboo, that had fallen halfway to the ground. The camp was empty, but we sent the farmer into each hooch and the bunker to see if there was anything that might give us some information about who had been held here. Uniform buttons, a shoe, a Bible hidden in the thatched roof of a hut, anything that might give us some information would have been useful, would have made the op worthwhile, but there was nothing left behind. The camp had been scoured clean. There was a pile of ash and burned-up odds and ends in the center of the camp, evidence that whatever they couldn't take with them had been torched. Even if we hadn't known that this was a POW camp, it wouldn't have been hard to figure it out from the double bamboo fence, six-foot-deep isolation pits covered with corrugated tin to keep the prisoners from escaping, and three broken-down bamboo cages that had once held prisoners now long gone, or dead. There was no question that this was the camp we had been looking for, but the intel was just too damn old.

It was getting late in the afternoon, and we didn't want to spend the night anywhere near here, so we formed up an assault line and moved out. So that we could move slowly and cautiously but not need to waste any time searching for booby traps, we went out the same way we had come in. We were sure that the word had gone out in the countryside that we were in the neighborhood, and we didn't want any surprises that we could avoid. When we reached the edge of the rice paddy, we let the farmer go back to his hamlet and decided that we didn't want to extract from the place where we had inserted. With a couple of hours of daylight left, we patrolled inside of the tree line toward a remote corner of the field where there would be enough room for the helos to land and load us aboard. We hadn't moved more than fifty or sixty yards when we halted and Lieutenant Moran signaled back that he could see enemy forces ahead. Down on one knee, with the muzzle of my Stoner covering my field of fire, I looked out across the field and could now see why Fallon and Fong had halted the squad. The VC were all well back, inside the tree line, but now I could see movement on the far side of the paddy just inside the cover of a banana grove.

The VC were forming up an ambush of their own, hoping that we would return to extract from the same area where we had inserted this morning. I could see Fallon looking toward the paddy through the powerful spotting scope he always carried. We moved quickly into a 360-degree security perimeter and waited to be told what was going on across the field. He turned around, staying behind the tree he was using for cover, and used hand signals to let us know that he had seen a minimum of seven VC with weapons.

Lieutenant Moran and Boomer were huddled in the center of our perimeter making sure that we had radio contact. Pulling the security perimeter tight, Chief Moncrief told us that it looked like the VC were setting up an ambush on the spot where we had inserted this morning and hadn't seen or smelled us yet. With the advantage of us knowing where they were, and them not even knowing that we were in the same grid square on the map, Lieutenant Moran decided to keep it that way. He got on the radio and called in a gunfire support mission. Even before he was done sending, a single Black Pony, who luckily was carrying a full load of munitions, told us that he would be covering our backside within fifteen minutes. Moran told the pilot that he would appreciate it if he came in for his run right over our heads; we would lay down an LZ marker with the top of the *T* in the direction of the VC and would lay down tracer fire in their direction when we heard his approach.

With the Black Pony on its way, we found as much cover as we could, formed up the squad for an ambush, and watched the movement in the banana grove. The paddy dike would give the VC some cover, but the banana plants were leafy and not much good for stopping bullets or shrapnel. The banana plants wouldn't be worth jack shit for cover when the Black Pony opened up on their position with rocket and machine-gun fire from two hundred feet off the deck. We might not have found the POWs, but we were, as sure as shit runs downhill, going to turn that line of banana plants into a VC graveyard.

Boomer had just finished laying out the LZ marker when we heard the shriek of the engine of the Black Pony coming our way. As soon as we got a visual on the streaking dot, Lieutenant Moran opened up on the VC position with tracers, and the rest of us joined in to make sure that if there was anything left it wouldn't be much more than smoking rubble. With eight rifles and two machine guns firing full auto, there were multiple streams of tracers pouring into the VC. The Black Pony pilot didn't have to guess where we wanted him to lay down his load. The sound of his wing-mounted M-60s and the almost simultaneous explosion of half a dozen 2.75-inch rockets only added to the deafening roar.

It was amazing that there were any VC still alive, but as he pulled up for a second run, green tracers came arching from the VC position, chasing after him as he gained altitude. If there were VC still able to fire, we figured that we should help the pilot out and keep their heads down or make them KIA. Our 40 mm grenades just didn't have the range to get all the way to the banana grove, but my LAAW rocket could make that range easily. As I cocked the rocket I wondered if the leaves of the banana plants would be tough enough for the LAAW to detonate. I didn't think that I could get an airburst, but, much to my surprise, the LAAW worked perfectly, airbursting over their position, reducing the return fire to almost nothing. If there were any VC still alive and kicking, they were probably heading for parts unknown as fast as they could get there.

As the Black Pony made a second pass, we heard the rotors of the extraction helos whup-whupping our way. They were flanked by two gunships looking for something to blast to kingdom come. If there were any VC left fit to fight, this just might turn into a real war.

The army helos rolled in just above the treetops and dropped into the LZ only a few yards from our position. We loaded aboard, and the pilots put as much empty space between us and the ground as fast as they could. I was sitting in the open doorway of the helo, holding onto the D-ring in the deck and looking for targets for the fresh load in my Stoner, when the Black Pony made his last run, waggled his wings, and headed for home. The four door gunners on the gunships hadn't come this far to go home with all their ammo. They laid down a solid stream of fire into the tree line, making sure that there wouldn't be anyone shooting at us as we lifted off and headed out of the bush.

Otis and Victor made the thirty-minute helo trip with eyes as big as saucers; they never said a word. This was a new kind of warfare for these two Aussies, and it was one of several lessons that they would take back to their units with them. Lieutenant Berg and a couple of his crew were waiting for us with our ground transport back to base when we landed at the helo pad in Quan Long. I gave Otis and Victor a hand up onto a 4-by-4. Although their eyes had shrunk back to almost normal size, they still could barely talk. All they kept saying was that they had almost run out of ammo and that they had never seen that much ammunition used up so fast. I suggested that they might think about finding more magazines and carrying more ammo.

26

Dickey's Revenge

The end of our tour was only three weeks away, so we spent most of our time digging for more intel that might lead to another hot op and running sneak and peek and ambush ops whenever we got a sniff of where we might find the VC. Otis and Victor were quickly turning into almost regular members of our squad. They were becoming accustomed to delinking 7.62 ammunition to feed their rifles for a couple of hours every morning, then going out every night to set up an ambush for VC who didn't show up. They were as frustrated as we were after a long night with no contact and even started swearing as much, and with as much originality and fervor, as even the "saltiest" SEALs. They even started buying us drinks when we extracted with almost nothing to show for the long night but more mosquito bites and the suspicion that the VC were getting more intel about us than we were about them.

Although the VC had eluded our ambush, Otis and Victor did learn a little about wildlife and the indigenous species of the canals of Vietnam on our last dry op. The PRU had captured a low-level VC recruiter, and he had spilled his guts when the interrogators had started sharpening their knives and smiling at him with a wicked gleam in their eyes. The intel was that the VC would be running three or four sampans loaded with mortar tubes, munitions, and food down the canal that night. This recruiter had arranged for twelve locals to meet the sampans and, with the help of the VC on the sampans, they would transport the load to several pre-dug caches and hide the supplies until they were needed. It looked as if we had fresh intel, but when the source of your intel was only one low-level VC who was trying to make sure that nobody would be slowly slicing off the most important parts of his anatomy, it was anything but a sure bet that it was worth chasing. With only a few weeks left before the long ride home, we decided it was worth taking the chance; maybe he wasn't as full of shit as most of the low-level VC that had been interrogated by the PRU team.

Lieutenant Berg and his crew gave us a ride down the Song Ong Doc River on their MSSC, inserted us in a mangrove swamp, then pulled back into the river to await further developments or our call for extraction at daybreak. With no good cover where we could set up an ambush on the bank of the canal, we decided that we had no choice but to set up in the swamp itself. I didn't like the snakes or mosquitoes, but I really hated leeches. As much as I wanted to set up on dry land—hell, even in the mud would have been better—a few leeches more or less wouldn't change the situation. We would be spending the night up to our waists in the mangroves again. If the VC pulled another no-show, I was going to be really pissed.

We were well hidden, several yards deep in the mangrove trees, but we still commanded a good field of fire for about two hundred yards up and down the canal through the openings between the trees. We had formed up our ambush with Otis and Victor about six feet to my right and Fallon, upstream to my left, on point. The VC recruiter that had been taken prisoner told the PRU that the sampans would be heading from the canal toward the river, so we picked a tight turn in the canal to set up our ambush. The sampans wouldn't be moving very fast in the sluggish current, and they would have to slow down even further when they reached the turn to avoid smacking into the mangroves in the darkness. I was hoping that we would get lucky, that the VC would be playing their transistor radio and using lanterns to light their way through the swamp. If we got that lucky, their night vision would be nonexistent, and they sure weren't going to hear us.

We planned to spring the ambush when they were dead center of our field of fire. Even after hundreds of nights spent in the bush, the silence of a swamp at night was almost spooky. If a bird flew, we knew that something had disturbed it, and all eyes swiveled toward the sound, but we never looked directly in the direction of the sound. We had been trained to "look past" whatever it was that we wanted to see in the dark, to use our peripheral vision, where the rods and cones are concentrated and suck in even minute amounts of light, to give us another edge in the bush.

With the silence and darkness came the suspense. Would the VC show up, or were we just feeding the bugs and leeches again? If they did show up, could we grab a couple of them alive and could the PRU or TOC get some intel out of them that we could turn into a sledgehammer to use against their higher-level infrastructure? Would they actually have anything worth destroying or capturing, or would they be hauling just some rice, a few old, rusty, bolt-action rifles, and ammunition made before World War II? If we got very lucky, we might grab up someone on command level and his maps and documents bag. If nobody showed up, it was going to be another long night with no contact.

After working more than twenty ambush operations with our squad, our Aussie pals, Otis and Victor, had learned most of our SOPs. They had shown us that their fire discipline was 100 percent and that they were as reliable and fearless in a firefight as anyone but a fool could be. There was one thing that we had failed to teach them, though, and, as it turned out, tonight would be one more lesson that they would take back to their platoon. It was about five hours into the ambush, and I hadn't seen anything move or heard a sound. Then I heard a familiar grunt, and Victor let out a scream and started bashing the water with the butt of his FAL. He was so close and screaming so loud that I almost dropped my Stoner. Unseen and moving silently through the water, a nine- or ten-foot croc had floated up to the poor Aussie and let out a mating call. Almost scared out of his boots, Victor smacked him in the head with the butt of his FAL, then did his best to take a stroll across the surface of the canal to get to dry land.

The ruckus ended our ambush, and while we waited for Lieutenant Berg to come make the extraction, I let Victor know that the croc wasn't hungry; the sound he had heard was a mating grunt. That poor, love-starved croc was just looking for a girlfriend, and Victor had ruined his whole night.

Back at our base before daybreak, we cleaned our weapons and gear, got some rack time, grabbed some hot chow, and checked in with the TOC and the PRU advisers to see if any new intel had come in. After too many dead-end ops we were itching to get some real intel that we could use to catch the VC with their pants down. There was no good news, no good intel, so a little after noon we threw in the towel; no op tonight. We spent the afternoon taking care of all of the details that needed to be taken care of so that we were always ready to move out with little notice.

Ammunition supply check, munitions supply check, everything that we needed to operate was checked and double-checked. Now we could relax and eat a great dinner. Dickey Cyrus had sent us a couple of crates full of shrimp and steaks, and we all ate like kings. Then we opened the bar; the drinking light was shining bright, and we were ready for a long night of bullshit and tall tales of derring-do. I was just about to order the first of a dozen or two cocktails when Fallon came in and told me that he had something out on the gun-cleaning table that I had asked for last week. He had taken pity on Otis and Victor and had traded a case of five LAAW rockets and bottle of Hennessy cognac to the PRU chief for two cases of loose 7.62 rounds for the Aussie FAL rifles. In South Vietnam, cognac is like Scotch to Scotsmen, vodka to Russians, and Jim Beam to rednecks. When he was a PRU adviser, Fallon had traded bottles of Hennessy for just about anything he needed. A single bottle of Hennessy bought artillery support from the South Vietnamese 155 mm batteries, and even prisoners—a couple of village chiefs, district chiefs, and province chiefs who might have some good intel—somehow ended up in our care after two bottles changed hands. He had even swapped Hennessy for several sampans and junks that were used on our ops. With a couple of bottles of Hennessy and a good line of bullshit, Fallon could get just about anything that we needed to reach out and touch the VC. He always had a couple of cases of Hennessy stashed under his bunk, but he used them sparingly and only when he really wanted something special. To sweeten the deal, he threw in the LAAW rockets as a lagniappe, a bonus that we hoped would be put to good use by the PRU. I was sure that Otis and Victor would appreciate the loose ammo; their fingertips were always red and raw from delinking those thousands of rounds of 7.62 ammunition that we used in our M-60 machine guns.

With a few drinks under our belts and daylight fast failing, Frank and I decided that it was time to set up another ambush for King Rat. For bait Frank opened up a can of ham and lima beans—we didn't eat that crap anyhow—and set it out on the bank of the shit ditch. With the silenced grease gun in my lap, we settled in to wait for the rats to forget that we had just put out the C-rat bait and to come slinking into the area illuminated by the big floodlight that lit up our field of fire. It wasn't more than a minute or two before three small rats started skittering toward the open C-rats. They were being cautious, but it was obvious that none of the little bastards wanted their brethren to get to the can before they did. They were only a couple of feet from the bait when they disappeared into the night; King Rat was on the scene and he was hungry. Just as I started to raise the grease gun, Frank told me that he needed to take a shit and started to stand up. I told him that we might not get a shot at the king if he didn't sit his ass down and stay motionless. Frank, being the thoughtful kinda guy he was, took a dump in the empty ammo can he had been using as a makeshift stool, closed the airtight lid, locked it in place, and sat back down to wait for further developments.

King Rat must have sensed that the smaller rats were too close for his dining pleasure, because he started running around the shit ditch at high speed like a crazed chihuahua, chasing at shadows and making sure that the little rats knew that the boss was in town and he was gonna have his dinner before they even got a sniff of the ham and lima beans. He finally slipped down the embankment, and I saw his whiskers twitching as he sniffed at the C-rats. At the edge of the open can, he sat up like an overgrown prairie dog. Using both of his front feet like hands, he started stuffing his face with ham and lima beans. Only ten feet away from the muzzle of the grease gun, this poor critter didn't have a chance. I took careful aim and put a .45 caliber bullet dead center of the C-rat can, blowing its greasy contents all over the shit ditch and sending the can five feet into the air. King Rat almost turned himself inside out, and his clawed feet left dig marks in the dirt as he hauled his ass for the darkest piece of bush he could find. Frank and I were laughing like two inmates who got loose from an asylum. Frank slapped me on the shoulder and told me that he would have done the same thing. Now that he was wise to our ambush, King Rat would be even more difficult to hunt; it would now be a bigger challenge, and we would have even more fun the next time we went rat hunting. As we exited the rat bunker on our way to the hooch lounge and a few more drinks, Frank threw the ammo can up onto the top of the bunker. Back at the hooch bar with a couple of cold Ba Me Ba beers, we let the squad know that we had chosen to let the king rat live for another hunt; there wouldn't be a nice new rat-fur rug in the hooch anytime soon. While our marksmanship was being derided by the entire squad, Lieutenant Moran and Fallon put the damper on the evening by announcing that the drinking light was out and briefing would be at 0700 tomorrow morning. We had some new intel, and we would be going on a rare daylight hunting trip.

Breakfast was early and quick; briefing was short and sweet. A VC squad, at least according to the intel, was moving into a district west of Quan Long City and intimidating the villagers in the area. Once again Lieutenant Berg and his merry crew of ne'er-do-wells would be providing transport and entertainment in and out. We were going to go out in broad daylight and patrol through the entire area, several scattered hamlets and a fairly large village, just daring the VC to come after us. If we got lucky, maybe they were that suicidal; if not, we might just catch them asleep at the switch and toast their ass. Fallon was planning on getting really fresh intel by sweet-talking the local fishermen and farmers. Hell, it was their food that the VC were stealing and their sons and daughters that the VC were dragging away to "volunteer" their services to Uncle Ho. Maybe they had had enough and would spill enough of the beans to give us a start at tracking the VC down and making them dead.

It was unlikely that the VC would take the risk of engaging our squad in daylight, even if they outnumbered us ten to one, but we were tired of lousy intel, long nights twiddling our thumbs, crocs that wanted to make smoochy-face with our Aussie friends, and nothing to show for it. We started the day off by patrolling up the canal to the first village where Fallon wanted to have a friendly chat with the locals. Much to our surprise, Victor spoke fluent French and not bad Vietnamese. He had a little talk with a group of farmers who were on their way to the fields for a twelve-hour day of busting their hump trying to drag a living out of the dirt. They confirmed that there was a VC squad in the area that had been hitting up the hamlets and trying their best to forcibly take the VC taxes out of the village chief. With the first fresh intel we had had in weeks, we decided that it might be a good idea to head on into Long San village and have a heart-to-heart with the head man. Maybe he was fed up with paying the VC taxes and could give us the skinny on where the VC hung their hats.

Long San village was about two klicks away, so we decided that speed was more important than stealth on this operation; we followed the dikes and paths along the irrigation canals hoping that the VC might still be in the area and that we could catch up to them. Ron Rogers was on point with his M-60 and I was covering our back door with my Stoner as we made a beeline through another small hamlet without even slowing down. As the squad exited the hamlet, something told me to take one last look. I don't know what had spooked them— if they had just sat tight we would have disappeared in the distance—but when I turned around for a last look I saw three men with rifles come sprinting out of a hooch toward the canal. These had to be the dumbest VC in Vietnam. How fast did they think they could run across a canal? The canal was three feet deep, and the bottom was soft, gooey mud, buffalo shit, rotting vegetation, and who knows what else. Sure as shit, when they hit the canal they would be running in slow motion. I thumbed the safety off, waited until they were only a few feet from the canal, and opened up with a 150-round burst from my Stoner, and they became fertilizer. Lieutenant Moran, when he wrote up the citation, put it more gracefully; he said that I "denied the enemy from reaching the other side." Yeah, I denied them stone cold dead right there.

The squad put themselves in reverse and set up a quick security perimeter, and Tim Baron and Ron Rogers went to see what, if anything, of interest might be left. They dragged the two bodies, a ChiCom SKS rifle, and some grenades up onto the bank. Chief Moncrief decided that this was a great way to start the patrol, but that since these guys were not going to be giving us any intel we had better start looking for their pals because they were probably damn close. Lieutenant Moran called for a pair of gunships to come help us spot the rest of the VC squad, but we were not going to wait for air support. We changed our line of march to match the direction where the now dead VC had been heading and started humping as fast as we could.

As soon as we crossed the canal, we saw six or eight armed men trying to run across a rice paddy right in front of us. I had been wrong about the three VC I had nailed; the guys running away from us through a rice paddy had to be the dumbest VC in all of Vietnam. When they finally figured out that they were never going to reach the cover of the bush before we opened up, they opened up on full auto and started laying down a shitstorm of AK-47 fire. Rogers, Victor, and Lieutenant Moran on point opened up with full automatic fire as the rest of us moved up online. Even the grass around us was being cut down by the tracers coming our way. Fallon spun around like a top and dropped, but he was back on his feet and firing almost as fast as he fell. Lieutenant Moran was on the radio to the Seawolf gunships, and they wanted to know who was where on the battlefield. They could see men running everywhere and tracers flying, but from the air it was hard to identify the good guys. Moran popped smoke to ID our position, and the gunships started lighting up the VC. With four M-60 machine guns and 40 mm automatic grenade fire raking their position near the dike, the firefight didn't last more than ten or fifteen seconds.

As the Seawolf helos circled above the paddy, we moved out to the dike and found seven dead and dying VC. Our platoon medic, Doc John Myers, was up in Ha Tien operating with Eagle Gallagher, so Ron Rogers, our M-60 gunner, was filling in for him. Ron patched up Fallon's leg, which had been hit by a single round of AK-47 fire. It was a clean through-and-through that missed the bone and hadn't hit any major blood vessels. Since Fallon was still on his feet and giving orders, it didn't look like the bullet hole was causing him too much discomfort. With Fallon patched up and back on his feet, Ron tried his level best to save the lives of two badly wounded VC so that we could extract them for interrogation. He got IVs started and battle dressings applied, but they were bleeding out fast; blood was squirting from too many holes. Ron jabbed them with a couple of shots of morphine to put them out of their pain.

We gathered up the weapons and everything else that might have some intel value and started humping back to the Song Ong Doc River. Lieutenant Berg had been following all the action on his radio and was waiting for us. The Seawolves circled overhead, covering our extraction, until we were aboard the MSSC and headed back to base. The next day Lieutenant Moran would take the weapons we recovered, a CKC, a couple of SKS rifles, and two AK-47s, over to the Seawolf detachment as thanks for covering our ass and our extraction. The papers and documents we captured didn't have anything that could lead to another operation. It was a good op, and Fallon was healing up, so it was time to say so long to our Aussie pals with an all-nighter in the hooch bar and grill. Otis and Victor would be loading up on a Caribou aircraft the following morning and heading back to their platoon in the north.

Our time was really getting short on our own tour of duty, but Eagle Gallagher up in Ha Tein had been kicking so much ass that Dickey Cyrus sent down a request for a quick resupply of ammunition. He needed LAAW rockets, 7.62 mm linked, 5.56 mm linked and ball, claymores, grenades, and anything else that would go bang and wasn't nailed down. Before I put together an ammo shipment for Dickey, though, I drove Otis and Victor to the air base in the jeep that I had stolen for our use and saw them off in grand style with a precious bottle of Hennessy brandy. As I arrived back at the base I noticed that it was monthly cleanup day. A bunch of Vietnamese kids that we hired were picking up every piece of litter and junk that had accumulated over the last month.

As I pulled up in front of our hooch, I noticed that two kids were cleaning out the bunker next to the shit ditch. One of the kids threw down a familiar-looking ammunition can from the top of the bunker. It was the still sealed ammo can that Frank had used a couple of weeks ago to avoid spooking King Rat—it had been sitting in the sun for almost two weeks, and the sides were bulging. This could be dangerous. An ammo can, when closed and dogged down, is airtight. Inside that can was a biological by-product of Frank's digestive tract. It was just chock-full of all kinds of microbial agents that were turning the semisolid mess into an explosive gas that was now under high enough pressure to bulge the sheet steel sides of the ammo can. I knew instantly that this situation needed to be handled by an explosives expert, and who better than my old friend Dickey Cyrus? Nope, there was no question that Bravo squad in Ha Tien could handle this touchy problem with ease.

As I packed up Dickey's shipment of ammunition and munitions, I made sure that I left enough room to slip the ammo can with Frank's little deposit right in the middle of all of the other ammo cans on the pallet that a Seawolf would be delivering to the Ha Tien helo pad later that day. Luckily, both Fallon and Tim Baron went along for the ride and saw what happened; they gave me the blow by blow down to the smallest and most hilarious detail.

Knowing that the ammo resupply was on its way, Dickey was waiting for the helo and immediately started checking the inventory list that covered everything he had ordered up. Everything was as ordered, but there was one extra can of what the stenciled lettering said was linked 5.56 mm ammunition. Now Dickey started getting suspicious. This can wasn't supposed to be there, it was bulging suspiciously, and it could even be booby-trapped. Not to take any chances with the suspicious ammo can, Dickey ordered the helo pad cleared of all personnel, the kids that always showed up when a helo lands, and all of the ammo except for this one little can. With everyone else taking cover, Dickey was all by himself on the pad with the suspicious ammo can. Carefully, crawling on his hands and knees, Dickey cautiously felt around the edge of the airtight can for any trip wires. With no trip wires or other devices that could fire a booby trap discovered, Dickey slowly and carefully lifted the latch that holds the airtight lid of the ammo can in place. In a split second the latch, driven by the now enormous pressure of expanding gas, slammed away from the locked position, allowing the lid to be blown open, and a shower of what had begun as one of Frank Moncrief's finest dumps spewed forth, spattering Dickey from head to toe. The stench, as described by Fallon, who was fifty feet away, would have gagged a starving buzzard, but that wasn't the worst part. In half a heartbeat Dickey knew what had happened to him, and the realization that he was covered in reeking, weeks-old shit got his vomit comet running wide open.

Fortunately, Dickey Cyrus could always take a good joke, and the weekly shipment of goodies that he scrounged up or doggie-robbed at the resupply ships showed up right on time. Thanks to Dickey, we always got great food delivered weekly. Tonight we would be dining on fresh lobster and steak and Dickey had sent us a whole bushel basket full of fresh oranges. Such a rare treat deserved to be savored, so we stacked them on the bar, saving them for desert.

Stuffed to the gills and ready to toss back a few drinks, just about everyone was peeling one. None of us could wait to get that first big juicy bite. The oranges were perfectly ripe and juicy, and the smell of citrus oil from the peels was almost as alluring as the smell of a beautiful woman. As we all took a big bite and the juice ran down our chins, we realized that these oranges tasted awful. All of us looked around at the rest of the squad and were all thinking the exact same thing. Those beautiful, juicy oranges tasted like someone had pissed on them. We all broke up laughing as we spit out the orange pulp and grabbed for anything we could use to wash out our mouths. I don't know how long it took Dickey, but I'm sure that, using the syringe he talked Doc into loaning him, it took at least a couple of hours to inject every one of those oranges. Dickey had taken his revenge.

27

Fair Winds and
Following Seas

In a week the 9th Platoon would be saddling up and turning our base over to whoever needed some extra space or wanted to sleep in the rusty racks under ratty mosquito netting. When Clausewitz said, "War is a continuation of politics by another means" he hit the nail on the head. Politics would be the nail that sealed our coffin in Vietnam; no SEALs were being sent to replace us. Our ass was in the wind, and we didn't have a sail or a rudder.

In February of 1970, just outside of Paris, France, and away from the glare of media coverage and distractions of anything related to the reality of the war, Henry Kissinger had initiated secret meetings with North Vietnamese negotiator Le Duc Tho. After three years of negotiations in Paris, the only accomplishment had been hard fought and difficult; our brilliant negotiators had agreed on the shape of the tables where the delegates would sit. The war in Vietnam was becoming increasingly unpopular with the American people, and Nixon and Kissinger had bigger fish to fry; they were focused on what would keep them in the White House, rapprochement and détente with Russia and China. The half-million men and women who had put their boots on the ground and their lives at risk, who fought the war in Vietnam, were now no more than another pawn on a deadly chessboard. President Nixon had promised "peace with honor." He lied; Nixon and Kissinger had decided to put Vietnam behind them before the next election.

While American troops were protecting and defending the liberty and freedom of 150 million people and every sacred word of the Constitution and Bill of Rights, Nixon and his gang of co-conspirators were ignoring the two documents that make our nation worthy of any sacrifice. Nixon's men were preparing to commit political suicide by breaking into the Watergate Apartments. Politics in America had become a shit sandwich, and all of us who served in Vietnam were the meat in the middle.

With no SEAL platoon coming in to relieve us, it was time to say good-bye to all of the friends that we had made in the Twilight Zone. Normally we would turn over everything that we wouldn't be taking home to the next platoon, but with no platoon to carry on our ops, the booty would be distributed helter-skelter to everyone who had become one of our brothers. Lieutenant Berg and his merry men ended up with some new weapons and a couple of bottles of Fallon's stash of Hennessy, as did the Seawolf pilots and crew who covered our ass when the shit was flying. Lieutenant Roberts at the TOC got anything he asked for and could have had the fillings in our teeth if he had asked. My jeep, captured weapons, and all of the food that Dickey Cyrus had doggie-robbed and hadn't been devoured at our send-off party got spread around as equitably as possible. The hooch maids, most of them old enough to be my grandmother, got anything that wasn't nailed down or claimed by our friends. Even they didn't want the ham and lima bean C-rats. Not to be wasted, they were opened and lined up along the shit ditch for one last big chow-down for King Rat and his pals.

Flying over the dead zone of mud and brown vegetation on our way to Tan Son Nhut Air Base, it seemed almost as if I had been on another planet for the past three years. What struck me most was that even with the lack of virtually everything I looked forward to being back in the world, I had spent most of three years in a time and place of incredible privilege. The men sitting in the belly of the twin-engine Caribou, even Dickey Cyrus and his piss oranges, had become more than fellow warriors who would die protecting my back if needed. I had done what each of these men had. I knew what was required and demanded to earn the right to become a SEAL. I also knew that we had become more than any of us had dreamed we could become, and maybe that was what made us SEALs.

We had all volunteered for the SEAL Teams and UDT, but volunteering had been our privilege. We had been allowed to choose to serve. Somehow we had been given a gift that damn few men, no matter how much they wanted it or how hard they tried to achieve it, would ever receive. This wasn't just a gift that was given because you had made it, because you had survived the training, the hardships, and the fighting. It wasn't an even trade—you do this, you get that. Each of these men, and almost every man who has earned the trident, gives the gift or never truly becomes a SEAL. This gift goes far beyond blood, guts, honor, and life or death. It cannot, even by those in the teams, be explained well.

It is not a feeling of superiority, nor is it only the appreciation and acceptance of your teammates. It is, I believe, that you have been allowed to do your duty, to believe beyond all rational thought or comprehensible ideology that you are living a life, no matter how flawed, that matters, that is of value, in a world overpopulated by liars, bullshitters, bastards, dictators, and strutting demigods. At that moment, sitting in the Caribou, listening to the drone of the engines, and hoping that they'd keep on turning until we were on the ground at Tan Son Nhut, I realized that I was one of the luckiest men who had ever been born.

With nine hours to kill before wheels up on the first leg of our trip across the world to Wake Island, Midway, Coronado, and finally Norfolk, we had plenty of time to load up our gear and catch up on what had been going on while we were dragging our sorry ass through the bush. Even the *Stars and Stripes* was running articles about the antiwar protesters and demonstrations back home. Other newspapers mirrored these articles, and I started wondering what the hell these people could be thinking. If they gave a rat's ass about people on the other side of the globe and understood what was going to happen to the Vietnamese and Cambodian people if we pulled out our forces and left the North Vietnamese in power, they might have been singing in a very different choir.

It was a long trip home. The crowd waiting for us to land at the naval air station terminal swarmed the aircraft almost before the chocks were in place. At the base of the movable stairway, wives, girlfriends, family, and friends hugged, kissed, and welcomed everyone for their first night back at home. While most of the platoon got rides to the base with their families or friends, I decided to grab a ride back to the Amphib base on the bus. It had been a very good tour; we hadn't accomplished as much as we would have liked, and the POW camp raids hadn't freed a single prisoner, but we had done some very serious damage to the VC infrastructure, and we had all come home. The few minor wounds we had picked up along the way had been handled by Doc Myers. As we unloaded the truck and stacked our gear, I started thinking about all of the close calls that I remembered, and I realized that there were probably many, many more that I didn't even know had ever happened. I was on the roster for a slot as a PRU adviser, but there were several men senior to me that would get those slots. My chances at getting back to operate in the bush didn't look too good. Maybe it was time for me to settle in and stash myself away in the ordnance department of SEAL Team 2 for a six-month break. There was probably a lot I could learn, and maybe something interesting would turn up.

Back at the base, my 1966 GTO was right where I had left it, up on blocks next to the engineering building with the tires and battery, on a trickle charger, inside the building. We off-loaded our gear and didn't have anything to do until quarters at 0800 the following morning. The keys were still in the ignition, the rent on our apartment on the beach was all paid up, and there was going to be a serious party, so Mike and I reattached the wheels, bolted in the battery, fired up the GTO, and headed for the Casino for our welcome-home blast. Beer was always on the house for platoons returning from Vietnam, but I didn't want to spend this homecoming alone. I made a quick stop on the way to the Casino to make a call to Paula Suggs, a tall, slender, top-heavy beauty that I had met while out on one of my daily runs just before I left for my third tour in Vietnam. My prospects for the evening, as I was to quickly learn, had just topped out and gone off the charts. Paula was at home and had no plans that couldn't be changed at the last minute; she told me that she would meet me at the Casino as soon as she had freshened up. Now our homecoming bash was really going to be something special, one of those nights that SEALs remember when they get old and gray—if they're lucky enough to get old and gray.

I dropped Mike off to let him have some private time with his serious squeeze, Diane, and was the first SEAL to show up for the festivities. Even before I had a cold drink in my hand, Jack Squires and his wife, Barbara, banged open the swinging doors. Mike and Diane showed up about fifteen minutes later; then the crowd flowing through the doors started growing fast. Tom Baron and Ron Rogers came strolling in, then Harry Constance, Dickey Cyrus, and Oz Osborne with their wives. Doc Myers, typical of a navy corpsman, brought both of his girlfriends. Last, but far from least, the leader of the pack, Bob "the Eagle" Gallagher, blew through the door to keep us all in line. To add to the crowd of SEALs in attendance, two of my mentors, Master Chiefs Tom Blais and Jim Cook, decided to join the increasing revelry. This was going to be one hell of a great party.

When Paula walked through the swinging doors of the Casino, heads turned. Half of the men in the room, even the married men standing next to their beautiful wives, took a good long look; this was the era of micro-miniskirts. Paula and I were both twenty-seven, in great physical shape, and it seemed that there was close to nothing that could slow either of us down. We managed to hold our own when the toasts were called and the drinks were flowing. We were the last two people through the swinging doors when last call finally rang out. We invited everyone still in the parking area over, and what was left of the party moved to my place on the beach for a final two or three welcome-home toasts. Being a country boy, and unschooled in the finer points of alcoholic blending, I had never heard of Paula's favorite drink, a Rusty Nail, but she claimed that, when consumed in considerable quantity, they acted as an aphrodisiac. Damn if she wasn't right! The following morning, as I waited as long as I dared before I would be late for muster, I thought that it might be a very good idea to see what it would be like to wake up next to Paula every morning.

After 0800 quarters, we turned in all of our weapons, checked our gear out to the appropriate department heads, and met with our new commanding officer, Lieutenant Commander Bob Gormley, an icon of SEAL

Team 2. Gormley gave us the bad news—all SEAL operations in Vietnam were being phased out or cut back to advisory roles only. I didn't have much hope of grabbing one of these few slots, but I checked in with the Ops Department anyhow. It was clear that a lowly E-5 like me wasn't going to be going back to Vietnam. I was advised that the policy wasn't going to change just because there was still a war that needed to be fought and won. I figured that I had nothing to lose and played my best, and only, card. I told Bob Gormley that I had completed the PRU advisers course and was ready to ship out tomorrow. I got a smile and a look that told me that I wasn't barking up the wrong tree, there just weren't any trees left in the forest.

I got the message and figured that I had better widen my horizons. The SEAL Team 2 AO, area of operations, had been expanded to include Europe, the Mediterranean Sea, and Central and South America. Things were starting to look up; maybe the SEAL Teams would avoid the fate of the UDT teams after World War II. The UDTs had almost disappeared when the world, once again, thought it was at peace. The budget boys at the Pentagon didn't see any reason to spend money on that "old-fashioned" kind of warfare when they could be burning up tens of billions of tax dollars on nuclear submarines, aircraft carriers, and jet fighter aircraft. Like too many other military planners, the REMFs didn't understand that the delicate use of limited, up-close and personal, focused violence was like a scalpel. SEAL Teams could cut out the nasty infections before they spread or, if they had started to spread, cut off the source of the infection before it got any worse. It seemed as if our officers had made the case for the teams, and made it well, or we would not have been assigned a bigger, and jealously guarded, piece of geographic military turf.

I started looking for a slot that would suit my skills and interests, and one where I could continue to learn and gain more experience. Finding a good berth wasn't difficult, but getting ahead of everyone else that wanted that berth was going to be the hard part. There were too many really talented SEALs looking for a good spot to land, and I was still a lowly E-5. It was even starting to piss me off that the navy had required me to burn up time that I could be using to find another berth by scheduling another awards ceremony.

Dressed in my gleaming dress whites, with the flags flying and the navy band filling the air with the kind of music that stirs the soul of even the most jaded old warrior, I took my place for the award of my third Bronze Star, my second Navy Commendation Medal, and a Vietnam Cross of Gallantry. I was proud of what I had done, and proud to stand up there representing Team 2 and all of the men who had fought and bled at my side.

Paula, gorgeous and smiling, stood out from all of the other girlfriends, wives, families, and friends like a shiny new penny. She almost glowed like the sun rising over the horizon as I stood at attention to have the medals pinned on my chest. Being recognized by your peers and superior officers and singled out in the teams was special, but medals didn't add a penny to my pay or get me any closer to the head of the line for a new berth. Eagle Gallagher knew this and gave me one of the most precious gifts I have ever been given. Eagle put in Harry Constance and me for combat advancement to E-6, first class; we were now able to fill billets for LPOs, leading petty officers. Our world had changed for the better, and it was Eagle, one of the toughest, nastiest, most demanding, wonderful bastards I had ever had the honor to serve with, who had opened the door. I had a debt to pay, and for the next twenty-three years I would never forget that Eagle was looking over my shoulder.

SEALs never just keep moving and hope for the best. We study the terrain; every hill, valley, and wrinkle is examined, planned for, and turned to our favor. With the chances of getting back into the bush just about zero, one of my best friends, Bob Shamberger, and I started looking for the best terrain where we could put what we had learned to good use. We needed to find a billet where we could expand our knowledge, and maybe add to the skill set that the SEAL Teams would need in the future. We decided that EOD (Explosive Ordnance Disposal) was just what the doctor ordered. We volunteered and were accepted for a six-month class that would be held at Indian Head, Maryland. I don't know if Bob knew how tough this class would be, but it was the toughest I experienced in my entire career. To finish third in a class of seventeen men, I almost lived in study hall. Three hours a night I was pounding the books just to pass the exams that were given every three days. Bob and I graduated from EOD

School in 1974. Of the six SEALs who went through EOD, Bob and I were the only ones who went back to the teams; the other men were assigned to the navy's EOD command.

The SEAL Teams were changing, evolving to meet the new threats in a world where a nuclear device could be packaged into a suitcase, and I was not going to stand down and let moss grow under my feet. I took my newfound ability to learn and study and passed the test to become a navy chief, E-7, as an aviation ordnanceman. For the next year I was never in one place for long. I spent a year running around the Mediterranean Sea and then worked with our SEAL counterparts in Great Britain, Greece, Turkey, Spain, and France. Back home and on leave, I took a breath and looked at the terrain again. I had the habit of putting a new pin in the map hanging on the wall of my place on the beach whenever I returned home from another assignment. It looked like a pincushion. I had been almost everywhere, but there was a whole continent that had escaped my attention. The following morning I volunteered for an MTT, a military training trip, to Colombia, in South America, and asked Paula to marry me. I hated to sleep alone, and she was the love of my life.

I had done everything I could to become a frogman. I pulled strings, finagled and strong-armed anyone I could, and begged favors when there was no other way to get into BUD/S. Although I can't prove it, I'm sure that my father pulled a few strings of his own behind the scenes. When I showed up for BUD/S, I was a young man who knew only one thing for sure: I was going to earn my own way onto the teams or go down swinging. I wouldn't quit, and I would never accept anything but success. No matter how small, I would play my part in developing the most advanced, smartest, deadliest, and fearsome warriors to ever fight, kill, and die for the country that they chose to defend and honor with their service.

Until my retirement on 18, September, 1992, I continued to operate anywhere I was needed, performed whatever duty was asked of me to the best of my ability, and trained more young men who I hoped would take all that I could pass on to them and improve on it. I believe that I did my best to teach them everything that I knew so that they would become better SEALs than I had been. Few disappointed me.

Vietnam was the first tenuous, treacherous step up a mountain that even the best of us have yet to crest. The SEAL Teams will soon celebrate our first fifty years of service, and while we have grown, learned new skills, and taken on more dangerous and demanding duties, not much has changed. Every warrior who served in the teams, and who serves in them today, carries on a tradition and a warrior ethic that remain unequaled. The only easy day was yesterday.

Tango Kilo—Out!

Glossary

This section isn't what you might expect. I put this information in here because I thought that a firsthand description of some weapons, places, and other guerrilla warriors that fought with us, or against us, might give you a better look at what the SEAL Teams ran into during my three tours in Vietnam. I have tried to keep my comments on each term as short and to the point as I could. I am definitely not a compendium of every piece of information about Vietnam or about what happened in Vietnam, I just wanted to put together some of my personal observations and definitions. These definitions may not agree with what you will find on the Internet, or even in other books. For good or bad, there has been lots of time to redact and rewrite reality since the end of the Vietnam War. I thought that I owed it to myself, to my teammates, and to you to end this book with what is, to the best of my recollection, the way it was.

SMALL ARMS AND OTHER WEAPONS

AK-47
Trained in the use of all small arms, as all SEALs are, we knew all of the weapons used anywhere on earth. If I had to pick the single rifle that impressed us most it would be the AK-47. The AK-47 rifle was, and remains, the battle rifle that every other battle rifle is compared against. No other infantry weapon has ever been as successfully used in as many wars, insurgencies, counterinsurgencies, and dustups around the world. Even today, from Africa to Afghanistan, the AK is still the backbone of armies, insurgents, and terrorists just about everywhere

on earth. It is cheap, easy to mass manufacture, close to indestructible, and easy to tear down, clean, and maintain in the worst conditions found in the field. There are over sixty million AK-47 rifles in use today. The AK-47 and close copies, or "clones," continue to be manufactured in several countries, including the United States. The AK-47 has become the most famous and infamous rifle in the world.

Developed by Russian weapons designer Mikhail Kalashnikov, the AK-47 was based on earlier designs, including the World War II German Sturmgewehr 44. Firing the compact, low-recoil 7.62 × 39 mm round (see 7.62 × 39 cartridge) that was effective and accurate enough to engage enemy forces out to three hundred meters, the AK-47 could be used effectively by just about anyone, including women and children as young as ten years old. Even when used in full-automatic fire, the AK-47 was not very difficult to control.

When I was working for an EOD company in Fallujah, Iraq, in 2004, I had my choice of weapons. The rest of the men all chose to carry M-16s; I carried an AK-47.

Browning Machine Gun—.50 caliber M2 (Ma Deuce, BMG)

John Browning's big .50 caliber machine gun was officially adopted by the United States in 1921 and is still in service. Due to the 121-pound weight of the water-cooled M-2, and the "lighter weight" of the 84-pound air-cooled HB variant, as well as the very heavy ammunition it fired, the .50 caliber Browning didn't get much, if any, use by the ground forces in Vietnam unless they were dug in and expecting the enemy to come to them. Because it was so damn heavy, the M-2 was almost always used in a fixed position, from aircraft or helicopters, mounted on vehicles, or, as we did in the SEAL Teams, used on boats where the weight wasn't a problem.

The M-2 had a maximum range of four and a half miles and fired a 655-grain bullet at over three thousand feet per second, and if you didn't care about destroying the barrel from the heat of burning powder gases and the friction of the bullet, you could fire over 250 rounds per minute. Nobody doubted that the "Big .50" BMG was a decisive fight stopper. There was damn little that it couldn't shoot right through; brick or concrete walls didn't last more than a few seconds when the Browning started laying down fire. Only once did I ever see incoming from a BMG that had been captured by the VC. That experience still stands out in my memory like it happened yesterday. That was the day I really learned to respect the Big .50 more than any other "small arm."

CKC rifle

As near as we can figure out, the CKC is the Chiang Kai Shek rifle; since we transliterate from Chinese, it is also spelled Chiang Kai Chek, thus CKC, a.k.a. Type Zhongzheng, Type 24, or CKC 45. These were bolt-action rifles based on the Mauser Gewehr 98 and more than half a million were manufactured during the 1930s in China. This quantity would explain the reason why they were still around during the Vietnam War. In our research, we have also discovered that some people describe the CKC as a semiautomatic. Our best guess from what we've read is that people who call CKCs "semiautomatics" got an early version of the SKS. We have seen pictures of the early SKS with a spike bayonet; later versions used a blade bayonet. The CKC was also thought of as a ChiCom bolt action rifle; since the Communists won the Chinese Civil War, it's fairly likely that they sent captured and later obsolete CKCs to Vietnam. It only held five rounds, but if it could shoot and they could find ammunition, the VC used just about anything that would go bang.

Claymore Mines

The first claymore mines, named after the Scottish broadsword, a.k.a. the T-48, were used in Vietnam in 1961. They fired steel cubes and were effective to thirty yards, but they were still in need of further improvement. The M-18A1 claymore mine that replaced them became one of the most reliable and destructive weapons that we used to initiate an ambush or to slow down or stop pursuit as we extracted. When 690 steel balls blasted out of the front of the mine at close to four thousand feet per second, the Claymore covered a kill zone that was 165 feet long and just short of seven feet high at fifty yards. The hit probability within fifty yards was 30 percent—and even out at the maximum range of a hundred yards those steel balls could effectively kill or cripple. Made of waterproof green plastic, the claymore had the famous phrase FRONT TOWARD ENEMY across the front. On the bottom were three folding legs that could be used to position the claymore, but we liked to get them off the ground a couple of feet, so these little legs didn't get much use. Weighing only 3.5 pounds, the claymore was easy to hump, reliable, and deadly. Designed to be command fired with attached wires and an M-57 firing device that was called a "clacker," the claymore became a standard part of our load out on almost every op. With the detonator wires connected to the claymore and the clackers hooked up to the firing wires, our OIC could trigger one or both mines to start the festivities when the enemy was well centered in our field of fire.

Colt 1911 Pistol

My father carried a 1911 in World War II, and if that weapon was good enough for him, it was good enough for me. His 1911 pistol, ready for use, is still tucked away where I can put it into use in a couple of seconds.

Invented by the brilliant and prolific firearms designer John Moses Browning, the .45 automatic, which is actually a semiautomatic that requires the trigger to be pulled for each shot to be fired, has been issued to American fighting men in several different forms for almost a century. As more and more was learned about war and the weaponry used in warfare, the Browning was redesigned, and redesigned again, finally becoming "Pistol, Caliber .45, Automatic, M-1911A1" during the Vietnam War.

The cartridge that is used by the 1911 pistol fires a 230-grain, full metal jacket bullet at a velocity of eight hundred feet per second. Compared to the Magnum pistol cartridges now available, that seems to be a rather anemic muzzle velocity, and it is. However, at the close ranges for which the cartridge was designed, in a trench or across a room, that big, slow bullet is a reliable and deadly man stopper. The 1911 has always been reliable and easy to strip and clean, and recoil is more of a long, slow shove than a sharp, staccato slap, all attributes that have made the 1911 near and dear to fighting men around the world.

When it was replaced in the U.S. military by the high-capacity 9mm pistols that hold more than twice as many rounds in their magazines, it was believed that the 1911 .45 automatic Colt pistol round was going to fade into oblivion. Not so. There have never been as many different .45 ACP chambered pistols available from as many different manufacturers as there are today. Several different U.S. military services are once again issuing the 1911, and other versions of the .45 ACP pistol, to the troops. It is even rumored that the U.S. government has been looking at new designs of .45 ACP pistols and that the 9mm high-capacity pistol may be phased out.

FAL

Also known as the FN FAL because it was manufactured by Fabrique Nationale de Herstal (FN), the FAL (Fusil Automatique Leger; Light Automatic Rifle) was well liked and widely used by the Australian troops and the troops of several other NATO countries in Vietnam. The FAL was a selective-fire rifle that was chambered for the full-power 7.62 × 51mm cartridge (.308) that gave it longer reach and more effective lethality than the AK-47. The FAL was a sturdy, accurate battle rifle that was adopted by so many countries, including the NATO nations, that it got the nickname of "the right arm of the free world." Like the Heckler & Koch G-3 rifle, the FAL came in many different variants, including folding stock rifles, folding stock Paratrooper models with shorter barrels, and heavy barrel rifles for use in sniping or to help dissipate the heat of full-automatic fire. The FAL wasn't a better rifle than the U.S.-issue M-14, but we thought that it was its equal.

Full Metal Jacket (FMJ)

A full metal jacket (FMJ) bullet is one designed to penetrate an adversary and not to expand. Under the terms of the Geneva Convention, "soft nose" or "hollow point" ammunition designed to expand as it passes through flesh is inhumane and cannot be used in warfare. It has been assumed that FMJ bullets are "more humane" and are less likely to kill the enemy. This wasn't much of a problem for the SEAL Teams. To overcome the lack of expanding bullets we put so much fire on our targets, so fast, that the nonexpanding FMJ we fired shredded everything in our kill zone.

M-3A1 "Grease Gun"

The M-3A1 was a full-auto, blowback-operated submachine gun that fired from an open bolt. Every piece of the weapon was designed to lower cost and maximize production, not accuracy, and it sure wouldn't win any beauty contests. Welded together using stamped parts, the M-3 got the name "grease gun" because it looked more like a mechanic's tool than a weapon. Chambered for the .45 ACP cartridge, it could be converted to 9mm and issued to foreign troops who had a readily available supply of 9mm ammo but not .45 ACP. With a double-stack, detachable magazine holding thirty rounds, it was an easy-to-use, cheap, and basically reliable spray and pray weapon. With a silencer, it was capable of performing good service at short range. The reason that it didn't get more use was that it was a submachine gun—pretty much a big, heavy pistol.

Hush Puppy

Commonly referred to as a "hush puppy," the only silenced weapon that got much use by the SEAL Teams was the modified 9mm Smith & Wesson Model 39. The modified pistol gained its sobriquet because it was supposedly going to be used to silence guard dogs before they could detect us or give away our position. I never saw any silenced weapons used to silence dogs, but they could come in handy when a sentry, or a VC hiding in the middle of a family in a hooch, needed to be taken out quietly. To make it as close to silent as any firearm could be, the Model 39 was modified to use a silencer and a slide lock—and it fired specially loaded subsonic ammunition. As each round was fired, the slide had to be manually operated for follow-up shots, but since the slide didn't cycle, the Model 39 was really very, very quiet.

Ka-Bar Knife

I still don't know how we got our Ka-Bar knives—they hadn't been manufactured in decades—but we got our hands on crates full of them that were World War II surplus and still packed in Cosmoline. Like a general purpose tool, they came in handy for everything and anything that needed to be cut, pried, opened, or hammered. From opening C-rat cans and ammo crates to prying the C-4 out of a claymore mine when we needed some explosives to destroy VC weapons and supplies, our Ka-Bars served us well.

Mauser Rifle

Originally designed by Peter Paul Mauser in 1898, the basic bolt-action, magazine-fed rifle is still in manufacture and is still credited by many people around the world as the best bolt-action rifle ever made. In Vietnam we never stopped finding

VC armed with Mauser rifles from as far back as World War I. Those rifles may have been rusted and beat up, and their stocks might have been wrapped with wire or rope to keep them from falling apart, but the damn things still worked.

Mosin-Nagant Rifle

The standard bolt-action rifle of the Russian army since 1891, the Mosin-Nagant rifle was chambered for the rimmed 7.62 × 54mm cartridge, which is not very different in ballistic performance than the revered .30-06 used by the Americans in both world wars and every other conflict in which our country has been involved. Manufactured by several different countries, the Mosin-Nagant was built in the United States by companies as large as the Westinghouse Corporation. Like the Mauser, it was a bolt-action, magazine-fed rifle. Most of them we found on the battlefield were over fifty years old. After all those years of hard use they were in pretty poor condition, but, like the Mauser rifles, they were simple and strong and still worked. As long as the VC could find ammunition, those old bolt-action rifles were another deadly threat that we couldn't ignore.

M-16 Rifle

In the formal terminology of the Armed Forces, "Rifle, Caliber 5.56mm M-16" has become common, and so many semiautomatic AR-15 versions have been bought by civilians that it is now simply called "the Black Rifle." The earliest M-16s had so many problems that there were investigations. Nobody could deny that too many American fighting men had died with jammed M-16s in their hands. The reasons for the jamming problems were soon discovered, and new cleaning kits and instructions were issued, but that was only a quick fix. The problem with jamming always started during a firefight, and that is not the time when you want to tear down your rifle and get it all clean.

For a couple of years, the M-16 underwent a serious evaluation, and it was upgraded to eliminate the problems with jamming. To resist the corrosion and rust that attacks everything in Vietnam, or on any wet battlefield, the bore and chamber were chrome plated. It was also discovered that the cheaper "ball powder" that had been approved for use in the 5.56mm cartridge had two serious problems. When it was fired it burned dirty, leaving too much powder residue and crud in the chamber and the gas system. The burned powder residue also covered the bolt, gumming up the extractor and slowing down the speed of travel of the bolt. Sooner or later the bolt would just stop moving or a cartridge would jam when being slammed into the chamber or when being violently ejected by the bolt. The powder also burned very hot, baking the crud into a hardened mess that was close to impossible to scrub out. Chrome plating the chamber and receiver and switching to a new powder solved both of those problems, and the M-16 rifle family, including the A1, A2, A3, and A4, has become the longest "in-service" infantry rifle in American history.

M-60

In the dense bush the M-60 machine gun was a decisive weapon because it fired the 7.62 × 51 mm round that was three times heavier than the 5.56 round used in the M-16 and the Stoner light machine gun. The penetration of the heavier round and the rapid rate of fire could discourage or shred the VC and NVA even when they decided to hide behind trees, dense bush, or a stone wall. Although the M-60 was supposed to be a crew-served weapon, with a gunner, assistant gunner (A-gunner), and ammo carrier, the SEAL Teams and SEAL M-60 gunners modified the M-60 and turned it into a one-man weapon. Some M-60 gunners cut a few inches off of the barrel, some removed the bipod, and some removed the butt stock and replaced it with the rubber boot that was used by door gunners on helos.

The only real problem was the weight of the ammunition, fed from a disintegrating belt of M-13 links. The SEALs who humped the M-60 and all of the ammo they could carry in addition to their normal load out got the respect of every man in the team.

The manuals say that the M-60 is effective in suppressing enemy movement in an area out to a little over a thousand meters. A whole bunch of VC and NVA thought that they were too far away for us to engage them. They found out that a SEAL with an M-60 wasn't impressed with training manuals and could reach out well past a thousand meters with well-controlled, deadly fire.

Stoner Light Machine Gun

My favorite weapon in Vietnam was invented and put together by Gene Stoner, the same engineer who invented the M-16. Although it used the same 5.56mm ammunition that was fired from the M-16, the Stoner was a much deadlier weapon. It was belt fed from 150-round belts and had a drum magazine that held a full belt, keeping the ammunition clean and dry when we were dragging ourselves across canals or through the mud and bush. With three or four belts of linked ammunition wrapped across my body, it would take an overwhelming enemy force to deplete my supply. The only problem that some people had with the Stoner was that it required the kind of cleaning and maintenance that most people just didn't want to do. I never understood how you could neglect to clean and maintain the only thing that was keeping you out of a body bag, but most troops just wouldn't spend the time that was needed to keep a Stoner running like a fine-tuned killing machine. The SEALs understood that every weapon was only as good as the man who used it and kept it fully operational. All of the SEALs who carried a Stoner into combat proved that with good maintenance you could bet your life, and the lives of your teammates, on the Stoner 63 (the year it got it's final form). The stoner was also a modular rifle system, and depending on the assembly, could be used as a carbine, assault rifle, folding machine gun, or light machine gun.

7.62 × 39 mm Cartridge

Designed in the Soviet Union during World War II, this was the standard cartridge used in the AK-47 and SKS rifles that were the basic weapons used by the NVA and VC in Vietnam. The ballistics of the 7.62 × 39 is not going to set the world on fire: a 124-grain FMJ bullet at a nominal 2,200–2,300 feet per second muzzle velocity. However, the short case, only 39 mm long, allowed the SKS and AK-47 to have a short, and therefore lighter, action, and the reduced recoil of the slower bullet allowed good control of the firearm, even in full-automatic operation. That hundreds of millions of rounds of 7.62 × 39 mm ammunition are fired every year in combat and getting ready for combat is proof positive that this cartridge, and the rifles for which it is chambered, might still be in service when the twenty-second century rolls around.

5.56 mm NATO Cartridge

Called the .223 in civilian dress, the 5.56 mm NATO cartridge was developed by Remington and was based on the .222 cartridge Remington had introduced in 1950. Development was specifically done for the ArmaLite AR-15 and M-16 rifle. Allowing the M-16 to operate in either full-automatic or semiautomatic mode while spitting out lightweight 55-grain bullets that left the muzzle at 3,200 feet per second has several real advantages that have been either overlooked or ignored.

The lightweight bullet allowed high muzzle velocity to be reached with less powder than would have been required by a heavier bullet. Because both the bullet and the powder charge were lighter, we could hump more than twice as many rounds of 5.56 as of the 7.62 × 51 mm (.308) fired by the M-60. With the increased muzzle velocity, the trajectory of the smaller bullet was reduced, so that the average troops didn't need to worry about how far away the VC or NVA were. They could put the sights on the middle of the chest, squeeze the trigger, and, if they were within three hundred meters of the bad guys, get a hit in the center of mass, between the chin and the groin. If the bad guys were way off in the distance, all they needed to do was put the top of the front sight on the top of the head and squeeze. Even at six hundred meters the little bullet would land someplace between the chin and the family jewels.

The 5.56 got bad press from some people, mostly marines as I remember, because they didn't think that the little bullet could be as deadly or destructive as the .30 caliber bullet that weighed more than double the 5.56. That was true, but only to a small degree. What the detractors of the 5.56 mm round didn't take into account was that when a 5.56 mm bullet hits human flesh, it penetrates a couple of inches, turns sideways, and breaks apart at the cannalure, so now two projectiles, still moving at close to twice the speed of sound, tear two holes through flesh and bone. I heard stories about the "little" 5.56 mm bullets going right through the VC and the VC running away, but I never saw it happen. Maybe that's because I always figured that if I carried hundreds of rounds out into the bush I might as well use them. Hell, anyone worth shooting once was worth shooting three or four times.

.30 Caliber Cartridge

The 7.62 × 51 mm rifle cartridge was adopted as standard issue by NATO in the 1950s. It was shorter than the .30-06 cartridge that was once the standard U.S. military round. The 7.62 × 51 mm allowed shorter, lighter weapons with faster cyclic rates of fire to be developed. While the ammo weighed less than the .30-06, it was still twice as heavy as the 5.56 mm cartridge.

Used in the M-14 rifle, the M-60 machine gun, and the FAL, it was a reliable, very accurate heavy caliber that easily outperformed the smaller 7.62 × 39 mm cartridge used in the SKS and AK-47.

One of the most famous Vietnam-era snipers, Carlos Hathcock, nicknamed "White Feather" by the NVA, used a bolt-action Winchester Model 70 rifle to win the thousand-yard competition at Camp Perry and was awarded the Wimbledon Cup. During his service in Vietnam, Gunnery Sergeant Hathcock was credited with ninety-three confirmed kills and three hundred probable kills. Although he used the .30-06 cartridge, the precursor to the 7.62 × 51 mm, the men that he trained and the equipment that evolved from his experience have all used the 7.62 × 51 mm, also known as the .308 Winchester, among other, more esoteric cartridges. It has been widely reported that Gunny Hathcock is, more than any other man, responsible for the rapid development of the weapons, tactics, and skills needed by both military and police snipers.

.45 ACP (Automatic Colt Pistol) Cartridge

Invented and developed for use in the Colt 1911 pistol, the .45 ACP cartridge has proven itself to be a reliable man stopper in war and when used by police and organizations like the Texas Rangers for securing the border and keeping the peace. There is nothing special about the ballistics, but ballistics is a science that studies things in a laboratory and makes comparisons. SEALs listened to the ballistics people, then made our less than scientific studies in the bush and on targets that were usually shooting back. The .45 ACP cartridge, almost the antithesis of the 5.56 mm, gave yeoman service.

9 mm Parabellum Cartridge

The 9 mm pistol cartridge has been used by every nation on earth in pistols and submachine guns; even two-shot derringers have been made for this cartridge. Developed by Deutsche Waffen und Munitionsfabriken for the Luger pistol, it is often mistakenly called the 9 mm Luger. While there is no debate that the 9 mm Parabellum cartridge can be deadly, there has been much debate about how quickly it can incapacitate or stop an adversary. When it is used in a submachine gun, the rapid rate of fire almost ensures multiple hits at close range, increasing the stopping capacity of the FMJ bullet. When we used it in our "hush puppy" against a sentry, the target was almost always hit only once, in the head. In either case I can guarantee that the 9 mm cartridge is as lethal as it needs to be.

RPK Light Machine Gun

The RPK is a light machine gun that looks like an AK-47 on steroids. This magazine-fed gun filled the same combat role for the NVA and VC that the belt-fed M-60 did for the SEAL Teams. In Vietnam we ran into what must have been some experimental RPKs because, like the M-60, they were belt fed, but these were rare. With a heavier barrel to aid accuracy and dissipate the heat of full-automatic fire, the RPK was a robust, simple light machine gun that shared many of the best attributes of the AK-47.

SKS Rifle

The SKS was a semiautomatic carbine and the first military weapon chambered for the 7.62 × 39 mm round later used in the AK-47 and the RPK light machine gun. The sturdy SKS was used in first-line service for only a few years before it was replaced by the AK-47, but there were still more than enough of these ten-round rifles for probably hundreds of thousands of them to be issued to second-line NVA or VC troops. The biggest drawback of the SKS was that it held only ten rounds in a fixed internal magazine and had to be loaded from the top of the receiver with either stripper clips or loose rounds. In a firefight ten rounds doesn't last very long.

Sten Gun

The Sten gun was developed in England to be used as a quick replacement for all of the weapons lost during the evacuation at Dunkirk. The British had been buying every Thompson submachine gun they could get their hands on from the United States, but when the Americans entered the war the supply started to dry up. Designed for ease and rapidity of manufacture, the Sten gun was a simple, blowback-operated, selective-fire weapon that fired the 9 mm Parabellum cartridge. The Sten gun had a thirty-two-round magazine that stuck out of the left side of the gun, making it a real pain in the ass to carry in the bush. It also jammed frequently and had lousy, fixed sights. At close range, if it didn't jam, the Sten gun was probably as useful as our Ka-Bar knives, but maybe not. Even the British troops during World War II would dump their Sten guns for a captured German MP-40 whenever they could.

Swedish K (Carl Gustav m/45) Submachine Gun

The Swedish K submachine gun was developed after the Swedes took a long hard look at the German MP-40, the British Sten gun, and the Soviet PPSh-41 and PPS-43. Chambered for the 9mm Parabellum cartridge, it weighed about ten pounds empty, fired full auto from an open bolt, and had two different magazines, which held thirty-six or fifty rounds. The Swedish designers moved the magazine to where it belonged, under the front of the receiver where it wouldn't get caught in every bush, vine, or tree limb in the boonies. Because it had a slow rate of fire and weighed over ten pounds when loaded, it was easy to control during full-automatic fire.

The S&W Model 76, another submachine gun that we evaluated and added to our armory, was based on the Swedish K design. It was often silenced but, contrary to what some say, was not referred to as a "hush puppy."

Tracers

Tracers use a small pyrotechnic charge in the base of the bullet that is ignited when the cartridge is fired. When you are fighting at night, as we chose to do whenever possible, it is damn difficult or impossible to see the sights on your weapon. When we initiated our ambush, the blast of the claymores, the muzzle flash from my Stoner, and the flashes from the rest of the squad or platoon opening up dilated our pupils, making the sights worthless. With a tracer round loaded every fourth round in a belt or magazine, all we had to do to adjust our fire was to follow the red glowing line of tracers streaming through the night. The downside was that the VC and NVA could also see the tracers and return fire toward where the red tracers were coming from. To reduce the incoming fire, we figured that it would take at least five seconds for the VC or NVA to get their weapons into action. If we killed or severely wounded them all by then, we wouldn't need to worry about them using the source of our tracers as a target.

MUNITIONS

LAAW Rockets (M-72)

The LAAW was designed as a light antiarmor weapon, but we figured out that having one or two along on our ops came in handy, as it could have several other uses. The LAAW is basically a tube inside of another tube. In the inside tube is a rocket. The outside tube is watertight and protects the rocket until the two segments are pulled open when you are ready to fire. When you fire the LAAW, the rocket motor burns completely—even before the rocket leaves the tube. The 66mm warhead is fired out of the tube with very little recoil, the spring-loaded fins deploy, and most of the time before you can drop the empty tube the warhead explodes on the target. The LAAW was like having artillery along on every op, and we used it against hard and softer targets. A single LAAW could destroy a bunker or a hooch, and when I used the LAAW as an antipersonnel weapon and got an airburst in the treetops above entrenched VC or NVA, it usually stopped incoming fire quickly.

Recoilless Rifles

The BSUs (Boat Support Units) used 57mm recoilless rifles on their boats so that we could have the advantages of artillery close at hand and didn't have to depend on artillery from a firebase that could be far away and take a while to get the rounds going downrange. Technically, recoilless rifles have rifled barrels and are capable of firing artillery-type shells at a range and velocity comparable to that of a light cannon, but most of the time in Vietnam they were used to fire larger shells at lower velocities and shorter ranges. The almost complete lack of recoil gave the BSUs the advantage of mounting them on insertion or extraction boats, where they could do the most good when we had our backs against the wall.

Concussion Grenades

In Vietnam we used concussion grenades to disorient or disable people inside a hooch or other structures, and in canals where the shrapnel from fragmentation grenades would be slowed down or stopped by the water. If a VC jumped overboard from a sampan or another vessel, the blast and concussion underwater was almost sure to knock him out or collapse his lungs. In either case he was KIA and no longer a problem.

The Mk-3A2 concussion grenade didn't look like much, but with a half-pound charge of TNT inside of a waterproof cardboard body, it added another deadly capability to our ability to destroy the VC.

Fragmentation Grenades (Frags)

The old, heavy "pineapple" grenades used in World War II were replaced with the more effective, lighter M-61, which got heavy use in Vietnam. Made with a thin outer shell of sheet steel and a core of notched steel wrapped around Composition B explosive, it is sometimes called a "lemon" due to the shape. Upon detonation the outer shell and inner coil shatter and turn into high-velocity fragments that can kill anybody out to fifteen or twenty yards. The average SEAL could throw the M-61 at least forty yards, and probably more. When we were under fire from somebody fifty or sixty yards away we got very motivated; tossing those grenades an extra twenty yards right into their laps was not too difficult.

We used the M-61 on most of our ops and as booby traps for the VC or NVA. To set the trap, we slipped the grenade under or inside of anything that would hold the spoon closed, then very carefully removed the pin. Most of the time we hid grenades under the body of a dead VC, a sack of rice, or something else that they might pick up on the battlefield. When the spoon flew, they had four to five seconds to get out of the blast radius. After hearing that ping of the spoon flying free and thinking to themselves, "I'm screwed," they had about two seconds to run thirty yards and hit the deck. Not too many made it that fast.

We also had instantaneously exploding grenades that we used for booby traps or left behind for the VC to find in the bush. When the pin was pulled and the spoon was released, there was no delay in the explosion of the grenade. It detonated before it could be thrown.

XM-148 Grenade Launcher; M-203 Grenade Launcher

The M-203 single-shot 40 mm grenade launcher was the replacement for the experimental XM-148 that was developed by Colt Firearms during the Vietnam War. The M-203 was light and easy to use, and with HE rounds, direct fire buckshot, CS gas, smoke, and illuminating rounds available, it was a very flexible, useful addition to the underside of the M-16 rifle. Maximum range was 450 yards, but effective range was closer to 100 yards. The only drawback was that it was a single-shot weapon and slow to reload.

WP (White Phosphorous) Artillery and Grenade

White phosphorous is a smoke-producing incendiary round often fired by artillery as a spotting round. While WP can be used as an offensive antipersonnel weapon that causes severe burns, it is not very effective when employed in that role unless the explosion is contained in a small area such as a bunker or building. It was widely known as "Willy Pete" or "Willy Peter" in Vietnam.

General Terms

Black Ponies

In 1968, Admiral Elmo Zumwalt decided that the riverine forces and SEAL Teams needed more and faster air support than even the Seawolf helos could provide. It wasn't too tough to figure out that the OV-10A Broncos nicknamed the "Black Ponies" could get to where they were needed three times faster than the helos. The OV-10As were armed with high-explosive 2.75-inch rockets along with their 7.62 mm machine guns, 7.62 mm minigun pods, and occasionally 20 mm gun pods on the centerline. The rapid reaction time and heavy armament of the Black Ponies saved our ass on several occasions. In the middle of a firefight, the sound of their twin turboprop engines was music to our ears.

Chieu Hoi (Open Arms) Program

The Chieu Hoi program was one of the "psyops" or "psywar" programs created to demoralize the VC. Leaflets were air-dropped and spread across every town, village, and hamlet offering them a safe passage and retraining to help the Allied forces if they would defect. The CIA thought that the program was a success because over twenty thousand enemy combatants "defected" every year. The problem was that the VC used the program to disseminate disinformation and to ambush U.S. forces led by their planted agents. We never trusted the information from the program and always tested individual Chieu Hoi several times before we trusted them or their information. In the long run we did get some good intel, and some of the Chieu Hoi became trusted warriors, but those were few and far between.

Chinese Nung

When the Communists took over China in 1948–49, more than a hundred thousand Nung from the southern provinces emmigrated to South Vietnam. They joined the French in fighting the Communists until 1954. Many Nung fathers taught their sons to fight, and together they continued to resist the Communist takeover of Vietnam after the French pulled out. The Nung were guerrilla fighters in every sense of the word, and they were tough. They were so tough that they were hired to protect the U.S. Embassy and other sensitive installations and were recruited by Special Forces units as scouts and security forces. At the end of the war, 130,000 Vietnamese were evacuated and resettled in the United States, but no one seems to know how many of the Nung who fought at our side were left behind to be "reeducated"—tortured or murdered.

Dien Bien Phu

The French defeat at Dien Bien Phu in 1954 was the final French defeat of the First Indochinese War and led to the Geneva Accords, which divided the country into Communist North Vietnam and pro-West South Vietnam at the seventeenth parallel. Fourteen years later General Giap tried the same tactics when the NVA surrounded and besieged the forward base manned by U.S. Marines at Khe Sanh. The marines held their ground and inflicted devastating losses on the NVA.

DOR

Nobody but you makes you a SEAL. SEAL training and duty is many things, but it is always voluntary. At any time during BUD/S training, students can be injured and forced to leave, and some find that they just don't have what it takes to endure the physical and mental strain of training. Of the men who go into BUD/S training, 70 to 80 percent don't graduate; some of those men make the decision to drop on request, DOR. The tradition of DOR is simple and stops the pain immediately. To DOR, you just drop your helmet liner next to a pole with a brass ship's bell attached to it and ring the bell three times.

LDNN

The Lien Doi Nguoi Nhai—roughly translated, the soldiers that fight under the sea—were south Vietnamese UDTs that were trained by the U.S. Navy advisers as early as 1961. Later they would be trained further and fight side by side with the SEAL teams. The LDNN guys were real warriors and trained and fought as hard as we did.

Mike Boats/Mike 8 Boat (LCM-8) a.k.a. HSSC (Heavy SEAL Support Craft)

The earliest Mike Boats were converted LCM-6s, which would do nine knots. Designed for use as an improved mechanized landing craft on the rivers, the Mike 8 is still in use today. Made of welded steel and weighing 135,000 pounds, the Mike 8 requires a crew of four men and is powered by twin 12V-71 diesel engines that drive twin screws, which will do twelve knots. While it is slow, the Mike 8 can carry sixty tons of cargo and act as a floating gun platform.

MSSC (Medium SEAL Support Craft)

The MSSC was designed and built specifically for SEAL operations, and manned by MST-2 detachments. Thirty-six feet long, it was an aluminum-hulled catamaran that was low to the water and had a top speed of over thirty knots. It was one of the fastest boats on the river. The standard crew of an MSSC was seven men. The coxswain (boat driver) and the OIC sat in the cockpit just aft of the bow; the driver was on the left. On the OIC's side of the cockpit were the boat's radar and radios. The compartment aft of the cockpit and forward of the engine compartment held a SEAL platoon and the other five MST crew members manning the guns—and the MSSC was very well armed. On each side of the MSSC was an M-60 machine gun forward and a .50 caliber machine gun aft. The seventh crew member manned a minigun on the stern that could pour out seven thousand rounds per minute. To add to their firepower, the crew all carried M-16s, and the OIC might also carry a .45. When we were going out on an op, all of us were armed to the teeth and always ready, willing, and able to add to the number of rounds headed toward the VC or NVA when the shooting started. The walls of the "troop" compartment were lined with antishrapnel curtains, and the compartment was covered with a canvas canopy designed to deflect rockets. I'm glad that we never found out how well that canvas canopy would work!

PBR (Patrol Boat, Riverine)

Although the PBRs were used for interdicting the flow of men, weapons, and material in the Mekong Delta and the Rung Sat Secret Zone, they were also put to good use to insert and extract the SEALs. With a fiberglass hull and a water-jet drive, the PBR could operate in very shallow water. If there was even a lousy two feet of water under the hull, we were good to go. The Jacuzzi water-jet drives, powered by dual 220 horsepower Detroit Diesel engines, let the boat drivers turn the boat completely around in its own length and bring it to dead in the water in just a few boat lengths. With very quiet drives and a top speed of close to thirty knots, PBRs were armed with twin M-2 HB .50 caliber machine guns, an M-60 machine gun, a Mk-19 grenade launcher, and, when the op might get very hairy, a 20 mm cannon. They were also provided with ceramic armor that protected the machine gunners and conning tower. A SEAL platoon inserting in their backyard from a PBR must have been one of the VC's worst nightmares.

PRU (Provisional Reconnaissance Unit)

The PRUs were tied to the CIA Operation Phoenix program and were well trained and well armed as a consequence. Basically light infantry units, they were rumored to be tasked with assassinations of key NVA, VC, and even Cambodian officials who collaborated with the North Vietnamese Communists.

Seawolf

The UH-1B "Huey" helicopters used by the U.S. Army were retrofitted and refitted and made ready for use by the navy in Vietnam in 1967. The Seawolves carried 7.62 mm machine guns, .50 caliber machine guns, 2.75-inch rocket launchers, and grenade launchers.

STAB (SEAL Team Assault Boat)

Even with a full crew of three running the boat and six SEALs with full load outs aboard, the STAB was a rocking and rolling river rocket. Driven by twin 110 hp Mercury outboard engines, the STAB could reach over thirty-five knots before your butt had hit the deck. Twenty-one feet long and eight feet wide, the STAB was lightly armed with one 7.62 mm machine gun. Originally modified Boston whalers, these boats didn't last long. They were replaced by LSSC (Light SEAL Support Craft), which, confusingly, were also called STABs (not officially by the U.S. Navy), but the acronym stood for STrike Assault Boats. The LSSCs were upgraded to the Mk II twenty-four-foot Utility Boats, then to the MSSCs, and finally to the Heavy SEAL Support Craft (Mike boats). The SEAL Team Assault Boat was an expedient interim measure; the fiberglass hulls and lack of armor rendered them unfit for long-term duty.

Index

U.S. Navy

Terry Roach

Thomas H. Keith retired as a Command Master Chief with thirty years of service in the U.S. Navy and twenty-nine years with the Navy's Underwater Demolition Teams and SEAL Team 2. During his three tours of duty in the Republic of Vietnam with SEAL Team 2, he received two Purple Hearts, three Bronze Stars with combat V for valor, two Navy Commendation medals with combat V for valor, one Navy Achievement medal with combat V for valor, two Presidential Unit Citations, and two Navy Unit Citations among his many awards. He devoted twenty-nine years of service to Naval Special Warfare and is still involved in active special operations in Iraq and Afghanistan as a civilian contractor.

J. Terry Riebling has been a shooter and hunter for over forty years and a competitive shooter for over twenty years. He is the winner of the Erskine Caldwell Award in Short Fiction and the author of "Sniper's Eyes." His articles have appeared in numerous firearms and hunting publications.